Visual Social Marketing

FOR

DUMMIES

A Wiley Brand

by Krista Neher

FOR

DUMMIES

A Wiley Brand

Visual Social Marketing For Dummies®

Published by: **John Wiley & Sons, Inc.,** 111 River St., Hoboken, NJ 07030-5774, www.wiley.com

Copyright © 2014 by John Wiley & Sons, Inc., Hoboken, New Jersey

Published by John Wiley & Sons, Inc., Hoboken, New Jersey

Published simultaneously in Canada

For general information on our other products and services, please contact our Customer Care Department within the U.S. at 877-762-2974, outside the U.S. at 317-572-3993, or fax 317-572-4002.

For technical support, please visit www.wiley.com/techsupport.

Wiley also publishes its books in a variety of electronic formats and by print-on-demand. Not all content that is available in standard print versions of this book may appear or be packaged in all book formats. If you have purchased a version of this book that did not include media that is referenced by or accompanies a standard print version, you may request this media by visiting http://booksupport.wiley.com. For more information about Wiley products, visit us www.wiley.com.

Library of Congress Control Number: 2013948032

ISBN 978-1-118-75348-4 (pbk); ISBN 978-1-118-77225-6 (ebk); ISBN 978-1-118-77226-3 (ebk)

Manufactured in the United States of America

10 9 8 7 6 5 4 3 2 1

Table of Contents

Introduction

A few years ago, I started noticing a shift in social media and Internet marketing. I've been involved in social media marketing since its inception, and rarely have I seen large shifts in social media trends. New tools and social networks come and go, but I was noticing a bigger change — a trend toward *visual* social marketing.

Visual social marketing is a way of using visual content, such as images and videos, to market your business online.

As I looked at trends, I saw that Flipboard, an application that visualizes news and social network updates, was the top downloaded application at the Apple App Store. Instagram, a social network that lets users shoot, edit, and share photos from mobile devices, was quickly growing and had just been acquired by Facebook, solidifying its position as a serious social network. Pinterest, which seemed to emerge from nowhere, was the quickest-growing social network and was generating a lot of buzz and interest.

Next, I noted the strategies that were working on my website and other social networks. On Facebook, posting images had become the primary way to attract the most interaction, with video close behind. Facebook, Google+, and LinkedIn were all increasing the prominence of images displayed on profiles and in posts. Blog posts with relevant images were generating significantly more traffic than those without.

All these signs were pointing in the same direction, toward visual content. Fast-forward, and now visual content is still getting results — and the world is experiencing the launch of micro-video sharing sites such as Instagram Video and Vine, where users can share short videos.

Successful online marketing and social media marketing now require *visual* social marketing.

About This Book

Visual Social Marketing For Dummies provides you, the reader, with an in-depth analysis of the strategies and tools that can enhance your existing efforts in social media and online marketing and help you benefit from new visual social networks such as Instagram, Pinterest, and Vine.

In this book, you see not only the strategies but also the specific techniques that lead to success, including exactly how to use each site. In addition, you'll see plenty of examples that show how businesses are now successfully using these strategies. Throughout the entire book, you'll find tips, tricks, and best practices to take your success in visual social marketing to the next level.

Visual social marketing can't be successful, however, if you don't supply stunning visual assets. Creating photos, images, and videos can seem to be an overwhelming task, but plenty of tools and hacks are available to use to create the necessary visual content even if you have no technical knowledge or expensive (and confusing) software. You can find plenty of resources that anyone can use, regardless of technical aptitude or design knowledge, to build visual content that gets results.

Visual Social Marketing For Dummies is laid out in a way that's easy to understand — and put into action. You'll even find specific step-by-step instructions to tackle some of the more complex aspects of social networks.

Foolish Assumptions

I make a few assumptions about you as a marketer or business professional in this book:

- ✔ You're familiar with social media marketing and social networks.
- ✔ You want to use visual social marketing to grow a business or fill a professional context.
- ✔ You're familiar with basic computer concepts and terms.
- ✔ You have a basic understanding of the Internet.
- ✔ You have permission to run a social media marketing campaign for your organization.
- ✔ You have permission to use any photos or videos that you use in your visual social marketing strategy and execution. (You may need to discuss this topic with your legal team.)
- ✔ You aren't necessarily a professional photographer, graphical designer, or video editor.

Icons Used in This Book

The Tip icon marks helpful information and shortcuts that you can use to your benefit as you get started.

The Remember icon marks information that's especially important to know — and retain. You may even want to highlight this information in some way because it represents important concepts.

The Technical Stuff icon flags information of a more technical nature that you may want to skip if you aren't implementing the technical aspects of your visual marketing strategy.

The Warning icon tells you to watch out! This vital information may prevent problems or save you from the headaches of trying to solve them.

Beyond the Book

This section describes where readers can find book content that exists outside the book itself. A *For Dummies* technically themed book may include the following elements, though only rarely does a book include all of them:

✔ **Cheat Sheet:** The Cheat Sheet for this book can be viewed online. You'll find a summary of the most important concepts and ideas from this book, along with checklists to keep in mind. The Cheat Sheet is a useful companion to the book as you begin to implement your visual social marketing strategy. Remember to keep the Cheat Sheet handy to refer to repeatedly, or to refer to quickly and easily when the book isn't nearby. To view the Cheat Sheet online, see

    www.dummies.com/cheatsheet/visualsocialmarketing

✔ **Dummies.com online articles:** To help you get more from this book, a number of online articles summarize the most important ideas and concepts from this book. These articles, which can help you extend and implement the information in this book, include links to interesting examples that you can further explore. The articles appear on the book's Extras page, at

    www.dummies.com/extras/visualsocialmarketing

✔ **Updates:** In social media, the situation often changes quickly, and some of the social networks covered in this book are still new and emerging. To help you get the most from this book, I periodically create updates where you can find the latest and most up-to-date information. Updates, which will be posted whenever a social network or a marketing strategy undergoes substantial changes, will be posted to the Downloads tab on the book's product page. On the book's Extras landing page, an article either describes the update or provides a link to open the Downloads tab for access to updated content:

`www.dummies.com/extras/visualsocialmarketing`

Where to Go from Here

This book is organized to help you get what you need quickly and efficiently. For this reason, you don't have to read the chapters in order as they're laid out in the book. You can jump in and out of the chapters and parts that are most relevant to you.

The first part of the book explains why visual social marketing is the key part of a solid Internet marketing or social media marketing strategy. It also covers how visual content can generate more traffic to your website. Though it's helpful to understand the important role that visual elements play in growing your business online, if you're already sold on visual social marketing and understand the implications to your online strategy, you can skip these sections.

I highly recommend that you spend at least a little bit of time reading Chapter 3, which tells you how to develop a visual social marketing plan. This plan applies to all the visual social networks you use — setting the strategy upfront can increase your ultimate success.

Part II is dedicated to taking photos and creating outstanding visual content. If you have a design team or an agency that will create visual content for you, you can skip these sections. If you want to see how to easily create stunning visual content, dive in and take note of the tools and tricks I cover.

Part III focuses on integrating visual elements into your existing social media marketing strategy. This section is relevant to businesses that are already using blogs or social networks such as Facebook, LinkedIn, and Twitter. If you aren't using these sites yet, you might not find much value in this section; if you *are* using them, this section can help you achieve better results from the networks you're already using.

The rest of the book explores the leading visual social marketing tools. If you aren't using many of them yet, read the first few pages of each chapter to understand how each visual social network works and how businesses are using it. This strategy can help you easily decide which social networks are right for you, and you can prioritize the chapters on the tools that you're most interested in using.

Here's to your success in visual social marketing!

Contact Us!

I'd love to hear from you, see your visual marketing successes, and share updates with you. You can find me and connect with me at these online locations:

- ✔ **Blogs devoted to social media marketing topics:** The page at `www.BootCampDigital.com/blog` contains a wide variety of social media marketing tips, tricks, and news. You can stay up-to-date with me at `www.KristaNeher.com/blog`, where I share my business tips, speaking engagements, and, of course, visual content.

- ✔ **Social networks:** Connect with me on LinkedIn at `www.LinkedIn/com/in/KristaNeher`, tweet with me on Twitter using @KristaNeher, and see my Facebook updates at `www.Facebook.com/KristaNeherIsSocial`.

- ✔ **Visual social networks:** I also love using visual social networks, and you can find me on these sites:

  Me

  - **Instagram:** `www.Instagram.com/KristaNeher`
  - **Pinterest:** `www.Pinterest.com/KristaNeher`
  - **Vine:** @KristaNeher
  - **YouTube:** `www.YouTube.com/KristaNeher`

  My company

  - **SlideShare:** `www.Slideshare.com/KristaNeher` or `www.SlideShare.com/BootCampDigital`
  - **YouTube:** `www.YouTube.com/BootCampDigital`

Good luck with visual social marketing. I'll see you online!

Part I

Getting Started with Visual Social Marketing

In this part . . .

✔ Understanding what visual social marketing is

✔ Discovering the marketing potential of visual content

✔ Exploring the copyright issues that arise from creating and using visual content

✔ Growing website traffic by harnessing visual content

Chapter 1

Marketing in the Age of Visual Content

A s social media marketing has grown and evolved over the past ten years or so, an exciting trend that has emerged is visual social marketing. I've been involved in social media marketing since its inception and have noticed in the past couple of years the phenomenon of adding visual content to the social media marketing space.

Visual social marketing is powerful because visual elements allow marketers to create deeper connections via social media. The expression "A picture is worth a thousand words" indicates that humans can process a lot of information relatively quickly by looking at an image.

While recently examining trends related to tablet devices, I saw that Flipboard, a visual news application, was the most frequently downloaded app for the iPad. Pinterest, an image-based sharing site, was the fastest-growing social network. Instagram, an application for editing and sharing photos on mobile devices, was gaining in popularity (and was eventually purchased by Facebook for a *billion* dollars). At the same time, social networks such as Facebook, Google+, LinkedIn, and Twitter are all increasing the prominence of images on their sites. Also, studies have begun to emerge, showing that images on Facebook were generating more clicks and engagements than any other content.

All these shifts, plus video, now continue — short-format video especially is growing in popularity. Twitter launched its Vine application, which allows users to share 6-second videos, and Instagram added video sharing to its popular photo-sharing application.

The growth in the popularity of visual content in social media is undeniable — it creates an opportunity for marketers to connect with customers on social media in the formats that customers are most interested in. Savvy marketers are creating visual content on visual social marketing sites and existing social networks in order to break through the clutter and connect with consumers in a deeper way.

With the proliferation of the iPhone and other types of smartphones, creating visual content such as photographs, videos, and drawings is easier than ever. Technology is no longer a barrier to creating stunning images or videos that connect with customers. In this age, every individual and business has the power to create powerful visual content at their fingertips by way of the smartphone.

In this chapter, I explain what visual social marketing is and why it's a vital part of any social marketing or communications strategy.

Defining Visual Social Marketing

In *visual social marketing,* you use images and videos to connect with consumers via social media. Visual social marketing can take place on visual social networks, such as Pinterest, YouTube, or Instagram, that focus primarily on sharing visual content, or on other social networks such as Facebook, Google+, LinkedIn, and Twitter.

Visual social marketing can include images or videos that a business purchases or creates itself or *user-generated* content, which anyone can create.

Visuals are images and videos (photographs, graphics, images, or videos) that are created to support visual social marketing.

Though some people believe that visual social marketing is only relevant to businesses that offer highly visual products in categories such as fashion, design, or food, that isn't the case. *All* businesses can benefit from participating in visual social marketing.

My company, Boot Camp Digital, provides social media training. It isn't a highly visual topic; however, my employees know that our customers are active on sites such as Pinterest and Instagram — plus, we need relevant ways to connect with our customers on Facebook, Google+, Twitter, and LinkedIn.

Boot Camp Digital employees create images with social media statistics to share on Facebook. These posts often generate more views than Facebook posts that have only text. We also use Instagram to share images from conferences and events. All these tools help build visibility with our target audience and benefit from our existing social media marketing.

Appreciating the Marketing Potential of Visual Social Marketing

Visual social marketing is a powerful way to grow your business presence on social networks. Because visual content is more powerful than text content, it can provide a number of benefits for businesses, including building deeper connections, increasing the believability of your marketing efforts, and communicating more quickly.

Building deeper connections

Visual social marketing allows businesses to create deeper connections with customers. A video or an image allows for a much more meaningful connection with customers than can simply sharing text.

For example, Pure Michigan is an effort by the state of Michigan to drive tourism and business to the state. Though it can use text to describe how beautiful Michigan is, nothing is more compelling than displaying stunning images. You can see the power of visual content in Figure 1-1 by taking a look at Pure Michigan's Facebook page. As a resident of a neighboring state (Ohio), seeing amazing photos of the lakes in Michigan makes me consider vacationing there, and it certainly changes my perception of the state. The images build this impression much more powerfully than text could have.

Images and videos can create deeper and longer-lasting emotional connections.

Figure 1-1:
The Pure Michigan Facebook page.

Increasing the believability of your marketing

Effective marketing influences perceptions, and visual content is a powerful way to show how a product works and to convince people to purchase it. A restaurant's site can tell you about its beautiful dining room, but seeing photos of it makes the claim believable. Visual elements allow customers to truly see how a product looks, works, or functions, which makes advertising and marketing claims more believable.

One of the biggest video marketing successes in the history of YouTube is the Will It Blend series by BlendTec (www.WillItBlend.com), a company that produces high-quality blenders. To show the strength and durability of its commercial blenders, BlendTec created a series of videos in 2006 showing its blenders blending items such as blocks of wood and even the iPhone and iPad. The video series increased sales of the BlendTec blender by 700 percent and even led to the creation of a consumer line of blenders. The blenders now have their own website, as shown in Figure 1-2, and most of their videos generate hundreds of thousands, if not millions, of views.

Visual marketing provides you with the opportunity to show customers the information that you want them to believe about your business — take advantage of this opportunity to create compelling marketing messages.

Figure 1-2:
The Will It Blend video website.

Communicating more quickly

In many instances, a concept may be communicated more quickly by using a video or an image rather than text. For example, if I wanted to teach you how to tie a bowtie, it would take pages of text to describe how to do it. Alternatively, I can *show* you in only a few minutes.

When used well, photos and videos can be a more effective and more efficient means of communication. For marketers, communicating by way of visual content often makes it easier to explain how to do something. This method is also appealing to consumers who are starved for time online.

Evaluating how viewers process visual elements

One reason that visual social marketing is becoming prominent is the way that people process images and other visual content. They can communicate more information, more quickly, by way of an image or a video than by text.

A number of studies show that the human brain processes visual information more quickly than it processes text. Images and visual concepts are processed 60,000 times faster in the brain than text. If you want to communicate quickly, therefore, an image can communicate the information faster than can text.

In social media, users typically scroll through news streams that have a lot of status updates and then choose to read the information that interests them. Because images can be processed more quickly than text, users of social networks are more likely to look quickly at an image than to read text.

Ninety percent of information that's transmitted to the brain is visual, so most of what you comprehend and understand comes from visual cues. When you omit visual content and use only text, you're eliminating a large percentage of information that can be consumed by way of an image.

Describing in print the photo of two men with computers in Figure 1-3 could take pages of text — especially their facial expressions. Viewing the image directly, on the other hand, communicates a lot of information quickly. Within a few seconds, you can comprehend their feelings and emotions much more accurately than by reading a text description.

Figure 1-3:
Two men
with com-
puters —
and easily
discernible
emotions.

Visual elements aren't just important — they're an effective and efficient way for people to consume and understand content.

Digging in to see how visual elements attract results on social networks

Visual content is generating tremendous results on social networks. Considering that people process images more quickly than text, you probably aren't surprised to know that, across social networks, images are generating more views and clicks than are other types of content.

The statistics in the following list indicate how images are garnering results on a few popular social networks:

- ✔ **Facebook:** The site reports that images generate 50 percent more inter-actions than other types of content; more than 6 billion photos are now uploaded to Facebook every month. Images on Facebook generate seven times more Likes and ten times more shares than links (on average).

- ✔ **LinkedIn:** A study by The Ladders (www.theladders.com) found that recruiters on LinkedIn spend more time examining a user's picture than the person's qualifications.

- ✔ **Twitter:** Images are the most often shared links on this site.

- ✔ **Blogs:** Posts and articles that include images generate 94 percent more views than posts without images.

As these statistics show, images are generating results across social networks, and they aren't important only for visual social networks such as Instagram and Pinterest. Images are an important part of *any* social media marketing strategy.

In any social media strategy, create a visual social marketing plan (described later in this book) to maximize results and drive interactions. If you're marketing or communicating on a social network, make visual content a part of your strategy.

A quick look at a variety of leading-brand social networks shows that many of them are harnessing the power of social media. Oreo received a lot of attention for its unique and creative Facebook images, creating 100 daily Facebook posts to celebrate its 100th birthday. Most of the posts included interesting and creative (and, sometimes, provocative) images, all of which featured the Oreo cookie, as shown in Figures 1-4, 1-5, and 1-6. During the 100 days of the campaign, the product's Facebook Likes grew from 26 million to 27 million and interactions increased *195 percent*.

Figure 1-4:
An Oreo Pride image, posted on Facebook.

JUNE 25 | PRIDE

Figure 1-5:
An Oreo post about the Mars rover.

AUGUST 5 | MARS ROVER LANDS

Figure 1-6:
Oreo celebrates Elvis Week.

Recognizing the challenges facing social media marketers

One daunting challenge for marketers is that social networks are becoming more and more cluttered — and marketers have to figure out how to break through and be noticed. According to Facebook, its average user has 130 friends and is connected to 80 groups, pages, and events. The average Facebook user is therefore connected to more than 200 elements on Facebook. If each of these is updated only five times a day, the user could be exposed to more than 1,000 status updates every single day.

If an average user can be exposed to 1,000 updates a day, how can marketers stand out and be seen? How can they attract attention and drive people to notice them?

To break through the clutter on social media, you have to be more strategic than ever about creating content that people want to see. As a business or an individual, if you want to gain attention, you must create content that people want and deliver it in a format that appeals to them. Otherwise, your posts will be filtered out with the noise.

As you start to consider the issue of overwhelming content and the challenge that businesses face to create the right content in the right format, one trend shows up again and again: Images, videos, and other visual content are increasingly what people want to see online.

Overcoming the clutter

Visual social marketing helps marketers overcome the key challenge of social media clutter and noise because visual elements such as images and videos can be processed more quickly than text.

Visual content overcomes the challenge of transcending social media clutter, for a number of reasons:

> ✔ **People process visual content more quickly than text.**
>
> As I mention earlier in this chapter, because our brains process visual content quicker than it processes text, visual content is a more efficient way for people to consume information. In cluttered social networks, where marketers are trying to stand out, it makes sense that images are more likely to be viewed than text.
>
> ✔ **Visual content generates the most interactions.**
>
> On many social networks, images and videos generate more Likes, clicks, and views than do text-only updates. These interactions increase the overall visibility of a post. For example, if you like a photo on Facebook, your friends may also see that photo in their newsfeeds, which makes visual content powerful for marketers — because the content generates more interactions, it also generates more views.
>
> ✔ **Ideas are distilled into the basic points.**
>
> Ideas communicated via images and videos are typically distilled into key points that omit extraneous text. For example, in Figure 1-7, the key ideas of a blog post are displayed directly in an image. The entire blog post or article will likely be significantly longer. Because the use of images to communicate ideas forces marketers to share their ideas more concisely, images helps to overcome the challenge of eliminating clutter.
>
> ✔ **Images catch the eye when you skim information.**
>
> People who are overwhelmed online increasingly skim content to find key information. When you skim content, good images stand out and grab your attention.

Visual content is growing in importance in the cluttered world of social media marketing because it's processed quicker than text, generates more interactions (leading to more visibility), forces marketers to distill their ideas into key points, and draws in users who skim social media content. You can see in Figure 1-8 that even in the LinkedIn newsfeed (the screen a user sees immediately after logging in to LinkedIn), images stand out.

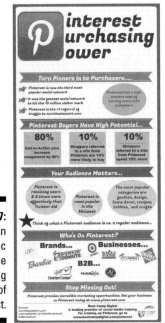

Figure 1-7:
An infographic showing the purchasing power of Pinterest.

Figure 1-8:
Images stand out in the LinkedIn newsfeed.

Adding visual content isn't simply a fad — it's a shift in social media that's based on the need of social networking users to quickly and efficiently process information in an increasingly cluttered world online.

Examining the Key Applications of Visual Social Marketing

Visual social marketing is generally applied in three ways: on social networks, on visual social networks, and to generate more traffic to a website. Though most social networks feature visual content, a visual social network is one that focuses on visual content such as images or videos. For example, Facebook includes visual content such as images and videos, but Instagram, a visual social network, focuses primarily on taking, editing, and sharing images.

Applying images on social networks

Images represent a prime opportunity to connect with customers on all social networks, not just on visual social networks. As described earlier in this chapter, images generate more views, likes, and clicks on most social networks than do text-only posts.

As a social media marketer, your visual strategy should focus on more than visual social networks such as Instagram and Pinterest. Your strategy should extend to all social networks in which you participate.

A solid social media strategy features a variety of content that includes images and videos. Additionally, existing social networks such as Facebook and Twitter are great places to post visual content.

For example, a photo taken on Instagram may also be used as a Facebook post or a Twitter status update. A video created to be shared on YouTube may also make a great post on LinkedIn or a strong blog post.

I describe how to integrate images into your social media strategy for nonvisual social networks in more detail in Part III.

Applying images on visual social networks

A visual social network is a powerful tool for visual social marketing because its primary content is *visual* — images and videos are the primary content that is viewed and shared.

Visual social networks are among the fastest-growing and most frequently discussed networks.

The primary image-focused visual tools that I cover in detail (in Part IV of this book) are described in this list:

- **Infographics:** A graphical representation of data tells a story in long-format images with charts.

- **Instagram** (www.Instagram.com): The more than 100 million users at this site (recently acquired by Facebook) shoot photos from their mobile devices, such as smartphones and tablets.

- **Pinterest** (www.pinterest.com): This online, visual "pinboard" site allows users to create boards based on any topic and to "pin" to them relevant images from their computers or from the web. It is now the third largest social network, and many similar sites have begun to emerge.

- **SlideShare** (www.SlideShare.com): People share PowerPoint presentations at this site, which is growing quickly and generating tremendous numbers of presentation views.

The following list describes the primary video social networks covered in this book:

- **YouTube** (www.YouTube.com): At *the* biggest video-sharing website — and the number-two search engine on the Internet — visitors can share any type of video.

- **Vine** (www.Vine.co): Using this new video sharing application (launched by Twitter), people can share six seconds' worth of short-format videos.

- **Instagram video** (www.Instagram.com): Users can create 15-second videos on Instagram and share them on Instagram or other social networks.

These social networks are all growing quickly and show the importance of visual social marketing.

Applying visual elements on websites

Visual content is vital to driving relevant and targeted traffic to a website. The importance of using images and videos on websites isn't new. What is new is that, as social networks have grown, they have emerged as indispensable places to promote content from websites. Social networks also drive significant amounts of traffic to websites.

As social networks become more visually oriented, visually optimize your website to take advantage of the traffic that can be generated from social networks.

For example, my website, www.BootCampDigital.com, has a free report on how to use Google+ for marketing. The page containing the report originally included *only* the report, and because the report was on the page, I didn't include an image of it.

The problem was that whenever customers read the report and received value from it, they wanted to share the report on Facebook. My site didn't display an image of the report, so whenever the page with the Google+ report was shared, no appropriate image accompanied it.

When I saw a customer share the report, I realized that I needed an image to optimize the report for sharing on Facebook, so an image of the report was created. Now, whenever customers share the report, an image of the report appears as a part of the post, as shown in Figure 1-9.

Figure 1-9: A Google+ report, shared on Facebook.

> Status   Photo / Video   Offer, Event +
>
> Check out our free report on Google+ for marketing.
>
> http://bootcampdigital.com/cmo-briefing-google-for-business-report/
>
> **Business Leader Briefing: Google+ For Business Report**   ×
> http://bootcampdigital.com/cmo-b...
> Social media, Internet Marketing and digital consulting from Boot Camp Digital, Cincinnati Ohio's premiere corporate training provider
>
> Upload Image
>
> Boost Post ▼   Post

After the image was added to the web page featuring the Google+ report, it began to generate more shares across social networks, more traffic, and more downloads.

This simple example shows the importance of incorporating images into your website design and marketing strategy. Images on a web page are increasingly important in generating shares and traffic via social networks. (I cover this topic in more detail in Chapter 2.)

Determining the Copyright Status of Visual Elements

Using visual content such as images and videos in your social media marketing creates a number of concerns about adhering to copyright law. My intent in this section isn't to provide you with a comprehensive legal overview of the countless copyright issues and model release issues that surround the use of visual content online; rather, I hope to provide you with an overall understanding of the issues to be aware of when you're using images and videos online.

Business owners can't simply search for images online and use any images they find. The owner or creator of an image holds the copyright to that image automatically. A business that uses a copyrighted image without permission may end up in legal trouble.

When you search for images to use for social media marketing, be *sure* that you have the proper permission to use the image legally.

You can also purchase the non-exclusive rights to use an image in your marketing to promote your business. Both free and paid sites provide businesses with licenses to use images commercially. Paid image sites generally have better selections, higher quality, and fewer restrictions than the free photography options.

Images and videos: Embedding versus uploading

One thing that blurs the use of copyright on the web is the difference between embedding and uploading an image or a video. Though some debate still exists in this area, in most instances, images and videos may be embedded on a site without violating the copyright, but they cannot be uploaded.

When an image or a video is *embedded* into your website, the source content is hosted on another site but is displayed on your site.

Suppose that someone at www.mashable.com writes an article about Facebook marketing, accompanied by a photo. To add the photo to the website, Mashable uploads the photo, and it is hosted on Mashable's servers. Then a few weeks later, as I'm writing an article about Facebook marketing on my blog at www.BootCampDigital.com/blog, I want to use the Facebook marketing photo from Mashable. I cannot simply download the Mashable photo to my computer and upload it to my blog post. Mashable owns the copyright to the photo it used, and I can't simply reuse the photo, even if I give proper credit. I can, however, embed the photo from Mashable into my blog so that the image is displayed. When a photo or video is embedded, it continues to be hosted on Mashable's servers, and I'm simply displaying its photo on my website.

The difference between embedding the photo and downloading the photo is subtle because, in both cases, the photo is displayed on my website. In downloading and uploading the photo, I'm hosting the image on my web servers and using the copyrighted image for my marketing purposes. If I embed the photo, I'm displaying the photo on my website but not copying, downloading, or reproducing it.

The bottom line: Embedding photos lets you use photos from other websites; however without proper permission, you cannot upload those same images to your website.

Avoiding legal issues when taking your own photos and videos

When you use your own images and videos online, you have to consider a few issues. Because a business's use of images and videos on social media is considered marketing, specific rules apply to the commercial use of images and videos. Consider the items described in this list:

- **Model releases:** When you take a photo of a person (even if that person is an employee or a customer), you may need to secure a *model release* — a form, signed by the person in the image or video, that allows the business to use the content for marketing purposes. A model release isn't required in every situation; however, if you're planning to use images of people, be sure to discuss this issue with your lawyer.

- **Property releases:** A property release may be required for images that include private property. For example, if you plan to create a video to promote your business and the video takes place in a Starbucks store, you may need a property release from Starbucks to show its store. When taking photos and videos on private property, determine whether a property release is important.

- **Trademarked logos or items:** When creating content to use for your business, consider whether your photo or video includes trademarks or logos from other companies. You may have noticed, in certain TV reality shows, that the labels on products are blurred out; that's because the use of other logos or trademarks to promote a business may require special permission. If you're planning to use other business logos or trademarks in your content, check with your lawyer about the potential implications.

✔ **Other copyrighted materials:** When creating your own photos or videos, avoid including other copyrighted materials in your content. For example, if you're creating a video to market your business, do *not* use copyrighted music in it. Whenever you use any content (photos, music, or video footage, for example) that was created by someone else, be sure that you have the appropriate permissions.

Consult an attorney to find out more about how all these legal issues impact your business. This section is intended only to give you an overview of the issues, not to serve as a substitute for legal advice.

Chapter 2

Generating Website Traffic from Visual Social Marketing

In This Chapter

▶ Analyzing how your website is shared across social networks

▶ Optimizing your site for visual assets to generate traffic and drive social sharing

*O*ne significant reason that visual social marketing has become popular is that it has been shown to drive traffic to websites. Many businesses participate in social marketing to drive traffic to their blogs or websites, and compelling website images can translate into more traffic from social networks.

A trend that has emerged across social networks — including Facebook, Twitter, and LinkedIn — is that images are being given more prominence, especially when links to websites are shared. When you *share* a website, you post a link to the website on a social network. For example, if I share a link to the website of a new café that I love, Facebook shows the link to the website and also displays the image from the web page beside the link.

Because images from web pages are shown on social networks, websites *must* have high-quality images to enhance posts and generate more clicks, which leads to more traffic. A click occurs whenever an Internet user clicks the mouse on a link, which opens a page on a website. Clicking links on social networks results in *traffic,* or the number of visitors to a website.

The use of high-quality, highly relevant images is increasingly becoming the key to driving clicks on social networks and traffic to websites. Obviously, most websites have a visually appealing design that includes images and communicates the brand identity and experience of the business. However, these website design images aren't the only ones that are important.

The importance of having images on your website extends far beyond the design appeal of your site. If you want your website or website content to be shared on social media, it must have relevant images that describe the content visually.

Examining How Websites Are Shared Across a Few Popular Social Networks

Websites are shared on social networks for a variety of reasons. People often link to websites when they're sharing their status updates on social networks such as Twitter, Facebook, LinkedIn, Pinterest, and YouTube. For example, I may post on Facebook about a new motorcycle jacket I bought and include a link to the product listing of the jacket at Amazon.com. Or I might read an interesting article about my industry and share a link to it on LinkedIn.

People who share status updates on social networks often include links to websites — a major source of website traffic for many businesses.

Traffic that comes to your website from another site on the Internet is known as *referral* traffic. For example, if I click a link to your website that was shared on Facebook, you would generate referral traffic from Facebook. Similarly, if I conduct a search on Google for your business and click the link to your site in the Google search results, you're generating referral traffic from Google.

Social networks can be major sources of referral traffic for websites. People click links on social networks that direct them to your website.

Referral traffic is linked to visual social marketing because images on web pages are often featured alongside the links that people click. Having powerful images can therefore lead to more clicks from social networks — and to more traffic to your site.

I noticed recently on Facebook that a friend of mine was sharing a blog post from my website. When I looked at the image displayed beside the website information, shown in Figure 2-1, I was surprised to see that it was neither my company's logo nor an image representing the content of the post. It was, instead, a picture of me.

Figure 2-1:
A blog post from Boot Camp Digital, shared on Facebook.

I immediately recognized a potential problem, because the photo displayed beside the link to the blog post didn't accurately represent my brand well. It seemed unlikely that people would click on the link or picture, because the picture didn't match the topic of the post. I immediately updated my website to include a relevant image so that my site could be shared by way of social networks with an appropriate photo.

Highly relevant images accompany all my content on social networks. Whenever I post visually interesting images that represent the content on my website, I generate more traffic to a post than when the image isn't relevant or I don't even post one.

Facebook has made a number of changes recently to increase the prominence of images that are shared with links. When you share a link on Facebook, the link is simply pasted into the Status Update area. Then Facebook scans the website that the link is referencing and prompts the poster to choose the appropriate image to accompany the link, as shown in Figure 2-2.

Figure 2-2:
Sharing
a link on
Facebook.

Notice that Facebook allows the user to choose an image to display beside the link. When the link is shared in the newsfeed, its eye-catching and relevant image is more likely to generate clicks on the link than a link that has no image or an irrelevant image.

To illustrate this difference, consider how images are displayed when I share links to two coffee shops.

When I link to Tim Hortons, as shown in Figure 2-3, I can choose a variety of images, many of which are beautiful pictures of coffee. The appealing image beside the link provides a strong visual representation of Tim Hortons products, and may even drive some viewers to grab an afternoon latté.

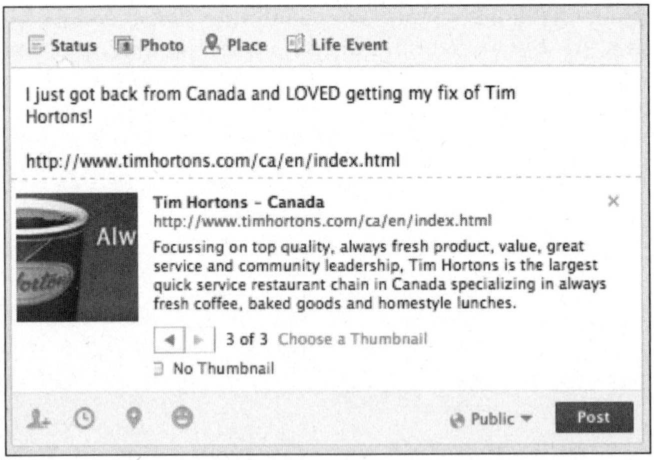

Figure 2-3:
Sharing a
link to Tim
Hortons on
Facebook.

Compare this example to a local coffee shop. In Figure 2-4, I'm sharing a link to my favorite spot. The company's home page shows neither a logo representing the business nor even a picture of coffee. The only images I can share are random pictures of awards that the business has won or a picture of what is presumably a coffee plant.

Figure 2-4:
Sharing
a link to a
local
coffee
shop on
Facebook.

Clearly, the link to Tim Hortons accompanied by a relevant and attractive photo is more likely to generate clicks than an unrelated image from my local coffee shop.

Posting high-quality, relevant, and attractive images on your website makes your links more prominent in the newsfeed and can generate more clicks to your website.

In the Status Update area on Facebook, paste a link to your home page, or to other important pages that people may want to share on your website, and then assess the strength of the images that are displayed.

Like Facebook, Google+ displays images prominently on its site. Figure 2-5 shows how a link that's shared on Google+ also displays a website image to draw attention to the post.

Check out these trends for 2014
http://bootcampdigital.com/3-social-media-trends-you-cant-miss-in-2014-infographic/
3 Social Media Trends You Can't Miss in 2014 [Infographic]
bootcampdigital.com
Remove
To:
Public
+ Add more people
Share
Cancel

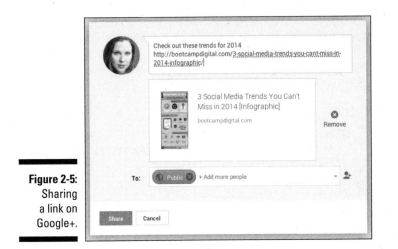

Figure 2-5: Sharing a link on Google+.

Similar to Facebook and Google+, posts on LinkedIn that link to a website pull an image from the website to display next to the post, as shown in Figure 2-6.

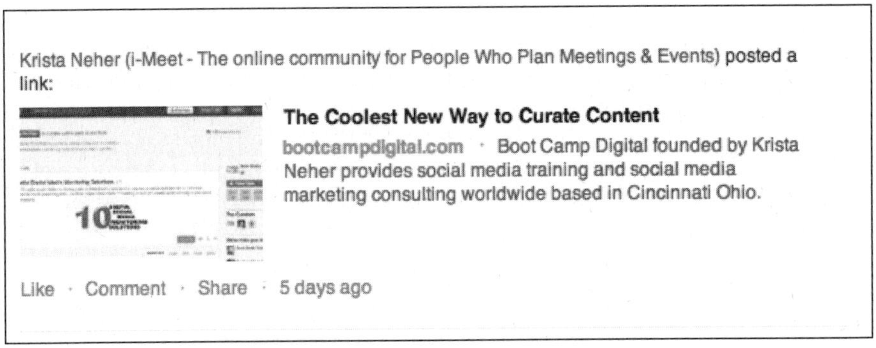

Krista Neher (i-Meet - The online community for People Who Plan Meetings & Events) posted a link:
The Coolest New Way to Curate Content
bootcampdigital.com · Boot Camp Digital founded by Krista Neher provides social media training and social media marketing consulting worldwide based in Cincinnati Ohio.
Like · Comment · Share · 5 days ago

Figure 2-6: Sharing a link on LinkedIn.

Optimizing your website to generate traffic from Pinterest

Pinterest deserves special attention in a discussion of how to generate website traffic from images. At Pinterest, users can create pinboards composed of pins of images that they share or from web pages. (I describe Pinterest in more detail in Chapter 10.)

Pinterest sends large amounts of referral traffic to websites, based primarily on the images on the site. Pinterest was reported to be the number-one source of referral traffic to MarthaStewart.com in 2012 and 2013, and many other e-commerce websites have generated sales directly from Pinterest.

For example, I may create a pin of a pair of boots that I spotted for sale on Amazon. Pinterest displays the image I selected of the boots from the web page, as shown in Figure 2-7.

Figure 2-7: Sharing a link from Amazon on Pinterest.

People who follow me on Pinterest, or who are searching for boots on Pinterest, may come across the boots that I pinned. Someone who wants to learn more about them, and see where I found them, can click on the image of the boots to open the page on Amazon.com where they can buy them.

Having interesting, relevant, eye-catching images on your site is important if you want to generate traffic to your site from Pinterest.

Creating pinnable images

One quality that makes links to websites on Pinterest different from links on other social networks is that Pinterest focuses almost exclusively on images. In Figure 2-6, you can see that LinkedIn pulls in the image but also pulls in some text from the website so that the image isn't the only descriptive information that's displayed.

When you compare Figures 2-6 and 2-7, you can see that the main image, the URL, and the description I write are the only pieces of content that are displayed with the pin.

For an image to be *pinnable* on Pinterest, it must tell a story all by itself. It must communicate, on its own, the basic information about the link being shared.

The prominence of images on Pinterest has changed the way many businesses think about the images on their websites, especially in blog posts. Figure 2-8 shows a pin of a blog post that recently appeared on my website, Boot Camp Digital. The image associated with the blog post doesn't relate only to the content; the image — on its own — tells you exactly what the post is about.

Figure 2-8:
This
pinnable
image
supports a
blog post on
Pinterest.

Pinnable images are not only important for blog posts but also relevant for any page on your website that may be shared on Pinterest. Figure 2-9 shows a pin of a free report from my site.

Figure 2-9:
This
pinnable
image
supports
a free
report at
Boot Camp
Digital.

Before I optimized this page for Pinterest, the page contained only a form to sign up for the free report. I noticed that my customers were pinning the report — but that a blank space was displayed instead of an image, because this page on my site didn't contain an image.

Posting pinnable images can increase the number of people who share your content on Pinterest and generate more clicks and traffic to your site. (Using pinnable images on my site has certainly increased the traffic from Pinterest.)

Viewing content that's pinned from your website

On Pinterest, you can see the content that has been pinned from your website, or from any other website. I frequently look at the appropriate page to see the content from my site that's popular on Pinterest, and to ensure that all my pages are optimized with images to generate traffic from Pinterest.

Go to www.Pinterest.com/source/*yourdomain.com* to see the content from your website that has been pinned to Pinterest. (Replace *yourdomain.com* with the website information from any domain that you want to view.)

In the earlier examples where I link to two coffee shops (refer to Figures 2-3 and 2-4), you can see how the presence of images on your website can change the visual impact when pages from your site are pinned on Pinterest.

In Figure 2-10, the content has been pinned from TimHortons.com. As you can see, a wide variety of images represent the brand. For example, pins referencing specific products, such as the Iced Capp Supreme, can use images of the actual product. The relevant and attractive images are likely to generate more shares on social networks, clicks on the images, and lead to more traffic. Also, because the images look appealing, they increase awareness of Tim Hortons and its products.

Figure 2-10:
Content from Tim Hortons that has been shared on Pinterest.

When you compare the content from Tim Hortons with the content from my local coffee shop (Coffee Emporium in Cincinnati), shown in Figure 2-11, the difference becomes clear. Because my shop uses images sparsely on its website, people who want to pin them on Pinterest have only a few images to choose from.

Figure 2-11:
Content
from a local
coffee shop
that has
been shared
on Pinterest.

Having images on your website that describe the content that people want to share, as in the Tim Hortons example, generates more traffic to your site. Every page, especially product pages, should have visual images that make it easy for people to share their love of your products on Pinterest.

Examining how search engines display images and videos

Images and video on your website are also relevant to generating traffic from search engines. Similar to social networks, search engines such as Google often display images and videos from websites beside links to the sites.

Figure 2-12 shows a search engine result where a video is present on the web page. As you can see, having a video on your website increases the visual appeal of your listing in search engine results, because a *thumbnail* (miniature) image of the video is displayed directly in the search engine results.

Figure 2-12:
How a video
on a
website
appears
in Google
search
results.

————— Video thumbnail

Add video to your website to increase its visibility in search engines and drive more search engine traffic.

For a video link to appear in the Google search engine results, it must be coded correctly.

Preparing a Website to Generate Traffic from Visual Social Marketing

Across social networks and even across search engines visual social marketing can grow your business. Photos and videos can help generate additional views of your content and traffic to your website. To take advantage of this opportunity, you must ensure that your website includes the right visual content to promote your business.

Assessing the pages on your site that may be shared

The first step in preparing your website to generate traffic from visual social marketing is to assess the pages on your site that may be shared — and that therefore require pinnable images.

An easy way to see the image options that are available for any page on your website is simply to share that web page on a social network such as Facebook or Pinterest. Both sites let you see all the images that you can select when sharing a link to a web page.

Assess the pages on your website to determine whether you already have appropriate images or need to produce some, and then create a list of all pages that require images, as described in the following steps:

1. **Determine the images you need for your site's home page.**

   On most websites, the home page is the one that's most often shared and referred to. The home page is the introductory page of a website, typically it is the primary overview page of the site. Ensure that your home page has at least two workable sharing options. On your company's home page, place an up-to-date image of the company's logo and a visually appealing image that describes the company's products.

   For example, Starbucks has an image of its logo and a picture of a beautiful cup of coffee or latté. This way, both scenarios have a relevant image where a user may be referring to the business (for example, "Starbucks is great") or the product ("I'm addicted to the frappuccino at Starbucks").

2. **Find the pages that have already been shared.**

   Look at the pages on your site that are already generating social shares. If you have access to *website analytics,* which is software that provides statistics about your website, you should easily be able to see when pages on your website are generating traffic from social media referrals. These pages should be the next ones you work on, after your home page.

   Depending on the nature of your business, these pages may be product or service pages, informational pages, blog posts, or the About page.

   Because these pages already generate shares on social media, improving them should also improve the results from the social media sharing that is already happening.

   To see which pages of your site are being shared on Pinterest, go to `www.Pinterest.com/source/`*yourdomainname.com* (and replace the italicized characters with your domain name). You can see any content from your website that has been pinned to Pinterest. Other social networks (such as Facebook, LinkedIn, Twitter, and Google+) have no easy way for you to view the content that has been shared from your site.

3. **Inventory the remaining pages.**

   When you have listed the high-priority pages that are already being shared, create an inventory of all existing content on your site that requires images.

4. (Optional) Build a plan for future pages.

As you're assessing your website for images, you can also build a plan to generate images for pages that don't yet exist on your site. For example, the employees at Boot Camp Digital have a blog — and a plan for how to generate images for all our blog posts. A client we work with runs a variety of annual events, so it has a plan to generate images for the event pages that will be posted later in the year. Build relevant images into your strategy for your site.

Generating images for website pages

When you create images for the pages on your website, the images you add should enhance social sharing, not necessarily enhance the appearance of the page.

For example, a blog post on your website may feature a video in which you share tips for search engine optimization. The video is the content, so from the perspective of the design of the blog post, you wouldn't normally include an image. The problem is that when you share the blog post on Facebook, an irrelevant photo from the sidebar of the page is shown with the blog post.

To fix this problem, you must add an image of the video to display on Facebook beside the link. Be creative to come up with appropriate images for various pages.

When you create images for your website, create pinnable images. The more relevant the image is to the content, the more likely the image is to generate clicks to your site. For example, if you write a blog post describing ten tools to edit images and you include an image of a toolbox, it isn't directly related to the topic. Instead, you may start with the toolbox picture and then add text to it, such as *Ten Tools to Edit Images,* to make the image more relevant to the content.

When you add images to your website, strike a balance between adding the image to enhance social sharing and adding it to maintain an attractive website. You must continually balance these two objectives and determine what best fits your business.

Chapter 3

Developing a Visual Social Marketing Plan

As in any form of marketing, having a plan is crucial to the ultimate success of your marketing efforts. While working with thousands of businesses on their social media marketing strategies over the past few years, I've recognized one huge problem that many social media marketers face: They lack a clear plan of action.

In visual social marketing, having a plan for success is vital, especially because generating visual content may involve significant lead times, production times, and even production costs.

To create a solid visual social marketing plan, start by exploring the images that people are creating and sharing in your industry or business area. Then define your marketing objectives and the target audience so that you can approach visual social marketing strategically. When the objectives of your strategy are clear, creating and executing a visual content strategy is the next step — followed by measuring and adjusting it.

Many businesses aren't successful in their visual marketing efforts because they find that they have invested significant resources but aren't entirely sure why they're creating visual assets or what marketing results they hope to achieve.

This chapter shows you how to build a visual social marketing plan that gets results.

Researching Your Category or Industry

The first step in building a visual social marketing plan, as shown in Figure 3-1, is to understand the landscape and assess the images that are garnering results in your category or industry. This combination of listening, looking, and observing is the first step because you have the opportunity to learn from others before jumping in.

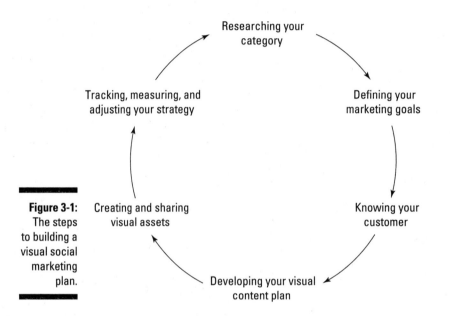

Figure 3-1: The steps to building a visual social marketing plan.

(Diagram, clockwise cycle): Researching your category → Defining your marketing goals → Knowing your customer → Developing your visual content plan → Creating and sharing visual assets → Tracking, measuring, and adjusting your strategy → (back to Researching your category)

Some of the companies that I work with, for example, spend months listening and observing before developing a plan.

The objective of the research step is to generate ideas and inspiration, to understand the content that generates shares and likes, and to assess the strategies used by others in your industry.

To get started, look for visual content in your category or industry. Consider searching for terms related to

- ✔ Your specific business or brand
- ✔ The category your product is in
- ✔ The industry you participate in
- ✔ The content that your competitors are posting

✔ The content that other businesses in your industry are posting

✔ Posts from leading businesses that want to reach the same target audience as you

You can also search in a number of different places for images and visual elements. On social networks such as Facebook, Google+, Pinterest, Instagram, and YouTube, search for both images and videos in general, but also search for accounts from competitors or other businesses in your industry or category.

Search for the topics I just mentioned on a variety of different visually oriented sites, such as in this list, to generate a wide range of ideas and inspiration:

✔ Facebook pages, image, and video search (`www.facebook.com`)

✔ Google Images search (`http://images.google.com`)

✔ Google+ page, image, and video search (`plus.google.com`)

✔ Instagram accounts, pictures, and videos (accessed from the Instagram mobile application)

✔ Pins on Pinterest that originated from your site (`www.pinterest.com/source/`*yourdomain.com*— replace *yourdomain.com* with the URL of your website)

✔ Pinterest search for pins, boards, and users (`www.pinterest.com`)

✔ SlideShare accounts and presentations (`www.slideshare.com`)

✔ YouTube accounts and videos (`www.youtube.com`)

As you create your content plan, refer to the best, most popular, and most inspirational images to help guide your strategy. During this stage, take notes or collect your ideas online. For example, you might create your own pin board on Pinterest with inspiration and ideas.

Defining Your Marketing Goals

After you've had a chance to discover how businesses are generating results from visual social marketing, the next step is to think about your marketing objectives and the goals you want to achieve. Consider your marketing goals and objectives so that you can build a strategic plan to generate results that help grow your business.

Define your marketing goals up front so that you can justify why you're allocating time, money, and other resources to visual social marketing. Your marketing goals for participating in visual social marketing may match your broader marketing goals or social media goals, or they may be specific to your strategies on social media.

Link to broader marketing goals

The first step in mapping out your marketing goals from visual social marketing is to look at your broader marketing goals or your social media marketing goals. For example, a yogurt company that wants to encourage people to try a new product might build a visual social marketing strategy that focuses on highlighting the specific new product.

Take a moment to evaluate your marketing and social media marketing goals, and whether your visual social marketing strategy can help to achieve those objectives. Depending on how specific your visual social marketing strategy is, you may have different objectives for each visual marketing channel.

You don't have to have a single objective or goal for all your visual marketing efforts. For example, your objective on Pinterest may be to drive traffic to your website; however, the focus of your efforts on Instagram may be to generate brand awareness. The goal of creating an infographic may be to generate links to your website to promote search engine optimization.

These are some of the most common objectives for participating in visual social marketing:

- ✔ Build brand awareness
- ✔ Attract website traffic
- ✔ Grow sales
- ✔ Engage customers
- ✔ Generate feedback

Build brand awareness

One common reason for participating in visual social marketing is to build *brand awareness* — the degree to which people are aware of your brand or business.

Brand awareness is a common marketing objective because people are more likely to choose businesses that they're aware of than ones they've never heard of. For example, in a grocery store a consumer is more likely to buy a laundry detergent that he has seen advertised on television over one that he's seeing for the first time. Whether you're choosing laundry detergent, an accountant, an IT firm, or a restaurant for lunch, you're more likely to do business with people and brands that you've already heard of.

Awareness isn't built by a simple single interaction with a business or brand. Think about a billboard you may have driven past today. Unless you travel the same route every day, you probably don't even recall seeing the billboard. To build awareness and familiarity, people typically have to be exposed to a brand or business more than once.

The goal of building brand awareness is therefore to expose potential customers to your brand repeatedly over time.

Visual social marketing is a powerful tool for awareness, especially if your customers are already using visually oriented social sites. For example, if my customers are on Pinterest, I can participate there with the objective of being seen by my customers (or future customers) to generate awareness.

Additionally, on social networks such as Facebook, Google+, LinkedIn, and Twitter, visual elements are generating increasingly more views and interactions, so a visual strategy for these networks can also lead to more awareness.

Attract website traffic

Chapter 2 shows you how images on websites can lead to increased traffic from social networks. If your website has relevant content that's sharable across social networks, the objective of generating website traffic from visual social marketing makes sense for your marketing plan.

The key to success with this strategy is that your website must have content that people are interested in sharing on their social networks. For example, I was asked to review the marketing strategy of a hospital that's using visual social marketing. Its objective was to generate traffic to the website, which had neither a blog nor other resources. As a result, the hospital had nothing to share on social media. The social marketing plan was failing at helping the hospital reach the objective of driving traffic to the website, because it wasn't the right objective to begin with.

For traffic generation to become a marketing objective, your website must have content that people want to share on social media. Adding visual elements to a website that has no interesting content doesn't generate traffic from social media.

Grow sales

Visual social marketing has been shown to generate sales, especially for businesses that sell products online. Because most products are visually oriented (and people like to look at them), they fit most naturally the objective of growing sales by way of visual marketing.

Pinterest in particular has been demonstrated to drive traffic and sales to e-commerce sites. Sephora, a company that sells makeup and beauty products (at www.sephora.com), found that its Pinterest followers spent 15 times more money than their Facebook fans.

The Sephora boards on Pinterest are shown in Figure 3-2. The prominence of visual elements on Pinterest is clearly a part of the increase in sales. The Pinterest boards present ideas to consumers visually to show what they can do with the products sold at Sephora, so it's no surprise that the company is effective in driving sales.

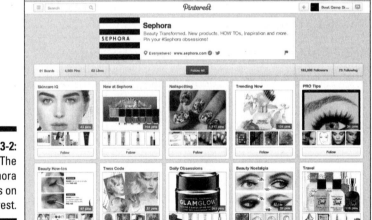

Figure 3-2:
The Sephora boards on Pinterest.

User-generated content, where customers and website users generate visual elements, has also been shown to increase sales. Lululemon, a retailer of high-end yoga apparel at www.lululemon.com, found that adding images from its customers to its home page increased the company's sales. Lululemon asked customers to share their workout photos with the hashtag #TheSweatLife. The best-looking photos were shared on the Lululemon home page, as shown in Figure 3-3.

Figure 3-3:
Photos tagged with #The SweatLife at Lululemon.

In a beta test, Lululemon saw a 5 to 7 percent increase in its conversion rate when it added user-generated images to its website. The *conversion rate* is the percentage of people who have visited the website and who ultimately purchased an item. An increase in the conversion rate means that a higher percentage of website visitors were converted into customers. Potential customers who were able to see real people wearing the clothes they were considering buying were more likely to buy.

The examples of Sephora and Lululemon show how exposure to visual social marketing can increase web sales.

Engage customers

Adding visual elements to your site can be a powerful way to engage customers with your brand or business. Customers who are engaged are actively participating with your business on social media. Customers typically engage with brands that they have a strong connection to, so driving engagement has the benefit of increasing brand affinity.

On social networks such as Facebook, images generate more engagements and interactions (such as likes, comments, and clicks) than other types of content.

Additionally, user-generated visual content also drives engagement. Many businesses have run small contests asking customers to share photos or videos for an opportunity to win a prize. For example, whenever reps from

Koyal Wholesale, a wholesale reseller of wedding supplies, attend a trade show, they post images on Instagram asking their customers whether items are "hot or not." They also ask "yay or nay," as shown in Figure 3-4, where they ask Instagram followers for their thoughts on a new product. (The post shown in the figure generated 187 likes and 19 comments.)

Figure 3-4: Koyal Wholesale is driving engagement on Instagram.

This process engages customers in the process of choosing items that the company carries. Customers who feel that they're a part of the process and who are engaged with the business are more likely to become loyal customers.

Knowing Your Customers

After you define your marketing goals, identifying the target audience and knowing your customers are the next steps in building a visual social marketing plan. Knowing your customers is important in understanding the type of content that appeals to your specific audience.

Sharpie, a brand that makes permanent markers, is targeting younger demographics with its visual marketing strategy. As you can see in Figure 3-5, the Sharpie Instagram account includes images that are likely to resonate with teens.

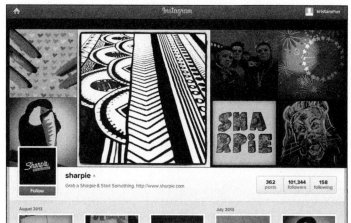

Figure 3-5:
The Sharpie
Instagram
account.

Your visual content strategy and execution should match the target audience you want to connect with. In the listening stage (the first step in a visual social marketing plan), be sure to look at brands and businesses that appeal to your target audience to get a feel for what they like.

Developing Your Visual Content Plan

The goal of an image content strategy is to clearly define what will be posted, when, and by whom. Rather than haphazardly share content when it comes to mind, having a solid content plan ensures that the right mix of content is shared at the right time. The goal is to be sure that content is created as needed and that the types of content match the strategic marketing objectives.

Depending on the size and complexity of your organization and the visual social networks that you participate in, your visual content plan may be more or less complex.

Consider these key elements in any content plan:

- ✓ The type of content
- ✓ The theme or category of the content
- ✓ Who will create the content
- ✓ When the content will be created

✔ Which approvals are required before sharing content

✔ When the content will be shared

✔ Where the content will be shared initially

✔ Where the content will be syndicated

✔ Goals for the content

A typical content plan for visual marketing connects to, or is included in, a social media content plan, and it often takes the form of a spreadsheet in Microsoft Excel.

The plan helps keep you on track, especially if you need to purchase, acquire, or create visual content, which can eat up more time than the schedule allows. To be active in any social network, you should post regularly. The content plan is the key to ensuring that you post regularly and that you post content supporting your marketing plan.

Evaluating the quality of the content you create

When getting started with visual content, many businesses struggle to determine the quality level that's required for the content they create. There's no single answer to the correct quality level of visual content.

The quality level of the content depends on these factors — consider these factors in your business to determine the necessary quality level in your visual marketing production:

✔ **The size of your business:** This statement may surprise you, but consumers have different expectations of media quality that originates from companies of different sizes. Consider what you would expect in terms of quality levels of media from a large fast-food chain versus a small restaurant. Larger businesses should generally have higher-quality content.

✔ **The type of business:** People have different expectations for different types of businesses. For example, a law firm is expected to share more professional-looking content than a bakery. Consider the quality level that consumers expect from a business such as yours.

✔ **Where the content will be used:** The production quality of the content you create should also be based on where the content will be used. For example, a video that will be shared on Facebook or a blog can have a lower-quality production value than a video on the home page of a business website. Images on web pages are also usually of a higher quality than images used on a blog post or for a Facebook update.

- ✔ **The objective of the content:** Depending on the purpose of the content, amateur content may be more effective than professionally produced content. For example a restaurant that wants to share the daily special on Facebook may get better results from an amateur photo that looks realistic than a professional photo that looks perfectly produced.

Let your competitors serve as benchmarks. You may also want to explore how similar companies manage their production levels.

Recognizing resources and constraints

As you formulate your content plan, list the resources and constraints that may limit your ability to execute the plan. The plan should be reasonable to achieve.

The constraints described in this list can affect your ability to execute a visual marketing plan:

- ✔ **Budget:** If your plan involves purchasing images or videos, hiring professionals, or acquiring equipment, first evaluate your budget for creating visual assets.

- ✔ **Time:** Creating visual assets can be quite time consuming. Even if you're hiring a professional, determining the scope and the creation of visual assets can take a significant amount of time. First decide how much time you have, and then prioritize the activities that are most likely to generate the best results.

- ✔ **Equipment:** If you're considering the do-it-yourself (DIY) approach, assess the equipment that's required in order to achieve the quality level you need. Some businesses find that they can produce photos of good quality on Instagram by using only an iPhone, for example, whereas others use a professional-grade camera. When recording video, you must consider many factors, including video, audio, lighting, and background.

Address any constraints before finalizing your visual marketing content plan, because they can affect your level of achievement.

Choosing between do-it-yourself and hiring a professional

One of the most common areas of questioning about visual social marketing is the quality level that's required of the content that's shared. For example, does a video need to be created by a professional? How professional? Does the video require professional equipment? Can I create it myself?

Choosing the DIY method over hiring a professional depends largely on the level of quality you want, the number of resources available, and the frequency with which you plan to create visual content. If you have more time than money and you plan to create videos regularly, you may more efficiently purchase equipment and record videos yourself. Alternatively, if you have more money than time and you're creating only a few videos, hiring a professional may be more appropriate.

Consider using a combination of creating your own visual content and hiring a professional. Often, a mix of high-quality production content and amateur content that looks more realistic is effective.

Figure 3-6 shows a sample from the Starbucks page on Facebook. Posts on the page include both amateur and professional photos.

Figure 3-6:
Professional and amateur photos on the Starbucks page.

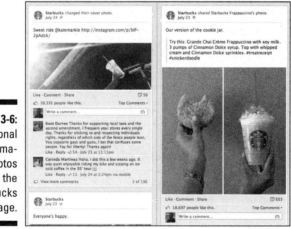

Selecting the right image-oriented social networks

When evaluating your resources and content plan, you may find that you lack the resources to participate in all the visual social networks. Prioritize your social networks so that you have sufficient resources to be successful.

When deciding which social networks to focus on, consider these factors:

- **Where your audience is:** You may have heard the expression "Fish where the fish are." The same advice applies to social media sites: Spend your time on the social networks where your target audience is spending their time. To be sure that you can reach enough people to justify your investment, calculate how many of the people in your target audience are using the social network.

- **A sufficient level of investment for success:** Certain social networks require that you spend a lot of time and effort to be successful, whereas others may require smaller time investments. Evaluate the resources required in order to be successful in a given social network, and weigh your findings against the possible benefits.

- **Marketing opportunities:** Certain social networks may seem to be perfect opportunities, but their terms of service or restrictions don't provide many opportunities for marketers to participate. Understand the restrictions or requirements for businesses to participate to be sure that you can achieve the result you want from social media.

- **Potential benefits:** Finally, appraise the potential benefits that you can generate from a social network. Determine what you can reasonably hope to achieve if all goes well. Weigh the benefits of participating in the social network against the cost to participate.

Assessing Your Visual Inventory

After you construct a visual marketing strategy and decide which social networks to participate in, the next step is to assess your visual inventory. I cover this topic in more detail in Chapter 4, but here's the bottom line: Assess the visual elements that you have access to, and compare them to the ones you require in order to execute your plan.

Depending on the size of your organization, this task may be simple or quite complex. Larger organizations may have multiple people with different types of images throughout the organization — simply taking inventory of the images can be a daunting task. On the other hand, in a small business, all the images may exist on a single computer. As you embark on visual social marketing, creating a central bank or library with clearly tagged and labeled visual content is important to being able to easily access and use your images.

Creating and Sharing Visual Assets

After building your plan and determining the images that you have access to, it's time to execute the plan. This step involves using best practices to implement your content plan. The majority of this book focuses on how to execute a visual social marketing plan across social networks.

When you create visual assets, you create the images and videos that are necessary for your visual social marketing plan. After you know what your visual content plan involves, you must create the visual assets to execute the plan. In a small business, this task can be as simple as taking photos; in a larger organization, the task might involve coordinating with an agency.

After the visual assets are created, you can post and share them online by way of social networks. Posting visual content on your website, and on the other social networks that your business participates in, is how you execute your visual social marketing strategy.

In later chapters in this book, I show you how to share images on social networks, including best practices.

Tracking, Measuring, and Adjusting Your Strategy

The final step in a visual social marketing plan is to track, measure, and adjust the strategy and execution. As you begin to implement your plan, tracking and measuring are important to increase your success. Identifying which parts of the plan are successful and which aren't allows you to adjust to continuously improve your results.

The visual social marketing plan in this section is vital to your ability to track and measure your success. Knowing what you want to achieve by first defining clear marketing objectives is necessary in order to determine whether you're successful after you begin to execute.

To effectively measure your visual marketing efforts, follow these steps:

1. Define your marketing strategies.

   Start by defining your marketing strategies and recognizing what you want to achieve. Knowing your goals and objectives is the first step.

2. Translate your marketing strategies into metrics.

   After you know what you want to achieve, the next step is to define the metrics that relate to your marketing strategies. For example, if your goal is to build awareness, your metrics may include number of views of a post. If your goal is to generate website traffic, the metrics may include referrals from visual social networks. The metrics you choose should be

   • Specific

   • Able to link back to your marketing strategies

   • Easy to attain

3. Set goals or targets.

   After you define the metrics, set your goals or objectives for each one. A goal can be a specific number or simply an improvement versus a current state.

4. Track the metrics.

   Set up documents to track progress over time.

5. Measure your success.

   Based on your goals and objectives, periodically measure whether you're achieving your objectives.

6. Analyze the results.

   Measuring isn't enough — turn the metrics into meaningful information by analyzing the results. Look for trends, and seek to understand the causes of the results.

7. Improve; rinse and repeat.

   Based on the results you discover in the analysis stage, look for opportunities to improve results over time. Then reevaluate your marketing objectives and begin at Step 1 again.

Assessing your results on the fly

One advantage that social media has over other types of marketing is that marketers have access to real-time information about the effectiveness of their marketing efforts. Most social networks provide businesses with analytics that let them see the number of views, clicks, and interactions generated by their content.

Analyze these basic factors as you implement your visual marketing strategy to determine what works and what doesn't:

- ✔ **Which posts do well and why:** Start by looking at the posts that are most effective at achieving the results you want. These may be the posts that generate the most views, likes, interactions, clicks, or traffic, depending on your specific marketing objectives. Determine what they have in common, and look to replicate your successes.

- ✔ **Which posts do poorly and why:** Evaluating posts that are underperforming is also valuable. Look for similarities in the posts that don't do well, and try to find opportunities to improve these posts — or simply cut them from your plan.

- ✔ **Which aspects you haven't considered:** Sometimes social media has unintended effects. For example, your initial marketing objective may have been to generate awareness, but you may find that you're driving engagement instead. Just because you're generating value that wasn't a part of the initial strategy doesn't mean that it isn't valuable. If you're achieving results that didn't match the initial strategy, you may still want to consider whether they're adding value.

Examine your analytics regularly to continuously optimize your execution. Each visual social network has different data available, so depending on which networks you participate in, you may have access to more or less data.

Building in testing

The reality of all social marketing is that a lot of testing and learning is required. Every business is unique, and sometimes strategies that work for one business don't work for another. Testing and learning are important steps in improving your visual social marketing results.

One way to continuously improve the results you achieve from visual social marketing is to continually test to find what works and what doesn't work. Plan to build testing into your visual marketing strategy, and track the results so that you can decide whether a particular tool or tactic is worth the investment.

If you have a strategy that you aren't sure about yet, creating a small test can be a good way to discover whether a particular visual marketing tool is right for you. For example, if you're unsure about using *infographics* (long-format images that visualize data) in your visual marketing strategy, start by creating one where you can test the results.

To build a test, follow these general steps:

1. Decide what you want to test.

   Start by determining what you want to test. You can test a strategy or a tactical implementation. For example, you may test to see whether Instagram is a strategic fit for your organization or whether a particular type of image works on Instagram.

2. Determine the metrics of success.

   If success is to be measured, it must be defined up front. Define the metrics that you will use as well as the goals you're hoping to achieve. Metrics can be both qualitative and quantitative, but they must be able to be measured.

3. Execute the test.

   Carry out the test and implement the element of your visual marketing strategy that you're testing. Use best practices to the best of your abilities to optimize the probability of success.

4. Analyze the results.

   You can complete this step during the test or after the test, depending on your metrics. Evaluate the results of the test based on the metrics you defined initially.

5. Draw informed conclusions.

   After you analyze the results, the next step is to determine what they mean. Was the test a success or a failure, for example? Did you meet your objectives? Did you deliver a positive return on your investment or improve its results?

When you assess the results of a test, be sure to look at all aspects of it to fully understand whether it was a success or a failure. For example, you may test how to create an infographic to decide whether that element should be a part of your marketing strategy. If the infographic fails to deliver the result you want, the cause might be that the strategy — or even the specific infographic you created — isn't right. Fully analyze the data you collect, and examine the results in-depth so that you make the correct conclusions.

Part II
Putting Together a Visual Social Media Strategy

Find Creative Ways to Get Great Photos to Market Your Business at www.dummies.com/extras/visualsocialmarketing.

In this part . . .

- ✔ Steps to building your visual social marketing plan.
- ✔ Understanding how visual content can meet your marketing objectives
- ✔ How to create content for visual social marketing
- ✔ Tools, tips, and tricks to creating visual content for your business

Chapter 4

Acquiring and Organizing Visual Assets

*A*fter you have a plan in place, the next step is to create the content for visual social marketing. Before diving into the technical aspects of using tools to create images (which I cover in Chapter 5), I show you where to look for images and videos and how to build a content library, and I explain creative ways in which businesses are creating visuals.

When you contemplate how to acquire visual assets, creating them yourself isn't the only option — you can instead borrow a number of creative strategies that other businesses are using with employees and customers to help build their inventories of visual assets. In addition, you can hire professional photographers or purchase images from photography websites.

After you have a plan to acquire the visual assets you need, you have to get organized. Many businesses have tons of photos and video footage that they can't locate or that they would have to spend tens of hours sorting to even begin to understand the scope of the content.

In this chapter, I show you resources you can use to acquire images, and I describe how to create and organize an image library so that you can find your assets when you need them.

Searching Your Resources for Visual Assets

The key to a successful visual social marketing strategy is, of course, the use of visual assets. Visual social marketing involves marketing your business via social networks, with visual assets. Many businesses struggle with visual social marketing because they can't find visual content to use on social networks. This section shows you how to assess the visual content that you already own and how to acquire new content.

Taking inventory of existing visual elements

Start by assessing the images you already have, and then build a plan to generate the images you need. When you create a visual marketing content plan (which I cover in Chapter 3), you should end up with a list of the visual assets you need to create.

Conduct an inventory of all the visual assets you already own, and organize them into a visual library. (See the later section "Building a Visual Library.") This strategy can help you easily find the visual resources you want.

Ask others in your organization to supply any images you might not be aware of. Many businesses I've worked with have discovered huge image libraries in their computer archives that they weren't aware of.

After you organize the images you already have, the next step is to evaluate your options and resources to acquire the images you need, as described in the following section.

Shooting photos and videos

The natural starting point for generating new visual assets is often to take photos and videos that can be used in visual social marketing.

To get started, you don't need professional-level equipment — start with the equipment you already have. You might be surprised at the high-quality images and videos you can take, even by using a typical smartphone.

If you have no equipment, you can borrow some — or start with a simple entry-level digital camera.

Look for opportunities to take photos in the course of your business activities. Whether you own a small business or you work for a large organization, you have countless opportunities to take photos that can be used in your visual social marketing efforts.

Consider using the types of settings described in the following list as photo opportunities to help your business get started:

- ✔ **Workplace:** Take photos or videos of the workplace, focusing on the intriguing or unique aspects that people might find interesting. Encourage your team or employees to get involved.

- ✔ **Product:** If you have a product-oriented business, take photos and videos of your product in its natural environment. People like to see real-life photos taken by real people. Show customers what they can expect, by displaying simple photos of your product in action.

- ✔ **Event:** Attending — or even hosting — an industry event is an opportunity to collect visual assets. You can generate them from training events, meetings, or even community events that you attend.

- ✔ **Customer:** Images and videos of your customers can be quite compelling. Record video testimonials or create pictures or videos of your customers using your product or service.

- ✔ **Employee:** Showing the real people who are working hard to provide a product or a service can also be quite compelling.

   Request permission from employees or coworkers before recording them.

- ✔ **Other interesting and related elements:** Find opportunities to build visual displays of interesting information that's related to your business, such as your neighborhood, suppliers, favorite books, or anything else that may interest your target audience.

Social media isn't about sharing everything — it's about sharing the *most interesting* information.

In addition to getting started by shooting videos and photos, you can start experimenting with creating images and videos based on text or illustrations, without live footage. For example, in Figure 4-1 and Figure 4-2, you can see images I created — in fewer than five minutes — by using a mobile application. (In Chapter 5, I show you the tools I use to create images like these.)

Figure 4-1:
A statistic, written in text.

Figure 4-2:
Supporting a page with a job posting.

Embrace the simple ways in which you can easily begin to build an image library yourself, by quickly taking or creating images that can be reused repeatedly.

Employees

Collecting photos and videos taken by employees can be a quick and easy way to build a visual library, which is covered later in this chapter. Because employees continually interact with your business and its customers, they're helpful as resources for images.

To generate images from employees, try these strategies:

- ✔ **Ask them to gather any existing visual elements** the company can use. Many businesses are surprised to find how many images and videos their employees have already taken.

- ✔ **Ask them to create visual elements.** Employees on the ground floor who interact with customers and products can be powerful resources. Ask employees to share their visual assets, and give them specific examples of the types you're looking for.

- ✔ **Run a photo contest.** Sometimes you get better results by adding a little incentive. I worked with a furniture company that was struggling to find compelling images for its Facebook page, so it ran a photo contest for employees in which the employee with the best photo at the end of the month was awarded a $200 prize. The store generated more than 500 interesting and compelling images to be used in its visual social marketing.

When asking others to produce and share visual assets, provide guidelines and inspiration. Let them know the types of visuals that will be helpful, and encourage them to be creative.

If you're asking employees to share visual elements, they *must* follow all copyright and legal guidelines. Also, as a business, you must have permission from employees to use their images in your marketing efforts, or else you may violate copyright and privacy laws.

Customers

More and more businesses are using their customers to support their visual social marketing strategies. Harnessing the creativity and passion of your customers is a useful way to generate a lot of compelling visual content for social marketing.

Businesses of all types and sizes actively look to their customers to create photos and videos that can be used online for marketing purposes. Here are some ways to generate photos from customers:

- ✔ **Search online for images taken by customers.** Many businesses are surprised to find that their customers are already shooting and sharing images and videos. Look on social networks such as Facebook, Instagram, and Pinterest for pictures that your customers may already be sharing. Or search for the name of your business at Google Images (`http://images.google.com`) or a similar search page.

Figure 4-3 shows a search at Google Images for one of my favorite coffeehouses, Coffee Emporium Cincinnati, that results in a wide variety of beautiful images. If you find images or videos that you're interested in using, contact the owner and request permission.

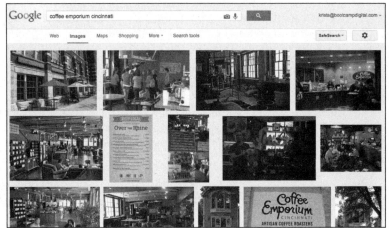

Figure 4-3: Search results for *Coffee Emporium Cincinnati.*

I'm on the board of a nonprofit that was desperately in need of images for its new website. No one had even hired a professional photographer. I did a quick online search and found three professional photographers who, collectively, had hundreds of fabulous photos from events. I contacted the photographers and requested permission to use their photos in exchange for credit on the client's website. One of the three granted us permission, one never responded, and the third asked for $100. The result was that we were able to acquire, for $100, hundreds of professional photos that the nonprofit could immediately use on its site and social networks.

✔ **Ask your customers to supply images.** Sometimes, all it takes is a request. Ask a customer to share her photos with you, and *be sure* to specifically request her permission to use the images in your marketing strategy.

Pure Michigan does this by asking people to share photos using the hashtag #PureMichigan. The site regularly features the best images created by its fans, and these images are shared on its Pure Michigan Instagram account (see Figure 4-4) and Facebook pages. The benefit of this approach is that Pure Michigan has a wide variety of stunning images to use without having to hire a photographer.

Figure 4-4:
The Pure Michigan Instagram account features user-generated photos.

✔ **Run a contest to get photos:** Photo and video contests are powerful ways to generate lots of images that can be used for marketing. The terms and conditions should specifically state that the images may be used in marketing.

General Electric (GE) ran a contest on Instagram asking people to shoot photos showing how GE inspires them, using the hashtag #GEInspiredMe, as shown in Figure 4-5. The winner was invited to a GE aircraft plant to take photographs to share online. The contest generated more than 4,000 submissions, and the images were shared on Instagram and Facebook and other social networks, driving customer engagement and awareness and giving GE photos to use in its marketing materials.

Figure 4-5:
Instagram photos, submitted to the GE Insta-grapher contest.

Hiring professionals

Hiring a professional photographer or videographer may be necessary to generate the quality of visual elements you require. If you require custom images or videos that need a quality level beyond one that you can achieve on your own, hire a professional.

My company has a green screen set up, and employees record amateur footage with their cameras at all company events. The videos we record aren't as high quality as the ones a professional can provide, however. I've hired professionals when the quality level I want exceeds the level I can achieve using company equipment.

When hiring a professional, you may be surprised by the range of prices that are quoted. A short, 2-minute video filmed and edited by professionals can range from $500 to $50,000. When determining how much you can pay for professional photos or videos, weigh the costs against the benefits based on the importance of the video to your business.

Exploring free, licensed image sites

One of the easiest ways to avoid copyright issues with images is to ensure that any images you use are acquired legally. A number of websites allow businesses to use images for free.

When using free image sites, you still have to ensure that the images can be used commercially and that no restrictions or requirements are placed on the commercial use of the image. For example, a common requirement on images that are free to use is that the creator of the image must be credited whenever the image is used publicly.

Review the license of any image used commercially to ensure that your intended use of the image falls within the licensing agreement.

Try the strategies described in the following list to find free images to use commercially in your business:

  ✔ **Free stock-photography sites:** Many sites were created specifically to provide free images for businesses and individuals to use, even commercially. A simple search for *free stock photos* at your favorite search engine shows many stock-photography sites that allow businesses to use photos for free. I recommend www.sxc.hu for free images, especially for blog posts.

When using images from free sites, check the license for the terms of use. Many of these sites may still require that the photographer be given credit or be notified whenever the image is used publicly or commercially.

The quality and selection of images on free stock-photography sites may be lower than at sites that charge fees.

✔ **Google Images or a similar search engine:** Search for commercially usable images.

You can't simply use any image that appears in the search results on your website or in your social media marketing efforts. An advanced search at Google Images (`http://images.google.com`) includes the option to find images licensed for commercial use.

Google Images is simply an option at the main Google search site (`www.google.com`) that lets you search specifically for images. To find images that are licensed for commercial use by way of searching Google Images, follow these steps:

    a. Conduct an image search for any term you choose.

    b. Open the advanced search settings by clicking the gear icon in the upper-right corner and clicking Advanced Search.

    c. In the Usage Rights section, toward the bottom of the Advanced Search page, select Free to Use, Share or Modify, Even Commercially.

    This option filters the image results from the search to show only images that allow for business use.

The images found in an advanced search at Google Images or a similar site may have additional requirements or restrictions. Though an advanced search shows images that can be used commercially, you *must* verify the license and its requirements by clicking through to the site where the image is hosted.

✔ **Commercial images at Flickr:** Flickr (`www.Flickr.com`), one of the largest photography communities online, uses a licensing system known as *Creative Commons* to provide licenses for the images on its site. This system allows photographers to choose who can use their photos and in what way. Many photographers who upload their photos to Flickr allow businesses to use their images commercially under the Creative Commons license.

To find images on Flickr that can be used commercially, search on Flickr and select the advanced search options. Then select the Creative Commons license option Free to Use, Even Commercially. The search results then display only images that can be used commercially.

As with other free-photography sites, check for restrictions and requirements before using the images for your business.

Paying via a licensed image site

Another way to generate images is to simply purchase images via a photography website. Many websites sell images for businesses to use, but (as I say elsewhere) review the terms of the license for the image to ensure that you're using it within the licensing agreement.

Before purchasing an image, examine the purchase and licensing options closely. Paying for images online may cost as little as a few cents per image to as much as thousands of dollars for a single photo, though most popular photo sites sell images for 50 cents to a dollar apiece when purchased in bulk. You may also have to purchase either credits to buy photos or a monthly subscription plan, because few of these sites allow users to purchase single images individually.

Here are a few of the most popular websites for buying images:

- **Bigstock:** www.bigstockphoto.com
- **Dreamstime:** www.dreamstime.com
- **Fotolia:** www.fotolia.com
- **iStockphoto:** www.istockphoto.com
- **Shutterstock:** www.shutterstock.com

Purchasing photos from these sites allows for the commercial use of the images — and you have a wide variety of high-quality images to choose from.

Given the importance of images across all aspects of social media marketing, I typically purchase images for my business from photography sites. Most of the images I purchase cost less than $1, and I try to buy versatile photos that I can reuse over time across social networks.

Building a Visual Library

The objective of collecting a variety of images from different sources is to build a library of visual elements that can be accessed over time. Every organization should have a central visual library where visual assets are clearly labeled and organized.

Here are some reasons that a visual library is valuable:

- It provides visual elements that can be accessed as needed.
- It's a central resource that multiple people in the organization can access.

✔ A visual strategy requires both professional and amateur images and videos, and both can be stored in one place.

✔ Visual elements can be reused over time and combined in different ways.

Store the visual library in a central location with a secure backup.

When you design a visual library, be sure that its images and videos can easily be found via search — the best visual libraries are well organized. Organize your visual library by adopting the organizational methods described in this list:

✔ **Use consistent file-naming methods.** It can be difficult to find images or videos when every file has a completely different name. Create a single, consistent approach for naming your files that is descriptive and makes them easy to find.

✔ **Maintain the dates on which the content was created.** All videos and photos should include the date on which the content was created, to allow you to search by date to find images from a specific period.

✔ **Add tags to content.** Most photo- and video-editing software lets you add tags or keywords to your content. Add keywords that describe the content of the video. Think about how you may search for content, and add keywords on which you anticipate basing your searches.

✔ **Use folders and subfolders.** Organize images into folders and subfolders so that you can easily browse and find the content you're looking for. A single folder named Video can get messy quickly. Instead, start with a Video folder and add subfolders that are named according to how you'll retrieve content from them. For example, if most of your content is related to events, you can create subfolders with dates and then event names. Alternatively, subfolders can be arranged by product. Create a system that's obvious and intuitive for you and your organization.

Turning Content into Visual Assets

One mistake that many people make when evaluating visual assets is that they consider only photographs or videos with live-action footage. Visual social marketing is based on much more — it focuses on creating visual content that makes your point more quickly and effectively and draws social media users to your content.

Many businesses don't consider the full range of content that can become visual — the reality is that *any* content can become visual.

Analyze all the information and content that you communicate. Most, if not all, of it can become visually oriented content, to make it more compelling. You can use visual marketing to make your business communications more effective.

This list describes several types of visual business communications:

✔ **Testimonials from customers:** HubSpot, a company that sells online marketing software, creates simple images to share testimonials that customers have left for them. The image includes a picture of the customer, the HubSpot logo, and a quote from the customer about the company. This strategy makes the testimonials highly visual and easy to consume. Plus, when you add an image of the customer, the testimonial becomes more believable.

✔ **Annual reports:** More and more companies are creating infographic annual reports or annual report illustrations. (An *infographic* is a long-format illustration that visualizes statistics and information.) Businesses can use visual annual reports to share the highlights of their annual reports without requiring readers to digest the entire report. For example, the Michael J. Fox Foundation for Parkinson's Research releases illustrations to share the key information in its annual report.

✔ **Résumés created by Re.Vu:** Users of the website www.re.vu can create visual assets from their résumés. Rather than have to slog through all the data on a résumé to look for trends, Re.vu shows trends and skill progressions visually, which makes the content of the document easier to process. Business professionals use this site to highlight their qualifications and accomplishments to business partners.

✔ **Business updates:** Any business information that you want to communicate can be delivered quickly and effectively by using visual elements. General Electric has started using its visual assets to communicate a variety of topics and raise awareness about them. Many topics can be found on the boards at General Electric's Pinterest page: www.Pinterest.com/GeneralElectric. For example, the company created a visual element to show how bad habits can increase the risk of cancer.

✔ **Press releases:** Companies have started creating visual press releases, too. Rather than distribute a standard press release in a text document, savvy businesses are communicating their news visually. In 2010, Electric Visual launched its new Smoke'n Mirrors glasses by distributing a visual release, as shown in Figure 4-6, that provides a highlight of the launch with images of the product and its specifications. The visual release, which is much easier to follow than a traditional press release, helps company news stand out.

Figure 4-6:
An image-
based press
release from
Electric
Visual.

Visual social marketing doesn't use only Instagram or only add photos to
Facebook posts — it helps you communicate in a more effective and efficient
way. Leverage the power of visual assets to communicate a wide variety of
marketing, public relations, and other types of messages.

Chapter 5

Tools, Tips, and Tricks for Creating Visual Assets

In This Chapter

▶ Creating stunning visual assets

▶ Creating interesting photos using tools you already have

▶ Leveraging free, paid, and mobile photo-editing software to create beautiful images

▶ Creating and editing your own videos that get results

*E*ven just five years ago, creating visual assets was a time-consuming and daunting task. To capture video or photos of decent quality, you needed professional-level cameras. Next, editing software was complicated and expensive, and only professionals had easy access to it.

Today, the landscape has changed significantly. Most modern smartphones can capture stunning photos and even decent-looking videos. At countless marketplaces, businesses can purchase high-quality photos and videos for less than $1. Editing software, which is readily available, comes preloaded on many computers. If that isn't enough, you can find plenty of free, or close-to-free, online tools for photo and video editing.

The reality is that anyone, regardless of their technical abilities, can create beautiful visual assets for their businesses.

It used to be that having "professional photos" meant hiring a photographer to create impeccable images with perfect lighting. Having great-looking photos now means having a wide variety of images, including photos taken quickly, on the fly. Consumers are skeptical of professional visual assets because the assets often seem staged and don't represent what a product may actually look like.

For example, I recently saw a television commercial for a hamburger from a fast food restaurant. The burger looked delicious: It was about three inches tall and peppered with fresh vegetables. In reality, most of the hamburgers I've ever eaten at this restaurant are flat (about an inch tall) and sprinkled with a few condiments. The reality isn't much like the picture in the ad.

This is partly why the trend is changing from perfect, professional-looking photos to realistic, user-generated photos. Consumers are displaying an appetite for real and authentic photos and videos, and the good news is that any business can create these elements. Though there's still a place for professional visual content, it's no longer the requirement for businesses.

In this chapter, I share with you some of the top tools, tips, and tricks that you can use to create attractive visual content. Most of these tools are intended to be used by consumers with no specific existing technical knowledge, which means that *anyone* should be able to start using these tools and get results.

Taking Outstanding Photos

When it comes to visual social marketing, you have to take great-looking photos. A visual social marketing strategy isn't complete without them, especially ones — taken on the go — of your business in action. Though you previously had to hire a professional photographer, now you can simply shoot your own photos that are unique, interesting, and engaging.

Taking photos is one of the simplest ways to start building an image marketing library. Regardless of the type of business you're in, taking photos is a helpful way to start creating visual marketing content. Some businesses might think that this option isn't a good one for them, because they have no physical product or service to market, but that isn't the case. Using a little creativity, any business can take photos as a part of its visual marketing strategy.

If you aren't a professional, don't worry — I'm not, either. The key to success in taking photos is creativity and taking advantage of interesting photo opportunities. The idea here is to start taking photos to begin building a library of images that you can use over time. You may not use all the images right away, but the bigger your library, the more you have to draw on when you need a photo for visual social marketing.

Though it's beyond the scope of this book to provide detailed photography tips, the key to success is to experiment.

When you're shooting photos, the primary issue is how good of a camera you need. A professional-quality camera produces better-looking photos; however, professional-quality photos aren't always necessary to best meet your marketing objectives.

When determining which type of camera you need, consider whether you need

- ✔ **Professional-quality photos:** If you're considering purchasing a professional-quality SLR camera, be prepared to spend between $500 and $1,000. This type of camera gives you a lot of flexibility in your photography, and you can use the additional options and controls to customize more aspects of the image. The downside is that you have to learn how to use the camera. Also, many professional-quality cameras take pictures that are too big to use on social networks — the images must be resized to make them small enough to upload to social networks, which is time consuming. Images can be edited; however, they have to be downloaded to your computer and uploaded into a photo editing application. Then they have to be uploaded to the social network on which you want to share them. The bottom line: Although professional-quality photos can provide more detail and better lighting, they're significantly more time consuming to take and upload to social media.

- ✔ **Point-and-shoot:** This type of camera costs significantly less than a professional-quality camera — you can purchase one for as little as $100. The benefits of using point-and-shoot are that you can easily get started and you have a lot more flexibility for taking photos with zoom and lighting settings. One problem with shooting photos from a smartphone is that you can't easily control the lighting, shooting mode, or zoom level. A point-and-shoot camera overcomes these issues. One remaining challenge is that taking pictures with a camera involves uploading them to a computer, editing them, and (potentially) resizing them before they're ready to upload to a social network, which can be time consuming.

- ✔ **The ability to shoot pictures from your smartphone:** Smartphones typically take the lowest-quality images, and the options for shooting photos are limited (though newer smartphones are improving the situation). The benefits of taking photos with a smartphone is that you can quickly take the photo, quickly edit the photo, and quickly share the photo. A number of photo editing applications for smartphones let you edit photos directly on your device. (Some smartphones even have these features built in.) Also, after you've taken a photo, you can upload it to a social network in a single click so that you don't have to download the photo to your computer and then upload it.

Although a professional-quality image from a high-end camera looks good, it may not be worth the time and effort, depending on how you're planning to use the image.

I own a high-end SLR camera with multiple lenses, a point-and-shoot model, and a smartphone with a camera. I find that when I'm creating visual assets for social media, the applications on my smartphone make pictures quick and easy to shoot and share. Also, newer editing applications let me make more interesting photos without having to worry about photo editing software. Depending on how I'm planning to use the photo, however, I sometimes prefer professional images. For example, the large cover photo on my Facebook page is of higher quality than a quick video I share from Instagram.

First plan how to use the image. After you know how you want to use it, you can better evaluate the pros and cons of different camera options. You certainly don't need high-end photography equipment to be successful in visual social media marketing.

Selecting Photo Editing Tools

Regardless of the method you use to get photos, whether you take them yourself, hire a professional, or purchase them, you'll probably need photo editing tools at some point in your visual social marketing image-creation strategy. You may simply want to crop a stock photo that you've purchased or remove the red-eye effect or add an interesting filter to make the photo more unique.

Even if you don't plan to edit photos to improve them, chances are good that you'll need to *resize* them. As I describe throughout this book, each social network requires photos of different sizes for various aspects of a profile photo. For example, on your Twitter profile, you need a background image, a header image, and a profile photo. Photo editing tools are mandatory if you want to be able to create customized image sizes to use on social networks.

You can choose from a variety of free, paid, and mobile photo editing applications to edit your photos.

Free photo editing tools

Free tools are useful if you're just getting started. Most free tools give you the basic editing functionality that you need in order to make adjustments to your images. Though they aren't as robust (or as complicated to use) as paid tools, they can generally handle the needs of an amateur photo editor.

Mac editing options

Most Macs come supplied with free, basic photo editing software, sometimes included in the preview feature. On the Mac, the Preview application often includes basic photo-editing functions. From the preview, you can crop, rotate, and flip photos and adjust their color and size. The app doesn't have a lot of functionality, but it can quickly meet your needs for basic adjustments.

In addition to simple preview edits, the iPhoto editing option comes supplied on most Macs. The photo editing software in iPhoto (which is quite similar to Windows Live Photo Gallery, described in the following section) allows users to fix red-eye and to rotate, enhance, straighten, crop, and retouch images. For basic amateur editing, the software is robust — it includes most of the editing capability you need. You can see the editing tools in iPhoto in Figure 5-1.

Figure 5-1:
Photo
editing with
iPhoto.

In addition to the quick fixes shown in Figure 5-1, you can add other effects and make adjustments.

PC editing options

You have two options on a PC computer. First, most PCs come with the standard Paint program, which lets you make basic edits to images, such as resizing, cropping, and adding text. Microsoft also has the Live Photo Gallery application, available for free as a part of the downloads in the Live Essentials package. The photo editing capabilities of Live Photo Gallery are much more robust than in Paint. For example, Live Photo Gallery lets you adjust for red-eye and for noise reduction, color, exposure, tint, and saturation. You can see some editing options in Figure 5-2.

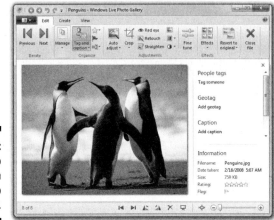

Figure 5-2:
Photo
editing in
Live Photo
Gallery.

Additional free photo editing software

In addition to the free tools that come supplied with computers, a number of other free tools are available. If you're interested in branching out, spend some time getting familiar with different tools and choose the one that's best suited to your needs.

Here are three popular, free photo-editing tools:

- ✔ **Picasa:** Google's photo sharing and editing application. The benefit of using it is that it connects automatically with other Google tools, such as Google+. Picasa is a free and easy way to edit and organize images, and it can be used on your computer or online.

- ✔ **Picnik:** One of the most robust online photo editors that you can get for free. Though its functionality is close to professional quality (which is more complex), it remains easy to use. The main downside of Picnik is that you have to upload images to the website before editing, so you have an extra step versus applications that work on your computer.

- ✔ **GIMP:** Works across operating systems, which makes it easy to use. The software has, for free, all the same functionality as many high-end, professional systems. The downside is that its expanded functionality makes it more challenging to use.

Paid editing tools

The number-one paid photo editing software is Photoshop, created by Adobe. It's the photo editing tool of choice of most professionals. The challenge is that it's more difficult to learn and use. Most free photo editing tools are simple and intuitive enough for users to learn on their own. Photoshop, on the other hand, usually requires instruction. An investment in Photoshop can pay off, however, because you can manipulate and edit photos dramatically. You can edit and otherwise correct photos down to the pixel.

Photoshop isn't an editing tool to pick up lightly. It's one of the more expensive applications to use.

In addition to the standard edition of Photoshop, you can use the Photoshop Elements version, which was created for hobbyists. Elements is easier to use and costs a fraction of the price of the full, professional version of Photoshop.

You can find other paid editing tools such as Corel Paint Shop Pro and Perfectly Clear; however, Photoshop is definitely the market leader in paid photo editing tools.

Mobile editing tools

With more and more people using their smartphones to take photos for visual social marketing, it isn't surprising that many mobile phone image editing applications are available.

Here are the benefits of using mobile editing apps:

- ✔ They tend to be easy to use.
- ✔ They usually cost less than $5.
- ✔ They have unique filters and editing options that can make your photos truly stand out.

Depending on the model of smartphone you use, different editing options are available to you. Start by exploring the photo editing options supplied with your phone. On my Android phone, I can apply filters, adjust saturation, and crop, rotate, and focus (and more!) directly from the Camera application.

In addition to using the tools built-in to your camera, other fun photo apps can be fun and interesting to use. To find these applications, search for them in the app store for your mobile phone. Again, not all applications are available for every device.

Check out some of these popular apps:

- ✔ **Adobe Photoshop Touch:** One of the more expensive mobile applications (at $9.99 for the tablet version or $4.99 for the phone version), it brings the amazingly powerful photo editing capabilities of Photoshop to your mobile device.

✔ **Aviary:** With a wide variety of editing tools for your mobile phone, it's easy to use and more robust than Instagram, without the complexity of Photoshop.

✔ **Instacollage:** Turn your Instagram photos (or the photos on your phone) into a collage.

✔ **Instagram:** Because Instagram is the most popular smartphone editing and sharing application, I devote Chapter 11 to describing it in more detail.

✔ **iPhoto for iPhone:** Apple brings the power of iPhoto (covered earlier in this chapter) to the iPhone.

✔ **Snapseed:** This photo editor for the iPhone, which has lots of editing functions, goes beyond the simple filters that Instagram offers.

Benefiting from Free and Simple Ways to Create Images

As you become more involved with visual social marketing, you soon realize that you need a wide variety of images. In some cases, you can take photos and edit them, but in other cases you need to buy photos or find unique ways to create the photos you need.

As visual marketing strategies move toward the need to create images that are *pinnable* (images that clearly represent their underlying content), the need to create good-looking images quickly grows.

You can create images to accompany your visual marketing strategy in many easy ways. You don't have to become a designer or download any special software to your computer. In the following sections, I share hacks and tips for creating great-looking images with no software.

Presentation software

Images with quotes and text are popular visual social marketing tools. The reason is that the text in the image can clearly communicate the message, though the visual design makes the content stand out. In this section, the term *presentation software* refers to software, such as PowerPoint and Keynote, that is typically used to create presentations.

Presentation software was built to make text content more visually appealing and engaging during a presentation, which makes it ideal for creating visual assets.

Creating visual assets in presentation software is a good idea because most computers already have this software. Also, it's quick and easy to use, and you can incorporate your branding.

Using presentation software for visual assets is appropriate when the image you're trying to create includes text such as a few key points, a tip, or a quote.

To create an image from presentation software, follow these steps:

1. **Open your presentation software and select a theme.**

   If you have for your business a customized theme that is visually appealing and represents your brand well, you may choose to start with that theme. Otherwise, browse the theme options in the software until you find a theme that can bring your idea to life in an interesting way.

2. **Create a presentation.**

   After you create a presentation, you see a square slide with the theme you selected applied to it.

3. **Drag, drop, and edit text on the screen.**

   After your canvas (the slide) is created, add a text box to the slide. Experiment with fonts, font sizes, and color schemes until the slide looks "just right." You can also add images to the slide to make it more interesting.

   The slide appears much smaller when you share it on social media, so create one that can be viewed in a smaller size with legible text.

4. **Export the slide as a JPG file.**

   Depending on the presentation software you're using, you may be able to export the slide as a JPG file by selecting Export from the File menu. After choosing Export, you see the Export As a JPG option. If you don't see it, follow Step 5.

5. **Take a screen capture of the image.**

   If your presentation software doesn't allow you to export to a JPG file, you can take a screen shot of the slide instead to be saved as an image. Depending on the type of computer you use, different steps lead to taking a screen shot. Look in the manual for your computer to see how to take a screen shot.

6. **Upload to your favorite social network.**

   You're now ready to share your image on social media!

This simple strategy makes it easy to create custom images for your visual social marketing strategy. A friend of mine who runs the site at www.girlfriendology.com uses this approach to make *quote images,* which are images with quotes overlaid. She has a custom presentation theme showing her branding, and then she creates her quote images in presentation software. You can see an example in Figure 5-3.

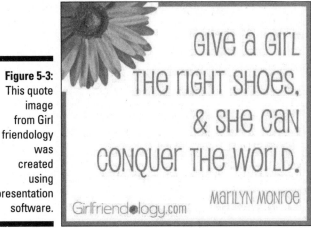

Figure 5-3:
This quote image from Girl friendology was created using presentation software.

At Boot Camp Digital, we too use this strategy to create quote images. We've customized our standard Boot Camp Digital branded template, which we use in presentations, to create visual assets for our social media quotes. You can see an example in Figure 5-4.

Figure 5-4:
This quote image from Boot Camp Digital was created with presentation software.

This approach to creating visual assets can extend beyond simply text images. You can import a picture into a presentation software slide (by either choosing Insert⇨Photo from the main menu or dragging the photo to the slide from your file viewer) and adding text to the image.

After the image covers the entire slide, add a text box on top of the image to add text to any photo. Adding text can make any image pinnable, because the text can describe what the image is about. We do this with images that we take ourselves and with photos that we purchase from stock photography sites, as you can see in Figure 5-5.

Figure 5-5: An image with text superimposed.

After you place the text box on top of the image, experiment with its size, font, color, and placement until the image looks interesting and relevant.

Smartphone or tablet

A number of mobile phone and tablet applications allow you to quickly and easily create visual assets that you can use on your site. The advantage of using these apps is that they're easy to use, they're inexpensive (or even free), and they can be uploaded to social media sites directly from your mobile device.

Two mobile applications for photo and visual creation are worth noting. If your goal is to create or edit photos, use the applications I discuss in the earlier section "Selecting Photo Editing Tools." The applications I cover in the two following sections can help you create interesting visual assets with text and photos.

Introducing Phonto

One of my favorite applications for image creation is Phonto, which can be downloaded from the application store on your mobile device. (It may not be available for all devices.)

You can use Phonto to take a picture from your device and superimpose text over the image. Phonto has some interesting and unique fonts that can help make your images "pop."

Using Phonto, you can add text to any picture on your mobile device to create an attractive image. If you want to share only text, you can also start with a plain or textured background versus an image. Sample photos that I've created with Phonto are shown in Figure 5-6. Phonto is free, or you can upgrade to a paid version to unlock more functionality. (I use the free app.)

Figure 5-6: Images created with Phonto.

In Phonto, you can easily create images; plus, Phonto is integrated with social networks so that you can share your images on social networks in a single click.

Discovering new mobile applications

If you're feeling creative, many other fun applications can help you create beautiful and interesting images. On my iPad, I have the Comic Book! application, which transforms a photo into a "comic" and adds callout boxes. In only a few minutes, I can create custom comic images from my photos.

The HaikuDeck application lets me create beautiful presentations with images and text from my tablet. HaikuDeck pulls in images from my phone, an image library, or my Google Drive to add to a presentation. Then I can add interesting text to the image to create an image-focused presentation.

If you want to take your visual assets to the next level, experiment with different image creation and editing applications to create visual assets that truly stand out.

Writing or drawing on paper or boards

Though the use of editing tools and software seems to be the obvious choice for creating images, don't forget about the option to draw or write on paper, a whiteboard, a chalkboard, or chart paper.

Use your physical surroundings to your advantage, and don't hesitate to draw or write. Variety is vital to keeping your visual social marketing strategy interesting, and real-life pictures can be a welcome change.

At Boot Camp Digital, we use a whiteboard in our office to create some of the images we use on social media. For example, you can see in Figure 5-7 how we create "handwritten" images.

Figure 5-7:
An image
created
from a
whiteboard.

Be creative and find different ways to create images for your visual marketing strategy.

Image sharing sites

As you consider the tools available for your visual social marketing strategy, don't forget the role that image sharing sites may play. The two most popular image sharing sites are Flickr (at www.Flickr.com) and Picasa (at www.Picasa.com). At these photo sharing sites, you can create a free account and then upload and share your photos. The sites give you basic photo editing capabilities and let you interact with other site users.

Though Facebook is the number-one site where photos are shared online, for the reasons described in the following list, you may want to share images on other photo sharing sites:

- ✔ **Images on sharing sites are search-engine-friendly.** Sharing images on a photo sharing site makes images more likely to show up in image search results at Google and other search engines. Because photos shared on Facebook aren't indexed by search engines, search engines can't see the images you share there.

- ✔ **Your photos gain increased visibility.** The reality is that not everyone is on Facebook (though a billion or so people are), so limiting your image sharing only to Facebook may prevent certain customers from seeing your photos. Sharing them on Flickr makes them available to everyone.

- ✔ **You can allow others to use your photos.** On some photo sharing sites, you can choose to license your photos so that others can use your images. If you want to share your images, or allow others to use or build on them, photo-sharing sites are the way to go.

- ✔ **You can participate in a community of photographers.** If you're interested in photography, photo sharing sites such as Flickr can be valuable resources. Many photographers use these sites to share images and connect with other photographers. You can discover, and connect with, other photographers on these sites.

- ✔ **You can find images to use.** Flickr allows photographers to select licenses for their images, and some of the image licenses allow images to be used commercially. Some images from Flickr can therefore be used in your visual social marketing strategy.

Some photos require attribution to the photographer, so carefully verify the license of any photo you use, to be sure that you have the right to use it commercially. I've used pictures from Flickr for my business in the past, and it's especially helpful for finding images of my neighborhood and local events.

Creating Videos

These days, videos are easier than ever to create. You can create videos from your smartphone, a webcam, or a point-and-shoot camera. If video is an important part of your strategy, you may also choose to hire a professional camera crew. In Chapter 14, I give you tips for creating videos and help you decide whether to choose to do-it-yourself or hire a designer.

If you choose to create your own videos, you can use a number of video editing applications to improve them. Alternatively, if you're planning to create your video primarily to upload it to YouTube, you may want to explore the video editing features that YouTube offers for free. (I describe YouTube marketing in Chapter 15, including an overview of the editing functionality.) The benefit of editing videos in YouTube is that you don't have to download additional software.

Free video editing tools

Many free video editing tools are available for basic editing chores. Though most of these tools are relatively easy to use, you may still need to follow a tutorial to be able to make the most of their functionality.

Most computers come supplied with basic video editing software that meets the simple editing needs of most users for free, as described in this section.

Mac computers come packaged with iMovie, which is Apple's video editing software. Using iMovie, you can upload multiple videos, combine them, add text and music, and apply basic editing techniques to the footage. iMovie is a helpful tool to fill the most basic editing needs.

PC computers usually come packaged with Microsoft Movie Maker. Similar to iMovie, Movie Maker allows you to import multiple video clips to combine them. In addition, you can add text and music and edit footage. Though the functionality is basic, it should meet the needs of most amateur video editors.

If these tools don't meet your needs, you can download one of these free editing tools:

- ✔ **Avidemux:** This program has been described as "the Instagram of video editing software" — it's quick, simple, and easy to use while having powerful capabilities. Using Avidemux, you can trim, edit, filter, encode, and add a variety of effects to your video.

- ✔ **Lightworks:** This powerful and complex video-editing tool, which offers both free and professional versions, may take some time to learn. Extremely robust, it can do many things that other free tools cannot. This software has also been used to make possible such Hollywood movies as *Pulp Fiction* and *Mission Impossible.* Using Lightworks, you can access professional-quality editing for free.

- ✔ **VSDC Free Video Editor:** This editor isn't as complex as Lightworks, but it has most of the basic functions you'll need without the challenges of learning to use a complicated editing tool. Common tasks such as changing lighting, applying filters, and cutting video are relatively easy to complete with little to no experience.

Paid video editing applications

Professional, paid video editing applications have a lot of power and functionality, but be prepared to invest time and money to fully learn how to use them. All these applications include lots of editing options and complete flexibility.

The most popular paid video-editing applications include the ones described in this list:

- ✔ **Adobe Premier Pro (about $20 a month):** This Adobe product connects with Photoshop and Illustrator, making it easy to use with other Adobe products.

- ✔ **Final Cut Pro (about $300):** This professional video-editing software has everything you need to create professional-quality videos, however it is only available for Mac computers.

- ✔ **Avid Pinnacle Studio (about $60 to $100):** This software has all the tools that most editors, from beginner to advanced, want. Though it doesn't have the same capabilities as many other professional programs, it's a step above most free editors.

Part III

Integrating Images into Your Social Media Marketing

Find out how images can engage your fans on Facebook at www.dummies.com/ extras/visualsocialmarketing.

In this part . . .

- ✔ How visual content on Facebook can improve your results
- ✔ Optimizing your Twitter profile and posts for visual content
- ✔ Incorporating images and videos into your blog to increase traffic
- ✔ Building images into your LinkedIn strategy to maximize your effectiveness

Chapter 6

Driving Engagement on Facebook with Images

In This Chapter

▶ Understanding why images are vital to your success on Facebook

▶ Optimizing the profile and cover photo on your Facebook Page

▶ Posting image status updates to increase engagement and interaction

▶ Generating more clicks by optimizing images in link posts

▶ Uploading and sharing videos on Facebook

*F*acebook is the social network with the highest number of users. It now has more than 1 billion users — half of whom log in every single day. Facebook is therefore a staple of any social marketing plan simply because it's the most popular social network.

Posting images is an important part of any Facebook marketing strategy. Over the past year, Facebook has introduced a number of updates that have increased the prominence of images on the site. For example, Facebook Pages for businesses now include a *cover photo,* which is a large image displayed at the top of the Facebook page.

Facebook has also increased the role that images play when sharing links in the newsfeed. As I show you later in this chapter, when you share a link to a blog post or web page on Facebook, an image from the post or page is shown in a large format in the newsfeed.

One reason that images are becoming more prominent on Facebook is that Facebook users *like* them. Studies show (see `http://blog.bufferapp.com/7-facebook-stats-you-should-know-for-a-more-engaging-page`) that photos generate 53 percent more likes, 104 percent more comments, and 84 percent more clicks than status updates consisting only of text. Facebook users are simply more likely to interact with posts that include photos.

In this chapter, I show you the types of photos you need to post in order to be successful on Facebook, and I describe how to optimize Facebook posts to generate more likes, comments, and clicks.

To read more about Facebook marketing and Facebook Pages for business, see *Facebook Marketing For Dummies,* written by John Haydon, Paul Dunay, and Richard Krueger (and published by John Wiley & Sons, Inc.).

Images Required on Facebook Pages

A Facebook *Page* is the official representation of a brand or business on Facebook. Figure 6-1 shows an example. As you can see, you need a variety of custom images to get started with your Facebook Page.

Figure 6-1:
A sample
Facebook
Page.

The vital images required for a Facebook Page are the profile photo, a cover photo, and — possibly — custom images for tabs. In this section, I show you exactly how to optimize each of these photos.

Optimizing profile photos

The *profile photo* is the small, square image that's displayed beside the name of the business on Facebook. Your profile photo is arguably the most important image on your page because whenever people see your posts anywhere on Facebook, they also see this image.

Figure 6-2 shows how a profile photo for a business page is displayed in the newsfeed on Facebook.

Figure 6-2:
How the
profile photo
is displayed
in the
newsfeed.

As of this printing, a profile photo should be square and should be sized at 180 x 180 pixels. You can upload or use an image of any size. Using Facebook's simple drag-and-drop tool, you can choose the area of the photo to display as your profile photo. The region you select must be a square.

To change or edit your Facebook profile photo, simply hover the mouse over the current profile photo while in Timeline view on your page. The Edit Profile Picture button appears. Then you can choose to upload a new photo or use an existing photo that you have already uploaded to Facebook. After you've selected the method, you can choose the image and adjust the crop region to display the section of the image that you want to display as your profile photo.

When choosing a profile image for your Facebook Page, consider these best practices:

✔ **Choose an image with a square shape.** The image you choose should be square, or you can edit it to a square shape using photo editing software. For example, the Boot Camp Digital logo is normally a rectangle; however, for the Facebook profile image, we created a square version.

✔ **Incorporate your logo or an easily identifiable item.** Your logo, or another element that easily identifies your business visually, is the best choice for your Facebook profile photo. The image should be professional-looking and stand out in some way.

✔ **Resist the urge to change your profile photo often.** Many Facebook users quickly skim their newsfeeds, looking for posts from the people and businesses they care about — and the profile image is what they look for in order to identify your posts. If the photo is continually changing, you face difficulty in building recognition with your fans.

These guidelines also apply to profile images for your personal Facebook profile, though people typically change their personal profile photos regularly.

Optimizing cover photos

The *cover photo* on Facebook is the large image that's displayed prominently across the top of the Facebook Page, or personal profile. Figure 6-3 shows an example from Project Blue Collar. The cover photo is your opportunity to set the tone of your Facebook Page.

Figure 6-3: Facebook cover image.

Cover photos on Facebook — which are public and can be viewed by anyone — must be at least 399 pixels wide. To lessen how long it takes for your cover image to load on your Facebook Page, Facebook recommends uploading a .jpg image that's 315 pixels tall by 815 pixels wide and 100 kilobytes or smaller.

When Facebook initially let business Pages add cover photos, it placed a number of restrictions on the images. For example, they could contain only 20 percent text. Facebook says that cover photos can't be "deceptive, misleading or infringe on anyone else's copyright." Also, you cannot encourage people to "upload your cover photo to their personal timelines." To find current information about Facebook's guidelines for cover images, visit www.Facebook.com/page_guidelines.php.

Businesses use Facebook Pages in a number of ways, such as these examples:

- **Brand a business:** The cover image can be used as a branding tool by showcasing your brand or business.

- **Showcase a product:** Some businesses showcase their products or services via their cover photos. For example, a restaurant might showcase its signature dish, or a dentist might show before-and-after pictures of a smile he helped to improve.

- **Recognize customers:** Periodically changing your cover photo to showcase or feature customers can be a popular way to make your page interactive and engage your fans. For example, a T-shirt company might use its cover photo to showcase designs from its customers.

- **Make special deals and offers:** The cover photo is a useful place to highlight special offers or deals. For example, a pizza restaurant may change its cover photo on Mondays to promote a Monday-night pizza special.

Images in Posts

When the standard images on your Facebook Page have been optimized, the next step is to optimize your Facebook posts or status updates for visual social marketing.

As mentioned in this chapter's introduction, images posted on Facebook as status updates generate more likes, comments, and clicks than text-only posts. People are more likely to engage with your Facebook Page when you post visual content — especially images. (I discuss videos later in this chapter, in the section "Sharing Videos on Facebook.") The more that people engage in your content, the more visibility you generate for your page.

Posting an image as a status update on Facebook is simple. When you're logged in as the administrator on your Facebook Page, the status update box is on the left side and at the top of Timeline view (directly under the About section of the page). Above the status update box, where you see the words *Photo/Video,* click to show the option to upload or create an album. Choose Upload Photos/Video and select the image from your computer.

Add text to describe the image, to interest your audience, and to encourage your audience, such as Click to Share This Image. After uploading, the words *Say something about this image* appear in the status update box, where you can add text to describe the image. Figure 6-4 shows a Facebook image post. You can see the image that's displayed and the text above it.

Figure 6-4:
Facebook
image post.

Any image shared on Facebook as a status update post (refer to Figure 6-4) is also saved on the Photos tab on the Facebook Page. To see the images associated with your Facebook Page, click the Photos tab at the top of the page to browse all the photos.

Editing Facebook post images

Facebook allows you to make basic edits and make other changes after posting a photo. To find the photo, click the Photos tab at the top of the page; or, if you see the image in the Timeline, simply click the image.

This action opens Image view, as shown in Figure 6-5, so that you can make changes to your photo. To make changes to the image, click the Options link underneath the post. A number of options appear.

Figure 6-5:
Image view
in Facebook.

This list describes your options for editing:

- **Edit Location:** Adds a location to where the image was taken. You can tag your own location if the image was taken in your place of business or other places on Facebook. You can also add a city as a location. To add a business or city as a location on Facebook, start typing the name of the place. A list of existing places appears that match the one you're typing. If you don't see the location you want, you can type the location name and click Add Place to create one.

- **Change Date:** Records the date on which your photo was uploaded. You can change it to any date in the present or past.

- **Rotate Left/Right:** If your image appears sideways or upside down, rotates it left or right.

- **Download:** Downloads images from Facebook to your computer.

- **Make Profile Picture for Page:** Simply makes the image you're viewing the profile picture for your page. After clicking the Make Profile Picture for Page link, you have the option to choose the square section of the image that will be displayed as your profile photo.

- **Move to Other Album:** Lets you change the album in which the photo is stored. After selecting this option, you can choose from existing albums to add the image or create a new album, which is an option at the bottom of the drop-down box.

- **Embed Post:** Creates code that lets you embed the Facebook status update elsewhere on the web. For example, I may select this option and copy the code to display the Facebook post on my website.

- **Delete This Photo:** Deletes the photo.

- **Enter Fullscreen:** Generates a full-screen view of the image.

In addition to choosing the options on the Options menu, you can click a few links to enhance your image posts — these are also displayed below the image:

- **Tag Photo:** Tags other people or pages in your photo by selecting them from a list after you start typing their names (after clicking the *Tag Photo* text). *Tagging* is simply a way to identify the people or pages that are in a photo. When using Facebook as a page (as opposed to using Facebook as your personal profile), you're limited in how you may tag people. For example, if I'm using Facebook as Boot Camp Digital (my business page), I can't tag my friends in photos. When I use Facebook as myself, Krista Neher, I can tag people in photos. Pages on Facebook can tag only the pages they have liked that are categorized as People, Brands, or Products.

✔ **Boost Post:** Lets you pay money for more people to see your posts (similar to an ad). If you want to increase the number of people who see your image post, you can click the Boost Post link and Facebook then guides you through the process of paying to promote the post.

✔ **Share:** Lets you share any photo (including your own) on your timeline. You don't typically share your own photos, because they have already been shared on your page; however you can share on your page a photo that you find on another page. When using Facebook as a person (not a business), you can share photos on your timeline or on the timelines of your friends or other pages you have liked.

Optimizing Facebook post images

When uploading an image as a status update on Facebook, you have a number of ways to optimize your post.

Be sure that the image is the optimal size. Images that are too large may be partially cut off, which can ruin how your image looks in the newsfeed and timeline. For example, Figure 6-6 shows how larger images may be cut off when viewed in the newsfeed.

Figure 6-6:
Facebook crops large images in the newsfeed and timeline.

The maximum size of an image that can be uploaded to Facebook is 2048 X 2048 pixels. When you share an image in Timeline view, Facebook displays an image in a "container" that allows an image size of 403 X 403. If your image exceeds this size, Facebook starts in the center and displays a portion of the image in the Newsfeed and Timeline views.

To optimize your photos for Facebook display sizes, make sure that the images you upload are square, if possible (because the space that displays the images is square). Alternatively, make your image sizes a maximum of 403 pixels high or wide.

Images Generated from Links

When you share a link to a website or web page on Facebook, an image from the page is typically displayed beside the post, as shown in Figure 6-7. For example, I may share a status update to a newspaper article I've read or share a link to the website of a new restaurant I've just tried. In either case, when my status update includes a link to a website or web page, Facebook searches the page for images and displays an image beside the link, as shown in Figure 6-7.

Figure 6-7: A web page shared in a status update on Facebook.

In Chapter 2, I discuss the importance of having relevant images on your website to generate more traffic back to your site. As you can see in the Facebook post update in Figure 6-7, when sharing a link to a website on Facebook, the image is displayed prominently below the status update. Over the past few years, Facebook has increased the size and prominence of the image displayed with a link.

A highly relevant image can increase the number of views of your post and clicks. In this way, a strong image beside a link can generate more traffic back to your website. You should have powerful and descriptive images on your website to accompany links that are shared.

Choosing the Image to Accompany a Link

After you have included a link to a web page in a status update, Facebook automatically searches the web page for images to accompany the link that's shared. This statement is true whether you're sharing content from your own website or from any other website. After a link is included in a status update, Facebook searches the site for images.

You may scroll through the image choices to accompany a link by pressing the arrow buttons below the initial image. In this way, Facebook lets users select the image to accompany the post. If you still don't find a relevant and engaging image, Facebook also lets you upload your own thumbnail image to accompany the post. For example, if I'm sharing a newspaper article that doesn't have a photo, but I still want to optimize the post, I can upload a relevant photo from my computer.

Optimize your website images for Facebook. Though uploading your own photo can help you create an optimized image for the Facebook newsfeed, when an article has no images, other people who are sharing your website, product pages, or blog posts probably won't take the time to upload their own image.

To determine the images that users can choose from when sharing your site, create a status update with a link to your website, and note the images that Facebook allows you to choose from. You may notice that Facebook doesn't recognize all the images on your page, or that it defaults to an image that isn't at the top of the page. Facebook chooses the images to be displayed based on how your website is coded, and how the images are coded and labeled.

A discussion about coding images for websites is beyond the scope of this book, though Facebook does have a "debugging" tool. You can use it to enter a URL and Facebook then shows you any page errors it recognizes, as well as the images it recognizes from the page. You can find the debugging tool at

```
https://developers.facebook.com/tools/debug
```

After you enter a URL, Facebook shows you any coding errors on your site and displays the images that it recognizes from your website. It's another way to find out whether your images are coded correctly in order to be recognized by Facebook.

Videos on Facebook

Videos can be shared by way of status updates on Facebook. Similarly to photos, videos often generate more views, clicks, likes, and comments than do standard text-only updates. People on Facebook enjoy watching videos, so share them as a part of your Facebook Page strategy.

Sharing a video on Facebook is a helpful way to mix up your content and provide customers with videos that they're interested in. The advantage of uploading a video to Facebook is that it's displayed in your photo gallery and people can view the video directly in the Facebook newsfeed. Users don't have to click a link and go to another site to watch the video — they can simply press the Play button and watch the video directly in the newsfeed.

You can see an example of how a video post looks on Facebook in Figure 6-8.

Figure 6-8:
A video shared in a Facebook status update.

Uploading videos to Facebook

Uploading videos to Facebook is relatively simple, but a number of advanced editing features are available as well. To upload a video to Facebook, it must be one that's already on your computer. In the status update box, click the Add Photos/Videos link directly above the status update box. From there, you're directed to choose the video to upload.

After you upload the video, Facebook may take some time to process it before adding the status update. When the video is ready, Facebook sends a notification so that you can continue to edit and optimize the video.

This list describes your video editing options, as shown in Figure 6-9:

- **In This Video:** In this text box, you can tag people who appear in the video. (To find out about tagging, see the earlier section "Editing Facebook post images.") Business pages can only tag other business pages that they have liked that are categorized as People, Brands, or Products.

- **Title:** Create a short (no more than 65 characters, including spaces) and highly relevant title for the video. The title should draw people in and entice them to watch the video.

- **Where:** Tag a business page or the location where the video was taken.

- **When:** Select the year, month, date, hour, and minute that the video was taken. You don't have to specify down to the minute; however, it's an available option.

- **Description:** Describe the contents of the video. Your description of a video can be lengthy (more than 1,500 characters).

- **Privacy:** Choose who can see your video, such as Public, or limit views to people who are connected to you.

- **Choose a Thumbnail:** A *thumbnail* is an image of a frame of the video that's displayed on the screen before a user presses the Play button to view your video. You can choose from a number of different options. Select an engaging frame that entices people to watch your video.

Figure 6-9:
Video editing options in Facebook.

To view the videos you have uploaded, follow these steps:

1. **Click Photos toward the top of your Facebook Page, just below the cover image.**

   This step opens a screen that displays your photos, with the newest photos at the top of the screen.

2. **Select Albums and choose the Videos album where all your videos are stored.**

You may have to scroll down to find the Videos album if you have a lot of albums. You can click an individual video to view it on Facebook. On the video viewing screen, you can find a number of additional options for editing and sharing your video. These mirror the options discussed earlier, in the section "Uploading videos to Facebook" and in the earlier section covering "Editing Facebook post images."

Sharing YouTube videos on Facebook

You can upload a video to Facebook for a status update only if the video you want to share is already on your computer. This usually applies only if you're sharing a video that you created.

You may want to share videos from YouTube or other video sharing websites on Facebook. You can share videos created by other people as status updates.

To share a video from YouTube (the largest video sharing network), find on YouTube the video that you want to share. After you're on the video's page, copy the URL (the website address) from your web browser; it should look something like this:

```
www.youtube.com/watch?v=vVw1aPUybB8
```

Go to your Facebook Page and begin typing your status update. When you finish, paste the copied URL of the YouTube video into the status update. Similar to sharing a link, Facebook finds the thumbnail image to display along with the title and part of the description from YouTube, as you can see in Figure 6-10.

Figure 6-10:
YouTube
video in the
Facebook
newsfeed.

Sharing a YouTube video in this way allows the user to play the video directly in Facebook. When the user clicks the image, the video plays instantly, so the user doesn't have to leave Facebook to watch the video.

Chapter 7

Generating Interest with Visual Content on Twitter

In This Chapter

▶ An overview of the images needed for your Twitter account

▶ Optimizing the visual appeal of your Twitter account

▶ Attracting engagement with photos and videos in status updates

*T*witter continues to be one of the most popular and important social networks, and visual content is an important part of your Twitter marketing strategy. Over the past few years, Twitter has made a number of changes to increase the prominence of both images and videos on the site. Images are now prominently displayed in Twitter profiles, and they can be viewed directly in the Twitter stream. In addition, Twitter launched the video social network Vine (which I cover in detail in Chapter 16). All these actions show that Twitter considers visual content to be important to driving engagement.

Visual content plays two different roles on Twitter. First, Twitter profiles are highly visually oriented, and optimizing your profile visually on Twitter can impact your success on the site. Second, images and videos are quite popular on Twitter. One study by Buffer (see www.mediabistro.com/alltwitter/ twitter-images-study_b51722) shows that images are the content on Twitter that people most often click to view. Images and videos should therefore be a part of your Twitter marketing strategy.

In this chapter, I show you how to optimize your Twitter profile visually and how to become more effective on Twitter by harnessing the power of visual content.

In this chapter, I don't go into the details of marketing on Twitter. To find out more about Twitter and how to use it to grow your business, check out *Twitter Marketing For Dummies*, written by Kyle Lacy (and published by John Wiley & Sons, Inc.).

The Images Required for Your Twitter Account

When you set up a Twitter account, you can customize a number of images to make it more effective and visually appealing. If Twitter is an important tool for your business, take the time to customize these images to optimize your profile.

As you can see in Figure 7-1, Twitter uses a number of image types on the profile:

- **Profile picture:** The image that's associated with your brand or business and displayed beside your *tweets* (Twitter status updates) in the stream

- **Header image:** The square behind the description of the account; can also be completely customized

- **Background image:** Displayed behind the entire Twitter stream

Figure 7-1:
Sample
Twitter
profile page.

All these images can be completely customized. In the following sections, I show you how to optimize and update the visual appearance of your Twitter account by customizing these images.

Optimized profile photos

Your profile photo is the small, square image that's displayed beside the name of your Twitter account. Your profile photo is arguably the most important image on your profile because whenever people see your posts anywhere on Twitter, they also see this image.

Twitter may occasionally refer to your profile photo as your *avatar*.

 Make your profile picture stand out, and make it instantly recognizable. Because Twitter users often follow lots of people and have a large number of tweets available to read when they log on, many people skim their Twitter newsfeeds rather than read every post. As they skim, they look for the profile images of the accounts in which they're the most interested.

You can edit your Twitter profile picture in two ways. First, when viewing your Twitter profile, click the Edit Profile button below the header image. When you click the pencil icon that appears over the profile image, you have these options: Upload Photo, Take Photo, Remove, and Cancel. To change the photo, select Upload Photo and choose a new image from your computer.

You can also edit your profile by clicking the gear icon in the upper-right corner of the screen when you're logged in and clicking Settings. Then choose Profile from the Settings options on the left. Your current photo is then displayed at the top of the screen, and you can click Change Photo and then Upload Photo to upload a new photo to your Twitter profile.

When you're choosing a profile image for Twitter, follow these best practices — these guidelines also apply to profile images for your personal Twitter profile:

- ✔ **Use a square image or optimize for a square shape.** The image you choose should be a square, or an image where a square portion of the image can be used for the profile image. For example, the Boot Camp Digital logo is normally a rectangle; however, for the Twitter profile image, I created a square version.

- ✔ **Incorporate your logo or another easily identifiable element.** Your logo, or another element that easily identifies your business visually, is the best choice for your Twitter profile photo. The image should be professional-looking and stand out in some way.

- ✔ **Use the image that best matches your strategy.** You may wonder whether a Twitter profile image should be a logo, an image of the person who manages the account, or a hybrid of the two. No single answer is correct, and many successful Twitter strategies have used different types of images. The image you use should match your strategy.

✔ **Make it professional and appropriate.** Make your profile picture match the image that you're trying to create professionally. A blurry logo that's cut off in the square-shaped profile image probably wouldn't reflect well on you professionally. If you choose to use a personal photo, the image should be a headshot that clearly shows your face. You can view sample profile images in Figure 7-2.

✔ **Resist the urge to change your profile photo too often.** Many Twitter users quickly skim their newsfeeds, looking for posts from the people and businesses they care about — and the profile image is the item they look for in order to identify posts. If the photo is continually changing, you face difficulty in building recognition with your fans.

Figure 7-2:
Sample
Twitter
profile
photos.

Changing header and background images and the color scheme

In the following sections, I explain best practices and optimization tips for header and background images.

To navigate to the place to change images, follow these steps:

1. **Click the gear icon in the upper-right corner.**

2. **From the drop-down list, click the Settings option.**

Changing the header image

To change the header image, follow these steps:

1. **Click the Profile button on the left navigation option.**

   When you click Profile, the profile editing options appear.

2. **Click the Change Header button.**

   A window pops up where you can select a header image from your computer. After you find the image you want to use, click the Open button. In the screen that appears, you can customize the image display.

3. **Position and size the header image using the interactive screen.**

   This screen shows you how the header image will look in your profile. Move the header image by dragging it with the cursor to change the positioning. To change the size, use the slider bar at the bottom of the screen.

4. **Click the Apply button.**

   The changes are saved to your profile.

5. **Click the blue Save Changes button at the bottom of the screen.**

   Enjoy your new header image.

Changing the background image

To change the background image, follow these steps:

1. **Click the Design button on the left navigation option.**

   After you click it, the design editing options appear.

2. **To use a premade theme, click on the theme picture at the top of the screen.**

   A premade theme customizes the background image and applies a matching color scheme to the profile.

3. **Click the Change Background button.**

   This step opens a pop-up window that lets you choose an image from your computer to use as a background image. Select the image and click the Open button.

4. **Select the Tile Background button if you want to tile the background.**

   In a *tiled* background, the background image is repeated. If the image isn't tiled (because you didn't select the Tile Background check box), the image is displayed only once.

5. **Select the background position.**

   You can choose between Left, Center, and Right. The background determines where the image is anchored to on the screen.

6. **Click the blue Save Changes button at the bottom of the screen.**

   The new background image is all set to go.

Changing the color scheme

To change the color scheme, follow these steps:

1. **Click the Design button on the left navigation option.**

   After you click Design, the design editing options appear. Scroll down toward the bottom of the screen to view the color editing options.

2. **Click the color box to change the colors.**

   To change the colors of the background and links, click the color that's displayed in the box. A color selection tool pops up that lets you choose the color you want to use.

3. **Enter the 6-digit HTML color number.**

   If you know the precise color you want to use, enter the 6-digit HTML color code in the box to the right of the color display box.

4. **Click the selector box to choose a black or white overlay.**

   The *overlay* color is the color that's displayed over the center of the Twitter profile. It essentially creates a box around the content in the center of the profile. Choose between a black or white overlay.

5. **Click the blue Save Changes button at the bottom of the screen.**

   This step saves your changes.

Header image

The header image is displayed at the top of your Twitter page, behind the profile information. It's another image that can be customized to improve your visual presence on Twitter.

Twitter recommends a header image that measures 1252 x 626 pixels, with a maximum file size of 5MB. Other image sizes may not be rejected, but Twitter recommends optimizing for this size.

In Figure 7-3, you can see some sample header images from leading brands, such as Coca Cola, Pepsi, Tim Hortons, and Girlfriendology. As you can see, the header image can improve the visual appeal of your Twitter profile. Be creative with your header image, and create one that makes your profile stand out.

Figure 7-3: Sample header images on Twitter.

A great-looking header image makes your Twitter profile much more visually appealing. As you can see in the examples here, brands use the header photo to extend their brand images, showcase their products, and make their Twitter pages more visually stimulating.

Background image and color scheme

One type of image that's required for your Twitter profile is the background image — it's displayed behind the Twitter profile. Twitter allows users to customize the color scheme that's displayed with their profiles. You select a color scheme in the same place where you select the background image.

The challenge in creating a background image is that different screen sizes may display more or less of the image. For example, if I have a narrower screen resolution, I might see only a small portion of the background image, and the body of the Twitter account occupies most of the screen.

When you create a background image, keep in mind that not everyone can see the entire image.

Twitter lets you fully customize the background image. Under Settings, select the Design tab to customize the look and feel of your Twitter account and set up a custom background image.

Premade background images

At the top of the Design Settings screen, Twitter allows you to choose from a number of premade themes. A premade theme applies a premade background to your Twitter profile and applies a matching background and link colors. You can preview premade themes by clicking them to generate a preview.

After you select a theme, click Save Changes at the bottom of the screen to save your changes.

In addition to the premade themes displayed at the top of the screen, Twitter provides an option to generate a premade background. Below the premade themes is the Check Out Themeleon link. Clicking it opens a new site that has thousands of patterns and color palettes that you can use to customize your Twitter account, as shown in Figure 7-4. You're prompted to log in to your Twitter account to get started on Themeleon. The background patterns and images are applied to your background, and the color palettes are applied to the other color settings on your profile. Select a background image and a color palette that are compatible with the rest of the visual assets in your Twitter profile.

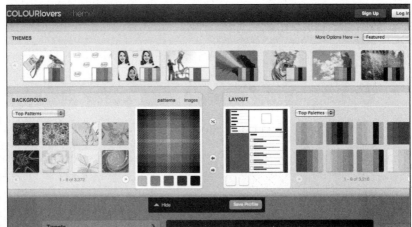

Figure 7-4: Themeleon background image and palette selections.

After you select the background pattern and color palette, you see the Save Profile button. If you don't see it, you may see one labeled Login to Twitter. If you're prompted to authorize the Themeleon application (from COLOURlovers) to access your Twitter account, choose to give the application access so that your selections can be added to your account. (You have to do this the first time you use the application.) After you authorize the application, click the Save Profile button.

After you save your profile, you see a notification that your stylish profile has been saved. The application should bring you back to view your profile.

Customized background images

Rather than use the premade background and color schemes, you may completely customize them. If you create a custom image, be aware of different screen sizes in your design. Many custom designs make use of the space on the left to share information, as shown in the Twitter account example shown in Figure 7-5.

Figure 7-5:
A Twitter profile page with a customized background.

The problem is that screens with different resolutions may not be able to view all the text on the left. When you scale down the width of your browser window, you will notice that the size of Twitter feed area doesn't decrease. Instead, it slides to the left to stay in the center of the screen, which can cover part of your customized background image.

When you create a custom image, the image must be in a PNG, JPEG, or GIF format and it must be smaller than 2MB. The image you create may be a single large image to display behind the entire profile, or you may tile a smaller image.

When you *tile* an image, it is repeated across and down to fill the space on the screen.

To create a single image to display behind the Twitter profile, you need to create a large image and remember that some of it will be displayed behind the Twitter account information.

The body of the Twitter screen is approximately 870 pixels wide; the average screen resolution is 1366 pixels wide on an average laptop, but may be as wide as 1600 pixels on a wider monitor. You should create an image sized at 1600 x 1200 pixels while optimizing it for viewing on a screen that is the average 1366 x 768 pixels. The Twitter body content is 870 pixels wide, which means that the design space for the background image is 248 pixels on each side of the Twitter stream. The primary design area for the Twitter background is typically on the left because that's where people tend to look when viewing a Twitter profile. If you're planning to add logos or text to the Twitter background that you want to be viewable, the space on the left is usually the primary design space.

You can download a number of free Photoshop templates online. Searching for the term *Twitter background template download* at your favorite search engine will display a number of websites with free, downloadable templates.

Customized color scheme

You can use the customized color scheme options to change the colors displayed with your Twitter profile. You can change the background color and the color of links, and you can choose between black and white overlays. You can find color customization options at the bottom of the Design settings page, which you open by selecting Edit Profile and then Design.

Visually stunning Twitter profile

The objective of customizing the images and color scheme on your Twitter profile is to create a visually stunning profile that supports your branding and attracts followers.

Follow these tips when creating your visual presence on Twitter:

- ✔ **Make it professional.** Your Twitter profile should look professional, such as when you choose custom images that use the same color schemes. Incorrectly sized images that are either pixelated or the wrong size create a bad impression. Make sure that all your visual content is professional-looking.

- ✔ **Be consistent.** All your visual content on Twitter should be consistent. Use the same colors and visual identity for all assets.

- ✔ **Matching matters.** Rather than view each image individually, look at how they all work together. The profile, header, and background images should all complement each other and match visually.

- ✔ **Get inspired.** If you're struggling to come up with a strong visual theme for your Twitter account, spend some time looking at other Twitter accounts. Viewing a variety of accounts will provide you with inspiration regarding the types of visual elements that can make your Twitter account stand apart from the rest.

Visual Content in Status Updates

Visual content is an important part of your Twitter content strategy. When you're planning what you will share on Twitter, visual content should be a part of the strategy. A recent study found that tweets with photos resulted in 120 percent more engagement and a 350 percent increase in clicks to the tweet.

Photos and videos shared by way of Twitter are also prominently displayed on the profile page, as shown in Figure 7-6.

Figure 7-6:
Visual content is featured on the Twitter profile page.

Photos in status updates

Photos can make for engaging status updates. A photo can be shared in a status update by uploading it directly to Twitter.

When writing a status update on Twitter, click the camera icon below the status update box. Then choose an image from your computer to upload to your Twitter status update. After you have uploaded the image, it appears as a link in the tweet. You can also do this from a mobile phone to add the image to a Twitter status update.

You can view an image on Twitter in a few ways. A user can click the link to view the image. At the bottom of a tweet with an image, the View Photo button is displayed. (Note that it appears only at the bottom of tweets with an image.) Clicking View Photo displays the image in the newsfeed, as shown in Figure 7-7. Users can then view an image directly in the Twitter newsfeed, without having to go to another website.

Figure 7-7: Photos can be viewed directly in the news-feed by clicking the View Photo button.

This applies only to images directly uploaded to Twitter or images shared from photo applications that are integrated with Twitter. Links to images on photo sharing sites that aren't integrated, such as Instagram, are simply displayed as links that don't include the View Photo button or are displayed with images in the profile. You can still share photos, therefore, from other photo sharing sites, such as Instagram, by adding a link to the image. The image however, isn't displayed on the profile page and isn't viewable with the View Photo button in the newsfeed.

Videos in status updates

Videos can also be shared in status updates by way of the Vine application or by sharing a link to a video that's hosted on YouTube or another video sharing site.

Twitter created the video sharing application Vine (which is covered in detail in Chapter 16). Videos can also be shared from video sharing sites such as YouTube. To share a YouTube video, copy the URL (website address) of the YouTube video, and paste it into the body of your tweet. You can also click the Twitter share icon under the YouTube video you want to share.

Videos shared from the Vine app and via links from YouTube are displayed in the Photos and Videos section of the profile page, and they can be viewed in the newsfeed by clicking View Media. In this way, Vine and YouTube videos can be viewed directly in Twitter.

Visual status updates

The visual status update can be a powerful way to engage followers on Twitter. A good mix of content includes sharing status updates; links to websites; images; and videos. To optimize your visual content for Twitter, keep these tips in mind:

- ✔ **Use an application that's compatible with Twitter.** When sharing visual content, either upload it directly to Twitter or use an application that's integrated with Twitter, to maximize the visibility of your content.

- ✔ **Make it relevant.** All the images and videos you share should be relevant to your audience.

- ✔ **Maximize the value of your visuals.** Make sure that your visual content is "worth a thousand words" and that it continues to tell your story and grow your brand image. For example, add your logo or branding to images that you share on Twitter and other social networks.

- ✔ **Let people know what you're sharing.** Because people on Twitter like to click on photos and videos to view them, point out that your tweet contains a photo or video to drive people to click on it and interact with it.

Chapter 8

Improving Your Blog with Visual Content

*V*isual content is a vital part of any blogging strategy. Studies have found that blog posts with images generate 94 percent more total views than posts without images. (See www.mdgadvertising.com/blog/its-all-about-the-images-infographic.) Images are therefore necessary to attract viewers of your blog posts.

In Chapter 2, I describe the role that images play in driving traffic to your website, and my description applies to blog posts as well. A blog post with images can be shared more easily on social networks such as Facebook, Twitter, Pinterest, and LinkedIn, which translates into more traffic to your blog posts and more views.

Since blogging first began, images and other visual content have been important pieces of the blogging puzzle.

It used to be that writing a blog post that was accompanied by a loosely relevant image was good enough to generate the benefits that images bring to blog posts. For example, if you had written a blog post titled Top Ten Tools for Blogging, you might have added an image of a toolbox. Now, with images being displayed more prominently across social networks, the standard has been raised. You can no longer have a loosely relevant image — the images must be highly relevant and tell the story of your post.

Posts with appealing images can be shared across social networks and drive traffic to the blog. Posts without images can't be easily shared and aren't as easy to read.

In this chapter, I show you why images are vital to your blogging strategy and how to use best practices to bring your blog to life visually. In this chapter, I don't go into the details of why and how to create a blog. To find out more details about blogging, check out *Professional Blogging For Dummies,* written by Susan J. Getgood, or *Corporate Blogging For Dummies,* by Douglas Karr and Chantelle Flannery (both from Wiley Publishing).

Driving Traffic to Your Blog with Visual Content

A *pinnable* image is one that, on its own, tells the story of the post. (I introduce the concept of creating pinnable images in Chapter 2.) Pinnable images, which can be shared across social networks with no accompanying text description, convey the key message of the blog post. A pinnable image can drive clicks and traffic to your blog, because the image entices people to click on your links and read your blog posts.

In the age of Pinterest, where the image is the focus of sharing a blog post or web page, you can't afford to miss out on the traffic to your site that images can generate. The idea is that the image alone tells your story.

As you can see in Figure 8-1, when a blog post from my blog at www. KristaNeher.com is pinned to Pinterest, the image alone must tell the story. An appropriate image attracts more clicks; a less relevant image attracts fewer clicks.

Figure 8-1:
A pinnable
blog post
image on
Pinterest.

Implementing best practices for adding images to your blog

To make the images with your blog posts pinnable, follow these best practices:

- ✔ **The image should tell the story**: The image alone should tell the story. Don't simply select a related image to accompany the post. Look at the image by itself, and assess whether it showcases the topic of the blog post.

- ✔ **The image should drive viewers to click**: The goal of pinnable images is to intrigue people to click on the image. The image should be intriguing and interesting enough to drive someone to click.

- ✔ **Images should be eye-catching**: All images should be interesting, intriguing, and eye-catching. Remember that the images accompanying your blog post may show up in a Facebook newsfeed. Make sure that it's eye-catching enough to make someone stop and click on it.

- ✔ **Image types should be mixed**: Some blogs and websites have an image template that they use on all their blog posts. To keep your blog posts interesting, mix up the types of images you use. Don't stick to a single format or template.

Planning a strategy for posting images on your blog

To execute on the strategy of creating pinnable images for your blog, you must have a plan. Every blog post should have a pinnable image that accompanies it.

Most business blogs follow some sort of editorial calendar that outlines the schedule for posting blogs. Depending on the size and complexity of your organization, the editorial calendar may be more or less detailed, though it should include who will post what and when. Images should be added to this calendar, especially if a graphics department is required in order to execute the image strategy.

 The reason that images should be included upfront on the editorial calendar is that they aren't simply afterthoughts. The image that accompanies your blog post can make or break the amount of traffic and the social media interest that your blog post generates.

Plan your images upfront. To successfully incorporate high-quality images into your blog strategy, follow these steps:

1. **Determine the key point of the blog**.

   Knowing the main premise, or theme, of the blog post is important in creating a pinnable image. Start by knowing what you want to communicate.

2. **Brainstorm image ideas**.

   Brainstorm different types of images that may represent your story visually. You may choose an image with a particularly interesting statistic or an eye-catching photo that's highly relevant with text written on it.

3. **Determine the image concept**.

   After brainstorming, decide on the image concept that best represents your blog post.

4. **Decide how to create the image**.

   After you know what you want to create, decide how you will create it. Perhaps the writer can create the image, or a designer may support the creation.

5. **Plan who will create it and when**.

   Decide who will create the image, and determine when it's needed. If your blog posts must first complete an approval process, you may need to have the image prepared in advance. Before publishing the image, be sure that it meets your requirements for a pinnable image.

6. **Add the image to the post**.

   Add the image to your blog post. Determine where the image should be displayed in the post and whether it should be in the center or on the right or left. Preview the post to be sure that the image displays correctly before posting.

7. **Analyze and improve**.

   All aspects of social media marketing include continuous improvement. Analyze how well different types of images perform for your blog. Look at the images that generate the most shares and clicks on social networks to evaluate the effectiveness of images. Continually refine and improve your image strategy.

These steps can be incorporated into your editorial calendar to ensure that you have enough time to create a stunning image.

Telling Your Story with Images

Telling the story of your blog post with images can draw more traffic to your blog. Adding images to your blog post shouldn't be simply an afterthought; the images should be relevant and interesting to attract readers to your blog.

After you have the image for a blog post, the next step is uploading it to the blog. When uploading images to a blog post, be sure that the images are uploaded correctly, to optimize the visibility of your post.

Uploading images to your blog

The precise steps for uploading images to a blog post depend on the blogging software you use. In this section I share the steps using WordPress blogging software, but the steps are similar for any blogging software you use.

You may choose to add the image at any point during the process of writing your blog post. I prefer to add images after I finish writing my post so that I can decide where in the blog post the image fits best.

To add an image to your post, you should see a button to add an image in your blog post editor. From there, you're prompted to upload an image. (You may also have the option to link to a photo, as covered in the later section "Linking to an image in your blog post.") After you upload the image, you have a number of settings to customize.

Figure 8-2 shows the options to customize the image upload in WordPress. Again, depending on your blogging software, you may have a different interface, but the options should be similar.

Figure 8-2:
Uploaded image cus-
tomization options.

Take the time to customize the fields on the image upload page. Customizing these fields is especially important for search engines. Many people search for images; updating these fields can help your images be found in search engines. You can customize the items described in this list:

- **Title**: The title is important because search engines such as Google can't understand the contents of an image; instead, they look to the title to understand what the image is about. Customize the title to clearly describe the image, and use keywords that people might search for so that your image shows up in search engines.

- **Caption**: The caption is displayed below the image when it's displayed on your blog post. The caption allows you to add text to accompany the image.

- **Alt text**: This text is displayed when the image can't be loaded. The alt text should describe the image in the event that the image doesn't load on the page.

- **Description**: The description provides the opportunity for you to describe the image contents in more detail. Search engines can view the description to help them understand what the image is about, beyond the text included in the title.

These fields should be complete to optimize the image.

In addition to optimizing the images with the fields provided, most blogging image upload software allows for additional editing of the image. In WordPress, the editing options can be found by clicking on Edit Image after uploading the image. Each blogging software will allow for different editing options, but most allow you to crop, rotate, and adjust the size of the image.

In addition to letting you edit the image, blogging software gives you a few options for displaying the image in your post. The options to display the image are described in this list:

- **Alignment**: Determines where the image is displayed on the blog post. You can align the image to the left or right or in the center of the text; choose None if you want the image displayed without text.

- **Link To**: Determines where a visitor goes after clicking on the image. For example, if I write a blog post about a training program and display an image of the training program, I may choose to have the link to the image lead to the page about the training program. By changing the Link To option, you can decide where someone is sent when they click on the image. The default option on WordPress and most other blogging software is to link to the media file. Someone who clicks on the picture sees a larger version of the image.

✔ **Size**: Adjusts the size of the image on your blog post. The optimal size for an image depends on the image itself and on the layout of your blog post. You can customize the image size when uploading the image, or resize it after it's in the blog post.

Customizing the options in this list affects the way the images are displayed in the blog post. Before publishing your blog post, preview the post to see how the image will be displayed when the post goes live. The blog post editor may not reflect how the image will look when the post is published, so preview the post to be sure that the image is positioned correctly in the post.

If the image isn't displayed correctly, you can continue to adjust the image size and alignment until it fits with your blog post. You can access the image editing and display customization options by clicking on the image to select it and then clicking on the image icon to be displayed in the upper-left corner of the image.

Linking to an image in your blog post

Uploading an image to your blog post isn't the only way to add an image to the post. Most blogging platforms also allow for a URL to be used for an image.

The basic difference is that when you upload an image from your computer, you're hosting the image on your servers. The image you upload from your computer must be one that you have the rights to use.

When you *link* to an image, you redisplay an image that's hosted on a different server or website. You aren't uploading the image to your website, so you can link to images from other websites that you don't have the copyright to display.

For example, if you find a helpful infographic that you want to display on your site, you can't simply download and then upload the image, unless it's explicitly copyrighted to allow commercial use. To get around this limitation, rather than download the image, you can link to it. The image is still displayed on the blog, but you aren't hosting the image yourself.

To display an image from a URL, choose the Insert for URL option (or a similar one) in your blog post editor and paste the link of the image you want to display. To display a URL image, follow these steps:

1. **Find the image that you want to display on your blog**.

   Choose a suitable image.

2. **Find the URL to the image**.

   The easiest way to find the URL is to right-click on the image you want to display and choose Copy Image URL from the menu that appears. This action places the URL of the image on the clipboard.

3. **Paste the image's URL on your blog in the Add Media section**.

   Find the input section on your blog to display an image via the URL. On WordPress, you click the Add Media button in the blog post editor and then select Insert from URL on the left side of the menu.

4. **Customize the display options**.

   As when you upload a photo, you may choose to add a caption and alter text and then select the alignment and the destination that the image links to.

After you insert the image into your post, be sure to preview your blog post before publishing to make sure that it displays correctly in your post.

When you use the Insert from URL image option, you have no control over the image. Because you're linking to an image that's hosted on another website, the website can remove or change the image, affecting how the image is displayed on your website. Though most websites don't remove or change images after uploading them, a risk still exists.

Engaging Readers with Videos on Your Blog

Adding videos to your blog can increase the engagement level of people viewing your post and extend the viewing duration. You may include videos that you upload from your computer or videos that you find on video sharing sites such as YouTube.

When videos are incorporated correctly in your blog, viewers can click Play to watch the video directly from your blog.

Uploading videos to your blog

Uploading a video to your blog isn't as simple as you might expect. Though blogging software makes it easy to upload images, videos are more difficult because blogging software lacks a video player. Though you can upload a video, the blogging software usually can't play the video. Adding a video player typically requires purchasing a plug-in or video player software to allow videos to play on your blog.

Though this problem may seem complex, a simple solution is to first upload the video to a video sharing site such as YouTube and then share the YouTube video on your blog.

One main reason that businesses prefer to upload their videos and use a separate video player is that you may have more control over the video display. Also, search engine results may include a small snippet of the video if you use a custom video player. (In Chapter 2, I show you a sample of how search engines display videos.) The benefit of having the video snippet in search results is that it can increase the number of people who click on your link.

Embedding a video on your blog

Rather than upload your own video and display it on your blog, you can embed a video from YouTube or another video sharing site. Though this section focuses on YouTube (the most popular video sharing website), the steps are similar for other video sharing social networks.

You may embed your own videos into your blog post or any video you find on YouTube. For example, I may find a YouTube video with an example of a commercial that I want to write about in my blog post. I can embed the YouTube video in my post, and viewers can watch the video directly in my blog, without having to go to YouTube. An example of a YouTube video embedded in a blog is shown in Figure 8-3.

Figure 8-3:
A YouTube video displayed in a blog post.

To embed a YouTube video into your blog post, follow these steps:

1. Find the video on YouTube and click the Embed link.

Start by finding on YouTube the video you want to share on your blog. Go to the page on YouTube that hosts the video. Below the video, click the Share tab and click the Embed link.

2. **Customize the embed code**.

   A small window with code is generated. You may want to customize certain aspects of this code before sharing it. YouTube lets you choose the size of the video player. You can also select the Select Privacy Enhanced-Mode check box so that YouTube doesn't store information about your website visitors unless they play the video. When you've selected the size and privacy settings, highlight the code generated in the display box and copy it to the clipboard. A sample of the code window is shown in Figure 8-4.

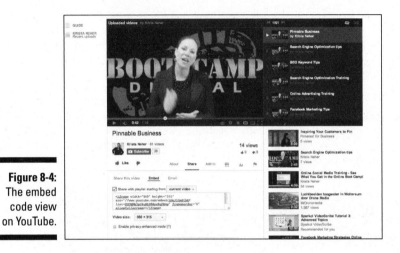

Figure 8-4:
The embed code view on YouTube.

3. **Go to the HTML/Code/Text entry on your blog**.

   The default editing screen on your blog is typically a visual editing screen that doesn't display the code for the blog. To embed the YouTube video, you enter the code editor/viewer of the blog post. Choose to view the code for your blog post. Scroll through the code to find the section of your blog post where you want to insert the video. Paste the code into the blog post. When you switch back to the visual view of your blog, you should be able to see a box that shows where the video will be displayed.

4. **Preview the post to see the video in the blog post**.

   Verify that the video is displayed correctly and is viewable in the post. Depending on your blog settings, the video may not be playable in Preview mode. Either way, Preview mode shows you where the video will be displayed and the size of the video.

Videos make your posts more engaging. Don't hesitate to embed a video directly into your blog post so that readers of your blog can view the video directly from your website.

Chapter 9

Drawing Attention to LinkedIn with Images

In This Chapter

▶ Making the most of images on your LinkedIn profile image

▶ Harnessing visual content throughout your profile

▶ Optimizing images on your company page

▶ Showcasing your products and services with images on LinkedIn

*L*inkedIn continues to be the largest professional social network, and it's a key component of many social media marketing strategies. As in other social networks, visual content plays a key role in your success.

A study conducted by TheLadders (see `http://finance.yahoo.com/news/14-terrible-linkedin-mistakes-you-re-making.html`) found that recruiters spend more time examining a LinkedIn user's photo than reviewing the person's qualifications. Even on a professional social network such as LinkedIn, images matter.

Additionally, when you're searching for people or businesses on a search engine such as Google, LinkedIn profiles and pages often show up at the top of the results. Your LinkedIn profile or page may therefore be the first impression you create, and the visual content is a fundamental aspect of this impression.

When you share your blog posts or website URL on LinkedIn as a status update or in a group, images from the website or blog post are displayed prominently in the post. (I cover this topic in Chapter 2, where I review the importance of images and links.)

This chapter focuses on the image assets needed for a personal LinkedIn profile and a company page. These images can make or break the visual appeal of your LinkedIn page. I show you the visual assets you need for your LinkedIn accounts as well as the best practices to follow to make them truly stand out.

Enhancing Your LinkedIn Profile with Visual Content

The images on your personal LinkedIn profile can affect how professionally you are perceived. Your profile photo is the most important photo on your LinkedIn profile because it sets the tone of your profile. LinkedIn also allows users to add images to the different sections of their profiles. This creates a unique opportunity to represent yourself visually and draw attention to your accomplishments in a unique way.

The well-known expression "A picture is worth a thousand words" also applies to your LinkedIn strategy. Professional images on your personal LinkedIn profile can continue to build your professional image and highlight your accomplishments in a unique way. Additionally, adding the appropriate images to your LinkedIn profile can help you stand out.

Adding or changing your profile image

Your profile picture is the most important image on your LinkedIn profile. It sets the tone for the entire profile and is displayed alongside your name across LinkedIn. According to LinkedIn, adding a profile photo makes your profile seven times more likely to be viewed by others.

As you can see in Figure 9-1, a LinkedIn profile displays the user's image at the top of the page.

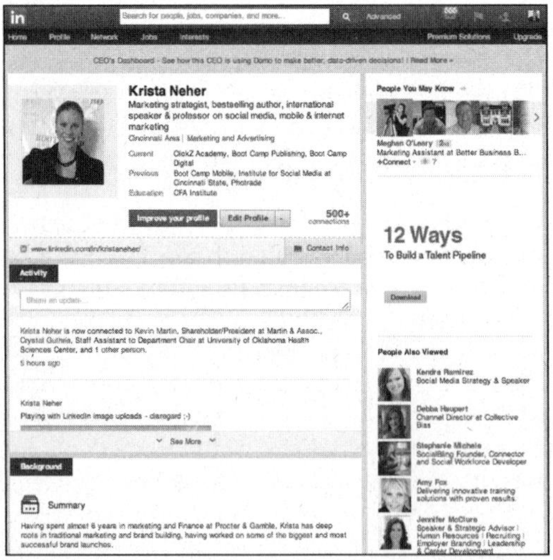

Figure 9-1:
Sample
LinkedIn
profile page.

Your LinkedIn image should be formatted as a GIF, JPG, or PNG file. The maximum file size is 4 megabytes. The image should measure from 200 x 200 pixels (the minimum) to 500 pixels by 500 pixels (the maximum).

To upload or change your profile photo on LinkedIn, follow these general steps:

1. **Navigate to edit the image.**

   Hover over Profile in the top navigation menu, and then click on Edit Profile on the drop-down menu. Click this button, and then all components of your profile can be edited.

2. **Upload a new photo.**

   After you click to edit the profile, a small camera icon is displayed on your profile page. Click the camera button, and you're redirected to the Upload a Photo page, as shown in Figure 9-2. Click the Choose File button and choose the image to upload.

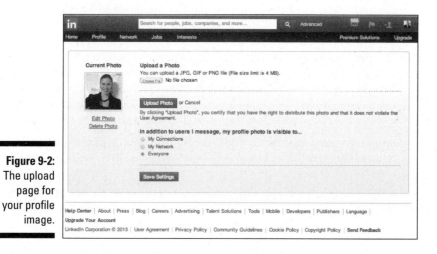

Figure 9-2:
The upload page for your profile image.

3. **Choose the portion of the photo to display.**

   After clicking the Upload Photo button, you're directed to a new screen that shows the image you uploaded. From there, you can crop the display of the photo to determine the square portion of the image that you want to display. When you're satisfied with the way the profile image looks, click Save Photo to be redirected to the Upload a Photo page.

4. **Determine who can see your photo.**

   You may choose to have your profile visible to your connections, to your network, or to everyone. If your goal is to use LinkedIn to expand your network, allow your profile photo to be viewed by everyone. Finally, click the Save Settings button to save the profile photo changes.

People are more likely to view your profile if they can see your image. If you choose to make your profile photo viewable only to those in your network, your profile will be less effective.

Optimizing your profile photo

To optimize your LinkedIn profile image, follow these best practices:

- ✔ **Make the image square in shape.** You can upload an image of any size, though you will have to crop it into a square shape. Uploading a square photo lets you control exactly what's displayed in your profile photo.

- ✔ **Make your face visible.** LinkedIn is about personal connections. Being able to see your face clearly in the photo helps to build a personal connection.

- ✔ **Remember that professionalism matters.** LinkedIn is a professional social network, so put your best foot forward with a professional profile photo — in the quality of the image *and* the professionalism of your clothing.

- ✔ **Your photo should look like you.** If you build your professional brand via LinkedIn, people who find your profile there should be able to get to know you. Don't use a photo that's more than ten years old or that doesn't quite look like you. Instead, find one that looks like you so that when you connect with people in real life, they know what to expect.

- ✔ **Only you should appear in your photo.** Your profile photo shouldn't include other people — but don't choose a photo that has other people cropped out.

- ✔ **Smile.** A profile photo should make you appear friendly and approachable (unless you're specifically trying to brand yourself in a different way). A smiling photo is more appealing to people.

Take the time to create a great-looking profile photo because it will likely be the first impression you're creating.

Adding images to the body of your profile

In addition to a profile photo, LinkedIn allows users to add images to the body of their profiles. You can add images to any section in your LinkedIn profile.

Adding pictures to the body of your profile can help to tell your story visually and to make your profile stand out. For example, I can write about the books I've authored, or I can add images of the books to draw more attention to them.

In addition to adding images to your LinkedIn profile, you can include videos, presentations, and documents. It's a powerful way to showcase your skills and expertise beyond just text. You can add YouTube videos and SlideShare presentations to truly highlight your skills and experiences.

To add visual content to your profile, start by hovering the cursor over the Profile in the main navigation on LinkedIn, and then click on Edit Profile. After you're in the Edit Profile section, follow these steps:

1. **At the top of the LinkedIn profile section to which you want to add visual content, click the blue, square box button with a plus sign on it.**

   At the top of each section of your LinkedIn profile is a square button with a plus sign (+) on it. You can click this button to add a video, photo, document, or slide show to your profile.

2. **Choose a method to add the image:**

   a. *Link to URL:* Links only to content that's on the list of approved content providers. LinkedIn specifies the sites you can link to for photos, videos, audio files, presentations, and other types of supported media. If you choose this option, your content must already be uploaded to one of the approved partner sites. To include content from an approved partner site on your LinkedIn profile, find the URL for the content you want to display and paste it into the URL box. After inserting the link and pressing Enter, a box appears in which you can customize the title and description of the content you post. You can see a sample of a YouTube video on a LinkedIn profile in Figure 9-3.

Figure 9-3:
YouTube video, displayed in a LinkedIn profile.

Professional Social Media Speaker and Keynote Speaker
Krista Neher
October 2008 – Present (5 years) | Cincinnati Ohio

Krista Neher is a sought-after professional keynote speaker on topics including social media, entrepreneurship, mobile and marketing strategy. Krista consistently receives top scores for her presentations because she is professional, easy to work with, educational, enthusiastic and engaging.

Krista has presented in North America, Eurpoe and Latin America to audiences as small as 10 to as large as 10,000. She isn't just a great speaker - she is a knowledgeble expert who shares engaging stories that leave audiences motivated and excited.

Krista's speaking engagements include keynote presentations, workshops, seminars, sessions, classes and courses. Krista has also worked with businesses and corporations, conferences, trade shows, conventions, annual meetings, company meetings and seminars and colleges.

Visit www.KristaNeher.com to learn more.

See why most conferences book Krista year after year! Satisfied audiences include Incisive Media, the United States Senate, 53 Bank, P&G, Presto Foods, SXSW, Chambers of Commerce, the Better Business Bureau, Remax and many, many more.

- 1 recommendation

  Ryanne Williams
  Digital Sales Assistant at Chico Enterprise-Record

Krista's presentation at the Chico Women in Business Meeting was very informative and helped me to better use Social Media at the Chico Enterprise Record. I enjoyed her presentation and would go see her again, hopefully she will come back soon! View)

Professional Social Media Keynote Speaker

b. Upload an image: Uploads the photo or presentation from your computer directly to LinkedIn. LinkedIn supports presentations, documents, and images. Images must be formatted as GIF, JPG, JPEG, or PNG files with a maximum file size of 100 megabytes. After you select an image or presentation to upload, you can customize the title and description of the content. Figure 9-4 shows how an uploaded image is displayed in the LinkedIn profile.

Figure 9-4:
Sample
image,
uploaded
directly into
a LinkedIn
profile.

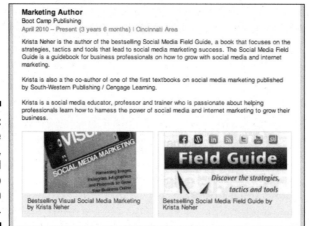

When uploading an image, be sure to examine how the image is displayed on your profile to be sure that it matches the way you intended it to appear. After a piece of content is uploaded to LinkedIn, it's displayed in the profile in a square box. Even if the entire image can't be displayed in the profile (an image gets cropped if it's too large), users can click on the image to view it in its entirety in the full-screen view.

Including images in status updates

On LinkedIn, people *and* pages can upload images, documents, and presentations to status updates. You likely already know that visual status updates generate more interactions on Facebook and Twitter, so it's likely that they can generate more visibility for posts on LinkedIn also.

To add an image to a status update by uploading an attachment, click the small paperclip icon in the Share an Update box. (You must be on your LinkedIn home page to add a status update.) Attachments can be images, presentations, or documents. LinkedIn doesn't support all file types; you can find a complete list of supported file types in the LinkedIn Help documentation.

After you select the attachment, you can add text to the status update and post it. Leveraging images can be a powerful way for your profile or your company page's status updates to gain more visibility in the newsfeed.

Optimizing Your LinkedIn Company Page with Visual Content

Visual content also plays a large role on your LinkedIn company page. A company page on LinkedIn is the official representation of a company. You can add a number of images to optimize the look and feel of a LinkedIn company page.

Businesses can use this powerful opportunity to showcase their products and tell their brands' stories. Fully using the visual content available to LinkedIn pages creates a more visually attractive page.

Harnessing photos on your LinkedIn company page

The LinkedIn profile page can display three types of images: home page image, standard logo, and square logo. Figure 9-5 shows a LinkedIn company page with a home page image and logo. As you can see, these images, as described in the following three sections, are a powerful way to visually brand your page.

Figure 9-5: Images on a LinkedIn company page.

Home page image

The home page image is displayed toward the top of the company page on LinkedIn. It's a powerful branding opportunity because the image is relatively large. The home page image should be a minimum of 646 pixels x 220 pixels and must be either a PNG, JPEG, or GIF file. The maximum image size of the home page image is 2 megabytes.

Logo image

The logo, which should be the official logo of your company, is displayed in the upper-left corner of the LinkedIn page. The logo also appears on a profile page to the right of the text *work experience* for your company. For example, if I list Boot Camp Digital in my work experience on my personal profile, the Boot Camp Digital logo is displayed to the right of the work experience listing. The logo image should be 100 pixels x 60 pixels, and it must be in GIF, JPEG, or PNG format with a maximum size of 2 megabytes.

Square logo

The square logo is used across LinkedIn as the equivalent of a profile photo. For example, when I see an update from a page in my newsfeed on LinkedIn, the square logo is used as a profile photo to represent the page. Because the *logo image* isn't square, the square logo is used in places where a square image is needed to represent a page. You can choose to upload an image of any size; however, it will be resized to 50 x 50 pixels. The images must be formatted as PNG, JPEG, or GIF files, and they have a maximum size of 2 megabytes. The square logo is shown in Figure 9-6, in the newsfeed.

Figure 9-6:
The
LinkedIn
square logo
appears
beside
status
updates.

Boot Camp Digital Boot Camp Digital CEO Krista Neher joins the Board of the Cincinnati Better Business Bureau. http://lnkd.in/2xMUST

Announcement: Krista Neher Joins the Cincinnati Better Business...
bootcampdigital.com
Boot Camp Digital founded by Krista Neher provides social media training and social media marketing consulting worldwide based in Cincinnati Ohio.

Like · Comment · Share · 13 days ago

Updated images on your LinkedIn page

All three of the LinkedIn company profile images can be changed and edited from the same location. To add or replace these images, follow these steps:

1. **Click Edit in the upper-right corner of the company page you manage.**

   This step opens a page where you can edit all elements of your LinkedIn page.

2. **Choose the image you want to edit.**

   As you scroll down the page, all three profile images are displayed.

3. **Click the Edit or Add Image button below the image you want to edit.**

4. **Choose to remove the existing image or upload a new image and select the file from your computer.**

5. **After you've selected the image, click the Save button to save your changes.**

6. **Click Publish to publish your changes to the company page.**

   This step saves your changes and publishes them to your page.

Including images in LinkedIn products and services descriptions

In addition to creating the LinkedIn company page, businesses on LinkedIn can list their products and services. This is another area where visual content can play an important role in creating a strong business presence.

A LinkedIn profile page gives you a spot to display a cover photo and the opportunity to update statuses, but the Products and Services page provides a number of opportunities to showcase your business visually.

To edit or add content to the Products and Services page (you might see instead only the Products page or only the Services page), select the Products and Services tab on the company page and click the Edit button in the upper-right corner. You then see a number of visual assets, as described in the following list, that you can add to this page to showcase your products and services:

✔ **Banner images:** You can add as many as three banner images to rotate. The images should be 646 x 222 pixels. Use images that represent your brand well. You can also customize the banner's URL, where people are sent when they click on your banner's image.

✔ **Add a YouTube video:** On the right side of the page is a space to add a headline and the link to the video. After you have populated these fields, you can preview how the video will look on your product page.

Figure 9-7 shows the products and services editing page, where you can add or remove the visual assets from your Products and Services page.

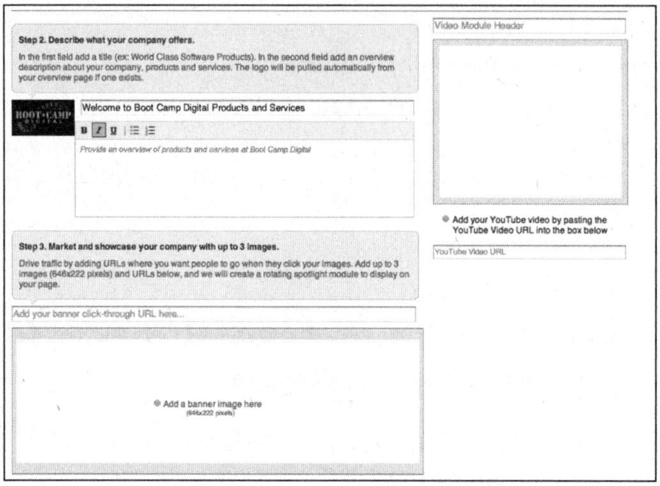

Figure 9-7:
The editing
view of a
LinkedIn
Products
and
Services
page.

Be sure to click Publish to add the changes to your page.

The Products and Services section of LinkedIn also allows you to upload visual assets for the individual products you add to your LinkedIn page. To edit an existing product, click on the product so that you're viewing the product page, click Edit in the upper-right corner, and then click Edit Page. To add a new product or service, click Edit and then Add Product or Service.

Regardless of whether you choose to edit an existing product or add a new one, you're now in the editing view of the Products or Services page. You can create two visual assets for this page. Add an image of the product or service. This image should be 100 x 80 pixels, and the file type should be GIF, JPG, or PNG. In the lower-right corner of the Add Products and Services page, you can add a title and a URL for a YouTube video to accompany the product or service.

Updating these pages is a powerful way to add visual content to your LinkedIn Products and Services page and to make your products or services more appealing. In Figure 9-8, you can see a Product page with banner and product images on LinkedIn.

Figure 9-8:
A LinkedIn
Products
and
Services
page.

Part IV

Marketing via the Visual Social Networks

Find out how three businesses are getting results from Instagram at www.dummies.com/extras/visualsocialmarketing.

In this part . . .

- ✔ Marketing your business with Pinterest
- ✔ Using Instagram to reach your customers and engage your fans
- ✔ Sharing presentations on SlideShare to grow exposure for your business
- ✔ Harnessing infographics to share your message online

Chapter 10

Growing Your Business with Pinterest

*R*ecently emerging as a must-have social network for many social media marketers, Pinterest is now the third most popular social network, and many websites, such as MarthaStewart.com and SparkPeople.com, report that Pinterest is the number-one source of social media traffic to their websites.

Pinterest is a visual social network because images are central to how content is shared and displayed on the site.

The network has demonstrated the ability to generate significant marketing results for businesses. They're using Pinterest to generate traffic to their website, build brand awareness, connect with customers, engage customers, and even drive sales.

The most popular categories of content found on Pinterest are design, recipes, diet, exercise, fashion, crafts, and DIY projects. But Pinterest is by no means limited to these categories. When Pinterest initially became popular, more than 90 percent of its users were women. Now about 70 percent of its users are female.

Businesses of any type can benefit from harnessing the power of Pinterest. Even industrial businesses such as General Electric are using Pinterest to connect with customers and build their brands in a fun way.

In this chapter, I show you exactly how Pinterest works and why it's a unique social network. You discover the marketing power of Pinterest and how to create a strategy for your business. I show you exactly how Pinterest works and how to create a strategy that gets results. I also tell you how Pinterest can generate more traffic to your website, and how to optimize your site to benefit from this traffic.

To find out more about how your business can use Pinterest, check out *Pinterest Marketing For Dummies,* written by Kelby Carr (published by John Wiley & Sons, Inc.), for more details on marketing strategies.

How Businesses Are Using Pinterest

Many businesses are using Pinterest as a part of their social media marketing strategies. It's a powerful social media marketing site because it has a large user base that spends a lot of time on the site.

Businesses use Pinterest for a number of reasons, to

- ✔ **Build awareness:** Pinterest is a useful tool for building awareness for your business. In this context, *awareness* means that people become aware of your business as they see it. Because Pinterest has a large number of users who are active on the site, Pinterest is a helpful way to build awareness and get in front of your target audience.

- ✔ **Generate traffic to your website:** Pinterest drives more traffic to websites than Google+, LinkedIn, Twitter, and YouTube combined. Used strategically, it can be a powerful source of traffic to your site. (I cover this topic in more detail in Chapter 18.)

- ✔ **Build brand equity and positioning:** *Brand equity* and *positioning* refer to the way your business is perceived. Pinterest can help bring your brand to life by showcasing the things that inspire your brand. For example, General Electric (`www.Pinterest.com/GeneralElectric`) uses Pinterest to show what General Electric is all about. It has boards such as #6SecondScience, Mind = Blown, and the Art of Innovation.

- ✔ **Connect with customers:** Pinterest can help businesses to connect with their customers on Pinterest and continue to grow their relevance. For example Home Depot (`www.Pinterest.com/HomeDepot`) uses Pinterest to connect with customers by sharing design and décor inspiration.

✔ **Provide a resource:** Pinterest can also make quite a useful resource center. Using a Pinterest board, you can create a collection of content from around the Internet. For example, at Boot Camp Digital, when people asked to see our infographics, employees used to suggest that they go to our blog and search for the term *infographics*. That wasn't easy. Now the company has a Pinterest board with its infographics, and people are directed to this board, which is well organized and easy to view.

✔ **Learn about your audience:** Many businesses use Pinterest to learn about their audiences. By searching on Pinterest and using analytics, businesses can discover the content from their sites that people are interested in sharing.

✔ **Drive sales:** Pinterest has also been known to drive sales. According to some studies, Pinterest users are 10 percent more likely to buy than users from other social networks, and they spend 70 percent more.

✔ **Help people discover unique products or ideas:** Many people use Pinterest as a searching and discovery tool. They use it to find and discover interesting products, tips, and tricks. By sharing your content on Pinterest, you can help your customers discover your unique products, services, or ideas.

✔ **Search engine optimization:** Pinterest can also help with search engine optimization, known as SEO. You use SEO techniques to help list your website or content near the top of search engines such as Google. Pinterest boards often show up at the top of search engine results. When you create Pinterest boards and descriptions with words and phrases relevant to your business, your boards can be discovered in search engines.

✔ **Pinterest contests:** Finally, a number of businesses are using Pinterest to run contests. Pinterest contests usually involve asking users to pin something and use a specific hashtag or to create a board based on a specific concept with a specific title and description. If your customers are already using Pinterest, a contest can be a helpful way to help them spread the word about your business, products, or organization.

Consider how Pinterest can meet your marketing objectives, and build a Pinterest strategy that matches them.

Before you start pinning, evaluate the topics that your audience truly cares about. Determine whom you want to reach on Pinterest and the topics they're likely to be interested in. If you pin only boring content from your website, no one is likely to take note of you. Start by putting your audience first, and tailor your boards and pins to them. (I explain boards and pins later in this chapter, in the section "Making Pinterest Boards That Get Results.")

One benefit of Pinterest is that everything posted is public and can be easily discovered by other users or shown in search engine results. The right content on Pinterest can, therefore, be discovered and shared by other users and bring increased visibility to your business and your content.

The public nature of Pinterest lets businesses search Pinterest for insights and find users with whom they may want to connect. Most social networks block or limit how businesses connect with individual users. Pinterest allows businesses to follow and interact with individuals, which makes Pinterest a unique opportunity. (Connecting with users on Pinterest is covered in detail later in this chapter, in the section "Pinning Images on Pinterest.")

Exploring Pinterest

Pinterest defines itself as an online pinboard. On Pinterest, users share content known as *pins*, which are images with descriptions, into grouped pages known as *boards*. The Pinterest profile, as shown in Figure 10-1, shows the basic elements of a Pinterest account.

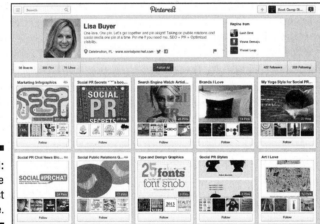

Figure 10-1: Sample Pinterest profile.

Understanding your profile settings

Similar to other social networks, getting started on Pinterest involves creating a profile. The elements of your Pinterest profile can be edited by clicking on your profile picture in the upper-right corner of your profile. Then navigate down to Settings and click on this navigation item. The screen displays all your account settings and information.

To explore your profile information, select the Your Profile and Pins option from the profile icon drop-down menu. Your profile is displayed with a small pencil icon in the lower-right corner of the profile information section, toward the top. Click the pencil icon to view the Edit Profile page. On this page, you can edit your name, picture, username, location, and website and fill in the About You section.

The elements of a Pinterest account include:

- **Account URL:** The URL or website address of your Pinterest account is set by default at `www.Pinterest.com/`*`YourUsername`*`.` (Replace the italicized text with your real username.) This is the unique website address where people can view your Pinterest account. Your username should match the username you use on other social networks, unless you use them for different purposes, and it should uniquely describe you.

- **Profile picture:** In the upper-right corner of a Pinterest profile page is the profile picture. If you're creating a Pinterest account for a business, this should be your logo. For an individual, it should be a picture that clearly shows who you are, and it should, ideally, match the profile picture you use on other social networks.

- **Name:** Beside your profile picture, your name (first, last) is displayed. This name is your username, not the one you enter in your profile information. If you want to remain anonymous or unable to be found on Pinterest, be sure to adjust how you complete the name fields in your profile settings.

- **About you:** The About You section, displayed below your name, is limited to 160 characters. Use them wisely, to clearly describe what you do in an interesting and appealing way. Also, keep in mind that Pinterest users often search for other pinners to connect with, and they may search by information in the contents of the About You section of your page. For this reason, you should use words that people search for in the About You section of your website.

- **Location:** The location displayed below your profile picture is based on the location that's entered in the Edit Profile section. Enter text into this field to describe your location; it can be your neighborhood, city, state, or country.

- **Website:** Whether you create a personal or professional Pinterest account, you can add a website. People can click on the website link to go to your website, and Pinterest gives you the option to verify your website. Verifying your website helps Pinterest confirm that you're the owner of the site you link your profile to. The benefit of verifying your site is that it then shows up on profiles and in search results. You need access to the code of your website to verify. To verify your site, click the Verify Website button on the Edit Profile page. Pinterest generates a verification file containing code that must be added to your website. Contact your webmaster to add this code to your site to verify it for Pinterest.

You can also verify by adding a meta tag to your website. To generate the verification meta tag, click the Verify By Metatag link at the bottom of the verification screen. The next screen generates meta code that can be added to the header of your website. After the code is added or the file is uploaded, click the red Complete Verification button to confirm that the verification was a success. A website that has been verified displays a verification next to the website on the profile screen. Adding a verified website to your profile also allows you to access analytics, which is covered later in this chapter.

✔ **Social networks:** Pinterest lets you connect your social networks to your account. Social networks are displayed at the bottom of the settings page. Your social networks are displayed in your profile beside your website. You can now connect Facebook, Google+, Gmail, Twitter, and Yahoo!. Connecting these social networks displays icons with links to your profiles. Connecting social networks to your profile can be completed on the Account Settings page. To navigate to this page, click on your username in the upper-right corner of your profile and select Account Settings from the drop-down list. Adding social networks happens about halfway down the page.

Knowing key profile statistics

Underneath the elements in your Pinterest profile on your public profile page are some statistics about your profile. It shows basic information about how active the account is and how many followers an account has. Here's the information you see displayed below the profile information:

✔ **Get Started:** Clicking Get Started lets you access tools that you can use to add Pinterest to your website. The first option is to install the Pin It button on your website. This button lets users pin your web page with only one click. The second option is to spread the word with the Follow Me button. Installing this button on your website lets users follow you with only one click.

The Get Started button is displayed only if you have verified a website as a part of your profile. If you haven't verified a website, you don't have access to these tools.

The Get Started button doesn't appear again after you have initially clicked on it.

✔ **Number of boards:** Shows the number of boards that the user has created. Clicking on the Boards button displays the boards created by the user.

✔ **Pins:** Indicates the number of pins that the user has pinned. Clicking on Pins shows you all pins created by the account.

✔ **Likes:** Shows the number of pins that the user has liked. A user on Pinterest may like pins created by other Pinterest users. Clicking on the Likes button displays all pins that the user has liked.

✔ **Follow All:** The Follow All button lets a user follow all boards created by the user. This button is displayed when you're on the profile page of another user. (I explain how to follow Pinterest users in more detail later in this chapter, in the section "Building Community on Pinterest.")

✔ **Followers:** Displays the number of users who are following the account, or all boards. On Pinterest, users can follow all boards from an account, or individual boards. The Followers number is the number of people following all boards. Clicking on the Followers link shows the user profiles of all people following the account.

✔ **Following:** Shows the number of accounts that the user is following. Clicking the Following link displays the profiles of the users that the account is following.

✔ **Invite Friends to Pinterest:** Inviting friends can make your Pinterest experience more social. Clicking the Invite Friends button lets you involve friends via e-mail or other social networks.

✔ **Find Friends:** Below the words Find Friends are Pinterest users you may be interested in connecting with. Clicking the text Find Friends displays the Pinterest profiles of people you may know based on your connections on other social networks.

✔ **Notifications:** Notifications are updates about how people have interacted with you on Pinterest. Beside your user profile image and name in the upper-right corner is a double pushpin button signifying your notifications. If a number appears in this space instead of the pin, the number signifies the number of notifications you have.

Making Pinterest Boards That Get Results

On Pinterest, users create *boards*, which are pages based around a specific theme. On these boards, users *pin* content (display images from websites or that they upload). A board typically has multiple *pins*. For example, on my personal Pinterest account, I have created a number of boards to represent the individual topics I'm interested in. Content is then pinned onto a board. A *pin* is an individual piece of content that's pinned to a Pinterest board.

A sample of Pinterest boards is shown in Figure 10-2. It shows Pinterest boards from SparkPeople, a fitness and weight loss site.

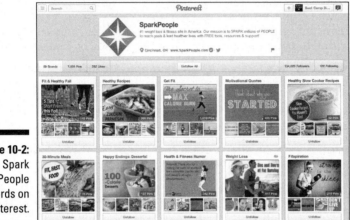

Figure 10-2:
Spark
People
boards on
Pinterest.

Creating boards

After your basic account is set up, the first item to create for your Pinterest account is a board.

To create a Pinterest board, log in to your account and follow these steps:

1. **Click the plus button in the upper-right corner of the screen.**

   Alternatively, if you're already on the Boards page of your profile, you can click the big button labeled + Create Boards (with the plus sign) on the right side.

2. **Click on Create a Board from the drop-down list.**

3. **Add the information for your board.**

   Next, you create the Pinterest board. Figure 10-3 shows the screen you see to create the board, and you fill in these items:

   • *Name:* The only required field for the board. In the Name field, enter the name that describes your board. Tips for optimizing your name are in the later section "Optimizing Pinterest boards."

   • *Description:* A text field, limited to 500 characters, that describes the board. Describe what the board is about and why someone may be interested in following it.

- *Category:* Possible categories that most closely fit your board's content. Adding a category to your board makes it easier to be found in searches on Pinterest.

- *Add a Map:* Selecting Yes creates a place board. A *place pin* has a specific location connected to it. A place board highlights all place pins on a map.

- *Secret:* Visible only to you and people you choose to invite to your board. A secret board doesn't show up anywhere else on Pinterest. Your secret boards can be viewed at the bottom of your profile. (Again, only you can see them.) You can now create only three secret boards.

You can make a secret board public, but you can't make a public board secret. Select Yes to make a board secret or No to make it public.

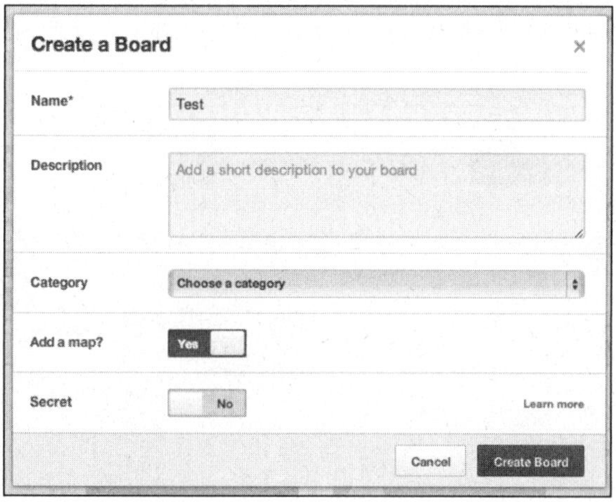

Create a Board	✕
Name*	Test
Description	Add a short description to your board
Category	Choose a category
Add a map?	Yes
Secret	No Learn more
	Cancel Create Board

Figure 10-3: Pinterest board creation screen.

4. Click Create Board.

Clicking this button creates your board and adds it to your profile.

The best boards on Pinterest are inspiring and interesting, and they draw people in with beautiful images. Pinterest is about interests and inspiration; rather than show only your products, show what inspires you to create them or what is most interesting about how they're used.

Creating group boards

Pinterest also lets you create group boards. Both public and private boards can be shared. A *group board* is a board that multiple people can pin to — you and other people whom you invite. Creating and participating in group boards on Pinterest is a helpful way to increase your exposure, reach new audiences, and interact with new people.

Group boards on Pinterest are identifiable by an icon of multiple people displayed beside the name of the board. If you contribute to a group board that's public, it's displayed on your profile page along with the boards you create. When someone is viewing a group board, the contributors of the board are displayed in the upper-left corner of the board page.

To contribute to a group board, you must be invited by the creator. If you're invited to join a group board, you receive an invitation in your notifications, as shown in Figure 10-4. You may choose to accept a group board invitation by clicking the red Accept button.

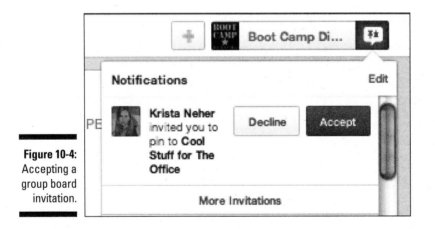

Figure 10-4:
Accepting a
group board
invitation.

You can also create a group board and invite other Pinterest users to contribute to your board. Follow these steps:

1. **Create the board.**

   First, create the board using the same steps described in the earlier section "Creating boards."

2. **Click the Edit button to edit the board.**

   From your profile, click the Edit button on the board to which you want to add contributors.

3. **Type a name or e-mail to indicate who can pin.**

   At the bottom of the Edit Board screen is an input box named Who Can Pin, as shown in Figure 10-5. As you begin to type the e-mail or username of the user you want you add, the person's profile appears in a drop-down list below the input box, and you can choose the user you want to invite.

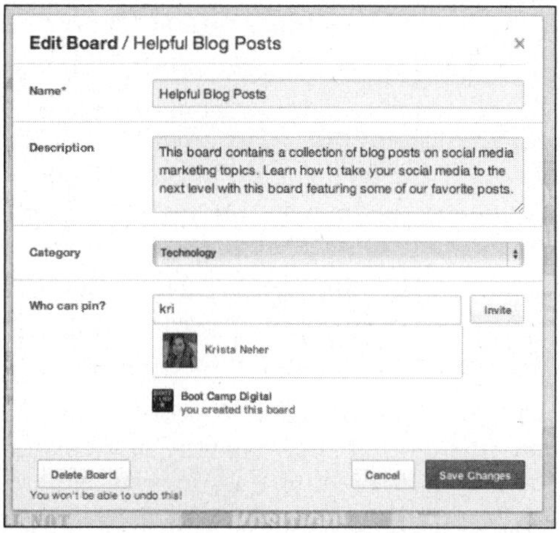

Figure 10-5: Inviting people to contribute to a group board.

You can also remove contributors by following Steps 1 and 2 in the preceding step list. However, when you reach Step 3, you see the current contributors below the Who Can Pin input box. Beside each username, the Remove button appears. Click Remove to remove a user from your group board.

Optimizing Pinterest boards

A board on Pinterest should be titled with the topic or theme representing the content that's pinned to the board. Follow these tips to optimize your Pinterest boards:

✔ **The more specific the topic, the better.** The more specifically your board is themed, the more traffic and attention it's likely to attract. For example, the title Healthy Slow Cooker Recipes would probably attract a more relevant targeted audience than Slow Cookers. If you're interested in healthy slow-cooker recipes, every single recipe pinned on that board is likely to be relevant to you. If you followed a Slow Cooker Recipes board, many of the recipes would be irrelevant.

A great deal of content is on Pinterest (along with a lot of viewers). The more specifically your pins are categorized, the more likely they are to be followed.

✔ **Keep board titles short.** Short titles work better for Pinterest boards because, when someone is viewing a Pinterest account, only a limited number of characters of the board title are displayed. Board titles should be written so that the primary concept of the board can be determined based on the characters that are displayed on the profile page.

✔ **Remember searchers in your titles.** When you're creating Pinterest boards, consider words that your customers might be searching for, and try to use them in your board titles. Pinterest boards often rank well in search engines such as Google, and Pinterest users often search Pinterest for relevant content. Using words that people search for can therefore increase the visibility and views of your Pinterest boards.

✔ **Make your boards unique.** Your Pinterest boards should all be different from one another. The title of each of your boards should be distinct so that your boards have a clear variety and differentiation.

✔ **Show your brand or business personality.** Pinterest is all about interests and inspiration. Create boards that showcase the unique and interesting personality of your business. Be creative and be yourself.

✔ **Include complete board descriptions.** Be sure to include board descriptions that fully describe the contents of the board using obvious words. When Pinterest users search for interesting content on Pinterest, they may search by the description of the board. Adding a longer description using words that people might search for increases the odds that your boards will show up in Pinterest search results — leading to more visibility for your boards.

✔ **Include at least five pins in each board.** The later section "Pinning Images to Pinterest" covers how to pin in more detail, but every board on Pinterest should be composed of at least five pins. When boards are displayed on your profile, five pins are featured on the board: the *cover image* (which is the larger pin in the top of the board) and four additional pins. If you don't have at least five pins on a board, these image spaces are blank.

✔ **Order your boards with the ten best boards at the top.** When viewing a Pinterest profile, the top ten boards are displayed at the top section of the page — so place your best boards at the top of the page. To reorder your Pinterest boards, navigate to your boards by clicking on the icon of your user picture in the upper-right corner and choosing Your Profile and Pins from the drop-down list. To rearrange the boards, click on the board you want to move, drag it to the location where you want to place it, and release the mouse button. It's relatively easy to drag and drop boards to reorder them to focus attention on your best boards.

Choosing the cover Pin of a Pinterest board

After you create a board and pin content to it, Pinterest selects a pin to be the cover of the board. The *cover* pin is the most prominently featured pin when your board is displayed, as shown in Figure 10-6. The cover pin should be a pin with a stunning image that represents the theme and content of your board.

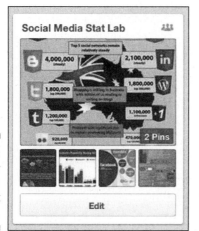

Figure 10-6: Cover image on a Pinterest board.

To easily change the cover pin, follow these steps:

1. **Move the cursor to hover over the cover image. When the Change Cover button appears, click it.**

2. **Choose a cover pin with the cover changer.**

   A screen launches with the cover changer. The screen initially launches with your most recent pin. You can click on the arrow button to the right. (The left arrow button also appears after you begin to scroll through your pins.) Click on the arrow to view your pins until you've found the one that you want to have on the cover.

3. **Move the image to fit in the cover image area.**

   The cover image is a rectangular shaped box. If an image is larger than this box or if it's shaped differently, you can choose the portion of the image that you want displayed on the cover. To reposition the image, hover the mouse over the image, and the cursor changes from an arrow to a plus sign with four arrows attached. Click the mouse and move the image around the screen until the section you want is in the white box displayed in the middle of the screen.

4. **Click Save Changes.**

The Change Cover Photo box disappears, and you return to your profile page.

Pinning Images on Pinterest

Every Pinterest board is made up of a number of individual pins. A *pin* is an individual piece of content that's then posted, or *pinned*, to a Pinterest board. Figure 10-7 shows some sample pins.

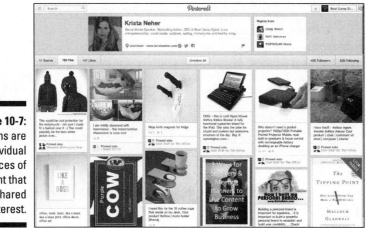

Figure 10-7: Pins are individual pieces of content that are shared on Pinterest.

As you can see, a pin is made up of an image, which is the primary focus of the pin, and a description below the pin. The image that's pinned can be either uploaded or selected from the website that's being pinned.

You can add pins to a board in one of five ways:

- ✔ Upload a pin.
- ✔ Pin a website.
- ✔ Click the Pin It button on a website.

✔ Install the Pin It browser plug-in.

✔ Repin other pins.

Uploading a pin

Uploading a pin adds an image from your computer to your Pinterest board. If the image you want to pin is on your computer, and not on a website, you upload a pin. Follow these steps:

1. **Click the plus (+) button in the upper-right corner of the screen.** (You must be logged in to your account to pin.)

2. **Select Upload Pin from the menu options.**

3. **Choose the image from your computer. Then click the red Choose Image button and select the image you want to pin from your browser.**

4. **Add a description to the pin.** After the image is uploaded, you see the pin screen, as shown in Figure 10-8. At the top of the screen, you can choose the board you want to pin to or create a new one. On the right side of the screen is the image that you selected to pin. Beside the image is a description box, where you can add a description of the pin. Though a description is required, it can be short. You can also choose to share your pin on a social network that you have connected to, such as Facebook or Twitter, by selecting the check box beside the social network. This action automatically shares your pin on the social network you selected. Click the red Pin It button to pin to the selected board.

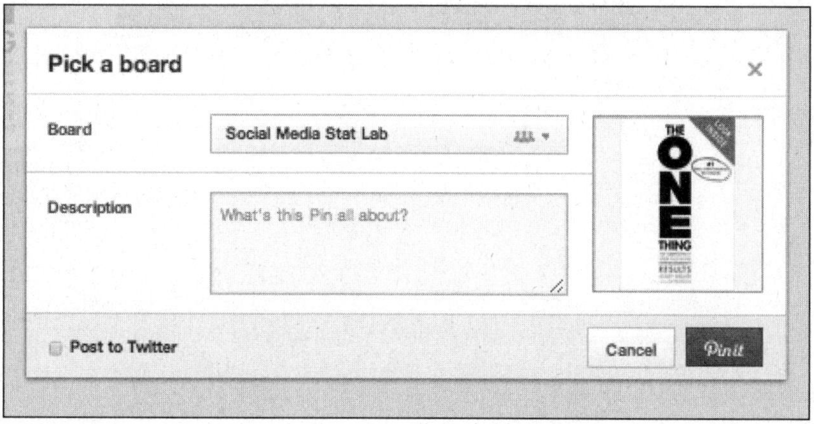

Figure 10-8:
The pin
screen.

Pick a board   ✕

Board   Social Media Stat Lab

Description   What's this Pin all about?

☐ Post to Twitter   Cancel   Pin it

Pinning a website (on Pinterest)

Pinning a website lets you pin an item from another website on the Internet. You may pin from your own site, or any other site on the Internet. To pin a website, follow these steps:

1. **Click the plus (+) button in the upper-right corner of the screen.**

   You must be logged in to your account to pin.

2. **Select Add from a Website from the menu options.**

3. **Go to the web page you want to pin, and copy the URL.**

   Find the web page you want to pin, and copy the website address or URL.

4. **Return to Pinterest and paste the website address.**

   Go back to Pinterest.com and paste the website address into the input field. The website address should start with the characters `http://`. If you have an incorrectly formatted website address, the warning *Not a Valid URL* appears in red text below the input box.

5. **Click the red Next button.**

6. **Choose a pin from the website.**

   As mentioned earlier, a *pin* is an image with a description. When you pin a website, Pinterest lets you choose the image that accompanies the pin. Many web pages have multiple images, and on this screen, Pinterest pulls in all images from the page you're pinning. If you find images on the page that aren't displayed on this screen, they likely aren't coded as images correctly and you should contact the webmaster. This screen displays the images that you can pin from the website, as shown in Figure 10-9. As you hover the mouse over the images, the red Pin It button appears. After you select the image you want to pin, click the Pin It button.

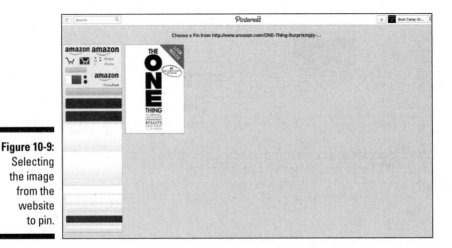

Figure 10-9: Selecting the image from the website to pin.

7. **Add a description to the pin.**

   This step is the same as Step 4 in the earlier section "Uploading a pin."

Using the Pin It button on a website

Using the Pin It button on a website is a quick and easy way to pin content on Pinterest. Increasingly more websites are including the Pin It button to encourage their customers to share their websites on Pinterest.

When you find content you like on the web, you can easily pin content if it has the Pin It button. This button now appears on most popular websites. An example of a website, Social PR Chat, with the Pin It button is shown in Figure 10-10.

Pin It button

Figure 10-10: The Pin It button on a site.

Clicking on the Pin It button on a site typically launches the pin screen. (Refer to Figure 10-8 in Step 4 of the earlier section "Uploading a pin.") The benefit of using this button is that the description of the pin may be automatically generated based on the title of the web page. (It depends on how the website owner has set up the Pin It button.) This makes it quick and easy to pin.

To add the Pin It button to your website, contact your webmaster, or add a Pinterest plug-in if you use a website development platform that supports plug-ins, such as WordPress.

Pinterest has a widget builder that creates Pinterest buttons for your website. To install a Pinterest button, you need to be able to access the code for your site. First, find the widget builder at

```
http://business.pinterest.com/widget-builder/#do_pin_it_button
```

and then create a Pin It button that's appropriate for your website. The widget builder lets you customize the button and generate code that you can copy and paste into your site.

Installing the Pin It browser plug-in

Another way to make it even easier to pin from around the web is to install the Pin It browser plug-in. The browser plug-in adds a small Pin It icon to your Internet browser and lets you pin any website with the click of a button.

To install the browser plug-in, follow these steps:

1. **Click the plus button in the upper-right corner of the Pinterest screen.**

2. **Click on the link labeled The Pin It Button.**

   The bottom of the drop-down list on the plus button says, "The Pin It button is the easiest way to pin things from around the web." Click this button to be redirected to the installation page.

3. **Click the red Install Now button.**

   The new tab gives you additional information about the browser plug-in. Click the Install Now button. Depending on your browser, you may receive an additional pop-up that requires you to select Add or Accept.

4. **A Pinterest icon should appear in the top of the browser.**

   After you have successfully installed the browser plug-in, you should see the Pinterest icon displayed in the top of the browser.

After the plug-in has been installed, it's easy to pin content that you find around the Internet. The browser plug-in makes it easy to pin because you can pin immediately from any page on the Internet, without going to Pinterest.com and copying the URL.

To pin a website using the Pin It button, follow these steps:

1. **Go to the site you want to pin.**

2. **Click the Pin It button in your browser.**

3. **Choose the image that you want to pin.**

   After you click the Pin It button, your browser brings you to Pinterest and the images from the page you want to pin are loaded. Hover the cursor over the image you want to pin, and click the red **Pin It** button.

4. **Update the description and choose the board.**

   The benefit of using the browser plug-in is that the description of the page from the website is automatically displayed in the description of the pin. You can still customize the description to make it more appealing and then choose the board to pin to.

5. **Click Pin It.**

   Click Pin It below the image in the lower-right corner.

Repinning other pins

One way to create pins for your boards is to repin other pins from Pinterest. Repinning a pin is similar to sharing a status update on Facebook or retweeting a tweet.

When you discover another pin on Pinterest and pin it to one of your boards, you *repin*. Repinning is one of the quickest ways to generate content for your Pinterest boards, and more than 80 percent of pins on Pinterest are repins.

To repin a pin, follow these steps:

1. **Find the pin that you want to repin.**

   I cover how to find and discover pins later in this chapter, in the section "Building Community on Pinterest."

2. **Click the Pin It button on the pin.**

   The red Pin It button is displayed when you hover the cursor over the pin.

3. **Customize the description.**

   Repinning can make pinning faster because the description from the original pin transfers into the description. Read the description to be sure that it's correct. You can still type in the Description box to customize the description.

4. **Select the check box to share the pin on other social networks.**

   Toward the bottom of the screen are check boxes beside the labels Post to Twitter or Post to Facebook. Select the check box if you want your repin to automatically be shared to these social networks.

   This option is displayed only if you have connected other social networks to Pinterest.

5. **Choose your board and click the red Pin It button.**

Repinning is also a good strategy to get noticed on Pinterest. When you repin another user's pins, that person usually receives a notification. This action can build awareness and views for your Pinterest boards, because the original pinner may check out your Pinterest account when she receives the notification.

Uploading versus pinning from a website

Pinning from a website is generally better than uploading a pin. The main reason is that people often want to discover more about the content that's pinned. For example, if you pin a picture of a smoothie you made, others may want to view the recipe.

When you pin from a website, Pinterest users can click on the image you pinned and go to the website from which it was pinned. The website often provides additional information about the pin, or it may even be the site where the pinned item can be purchased.

As a business, one of your biggest benefits from Pinterest is that it can send traffic to your website. If you upload a product picture for your pin, Pinterest users can't click on it and find your website. If you pin from your website, people can click on the image and go directly to your site and purchase your product. For these reasons, pinning from a website is often better then uploading a pin.

Optimizing pins

Creating appealing pins is the key to a successful Pinterest account. If your pins aren't interesting, you get no traction from your Pinterest account. The most important thing is to pin websites or upload pins with relevant images. If you find a site with information that you want to share but it doesn't have an image or it has a boring image, don't bother pinning it. Doing so can make your board look boring and unappealing.

- ✔ **Pin interesting images.** Because a pin revolves around an image, having an interesting and intriguing image is the key. Choose to pin content that includes interesting images that people are likely to want to click on. Boring stock photos don't cut it. The image is the center of a pin, so don't pin content with irrelevant or boring photos.

- ✔ **Pin the image that's most representative of what you're pinning.** Another factor in pinning inviting content is to choose images that are most representative of the content you're pinning. The pinned image should describe what the pin is about. For example, if I'm pinning an article about new Facebook contest rules, a picture of the Facebook logo doesn't truly describe the article I'm pinning. Instead, a picture with the words *New Facebook Contest Rules* and the logo is more descriptive of the content. When pinning websites, you're limited because you must select from the images on the website. Regardless, try to pin content from sites with images optimized for Pinterest.

✔ **Make sure your pins match your board.** Keep pins relevant to the boards you're pinning on. If needed, create new boards, but keep in mind that it takes at least five pins in a board for it to look complete on your profile.

✔ **Pin when your audience is online.** Your followers see your images when they log in to Pinterest and view their newsfeeds, which is the first thing they see when they log in. The newsfeed displays the pins from the people you follow and shows the newest pins first. If you pin when your customers are online, you're more likely to generate views.

✔ **Add long keyword rich descriptions.** Because many people search Pinterest for content they're interested in, adding a complete description is the key to discoverability. The longer your description, the more likely you are to be discovered. The description field is 500 characters long — use as much of it as possible. (Keep the description relevant.) If you want your pins to show up in search results, be sure to use keywords that people might be searching for.

✔ **Write catchy descriptions.** Though long descriptions are helpful for gaining exposure in searches, catchy descriptions encourage people to click and repin your content. Share what you love about the pin and make it interesting.

✔ **Use hashtags in descriptions.** Hashtags can make pins more searchable. To add a hashtag, you place the pound sign (#) in front of the words that describe the general theme of the pin. For example, if you want to make a more searchable pin of a motorcycle jacket that you like, you may add #motorcycle #jacket to the description.

✔ **Pin regularly.** The more often you pin, the more likely people are to see your content. Build pinning into your habits when browsing online. When you install the Pinterest browser plug-in, it becomes easy for you to quickly pin something you find interesting. The frequency with which you choose to pin depends on your Pinterest marketing objectives and on how much time you can dedicate to Pinterest. Plan to pin at least once a week to keep your account active.

Pinterest pins aren't *time-stamped*: The date and time that a pin was created aren't displayed beside the pin. People viewing your profile can't see the last time you were active on Pinterest, which relieves the pressure that many marketers feel to be constantly updating social networks. This doesn't mean that you can create your boards, fill them with pins, and ignore your Pinterest account. The more active you are on Pinterest, the better your results.

You can always edit a pin, even after pinning it. To edit a pin, hover the cursor over the pin. You see a pencil icon displayed in the upper-right corner of the pin. Click on the icon, and the Pin detail screen opens, as shown in Figure 10-11. From there, you can change the board that the pin is on, the description, or the source (the website from which the pin was created). You can choose to use this screen to change the website that the pin sends people to when they click on it.

Figure 10-11:
The pin editing screen.

Edit Pin ✕

Board   Cincinnati Social Media Training ▾

Description   Online Advertising training in Cincinnati Facebook Ads Twitter Ads and Google AdWords

Source   http://bootcampdigital.com/blog/

Delete Pin   Cancel   Save Changes

Promoted pins

Pinterest is now experimenting with promoted pins. *Promoted pins* allow businesses to pay to have their pins displayed to Pinterest users.

For example, a business may be able to promote its pins to the top of search results when users search for specific pins. Alternatively, businesses can target specific users and have their pins displayed in their newsfeeds.

Promoted pins are now in a limited beta test and unavailable for businesses to use. Find out more about promoted pins and stay up-to-date on updates at http://business.pinterest.com/promoting-pins.

Building Community on Pinterest

Creating an account and pinning content is only the beginning of the opportunities to market your business on Pinterest. The second step is to participate and engage on Pinterest. Participating on Pinterest is about interacting with other Pinterest users. Interacting with other Pinterest users can grow awareness for your account because whenever you interact with other users, they receive notifications in their Pinterest accounts.

At my company, Boot Camp Digital, actively participating on Pinterest by interacting with other users and their content dramatically increased the number of people following our account and interacting with our pins.

Exploring Pinterest content

To get started in participating on Pinterest, explore the content on Pinterest. Exploring pins, boards, and users helps you to find content and find users who share your interests.

I search Pinterest content as a source of inspiration for creating content for my business. Pinners pin the content that they find most interesting from around the web, so it's an excellent collection of the most visual and most interesting content that people are sharing.

Searching on Pinterest

Pinterest search is a powerful way to find content that you may be interested in, or to discover the content that your audience is already pinning.

To search on Pinterest, follow these steps:

1. **Type the term you want to search for in the Search box in the upper-left corner of the screen.**

2. **Click the magnifying glass icon.**

3. **Scroll down to browse pins.**

   The returned results show you pins that contain the term you searched for in the description, as shown in Figure 10-12.

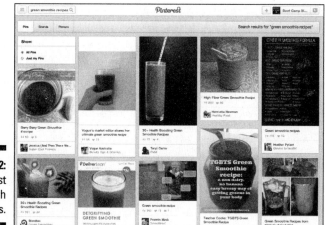

Figure 10-12:
Pinterest search results.

4. Click the Boards tab to search boards.

Searching pins shows you the pins that contain the search term, though you may want to see boards that are all about the content you're searching for. In the upper-left corner of the search, you see a tab named Boards. Click this tab to view boards that include the search term in the title or description.

5. Click the Pinners tab to find pinners.

To the right of the Boards tab is the Pinners tab. Clicking it displays pinners or Pinterest users who include your search term in their usernames or descriptions. It's a helpful way to find Pinterest users.

Browsing on Pinterest

In addition to searching to explore content on Pinterest, you can browse. Browsing is a useful way to explore Pinterest if you're unsure exactly what you're looking for or if you want to view pins from a broader category.

To browse on Pinterest, click the icon with three bars on it in the upper-left corner of the Pinterest screen. Then you see a drop-down list of categories, plus other choices such as Popular and Everything.

Browsing can help you to discover new pins. When browsing on Pinterest, you can only browse pins — not boards or pinners.

Interacting with Pinterest pins, boards, and pinners

After you've explored Pinterest and found users who share your interest, the next step is to interact with them. You can interact with pins, boards, and users. Interacting on Pinterest is one way to increase awareness, views, and interactions of your own Pinterest account.

When you interact with content on Pinterest, the creator of the content may be notified (depending on how her notifications are set up). When that person receives the notification, she sees that you interacted with her, and she may check out your account, boards, and pins. If she finds content she likes, she may interact with your content and in this way increase your exposure on Pinterest.

To see all options for interacting with a pin, click on the pin. After clicking on it, you see the Pin screen, as shown in Figure 10-13.

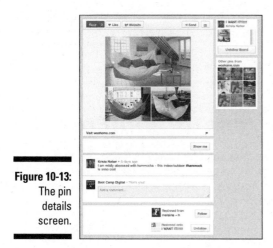

Figure 10-13:
The pin
details
screen.

You can interact with pins in a number of ways:

- ✔ **Pin It:** The Pin It button in the upper-left corner lets you repin a pin to your own boards. After clicking the Pin It button, you have the option to change the description and choose the board to pin to.

- ✔ **Liking a pin:** To like a pin, click the heart on the upper-right corner of a pin. After you like a pin, the heart turns red.

- ✔ **Website button:** Clicking the website button opens, in a new tab in your browser, the website from which the pin originated. This is where you can see the source of the pin.

- ✔ **Send:** Sending the pin lets you e-mail a link to the pin. The Send button looks like an airplane.

- ✔ **Share:** The button to the right of the Send button, with a square and an arrow, is the Share button. Clicking on this button lets you share a pin on Twitter or Facebook, or you can embed the pin into your blog or website.

- ✔ **Comment:** Below the pin is the Comment entry box. From there, you can leave a comment about the pin.

You can also interact with boards on Pinterest. When you find a board that interests you, you can follow the board. Then new pins from the board display in your newsfeed when you log on to Pinterest. To follow a board, click the Follow button displayed below the board.

In addition to following boards, you can follow users on Pinterest. To follow a user, click the Follow All button in the top center area of the User Profile page. When you follow a user, you see her new pins in your newsfeed.

Overall, the strategy for building community on Pinterest is to find users who share your interests and "get on their radar" by interacting with their content. Interacting with other pins, boards, and pinners can increase the visibility of your account, boards, and pins.

Driving Website Traffic With Pinterest

Pinterest is popular with marketers because of its ability to drive traffic to websites. Pinterest sends more traffic to websites than Twitter, YouTube, LinkedIn, and Google+ combined. Pinterest has the potential, therefore, to be a major source of traffic to your site.

People search Pinterest for topics they're interested in — recipes, workouts, design ideas, clothes, shoes, inspiration, and more. After they find a pin that interests them, they often click on it to view the website from which the pin was created. That's how Pinterest sends traffic to websites.

Optimizing your website for Pinterest can help you get more traffic from Pinterest.

Finding content pinned from websites

One of the first things you can do to understand how to generate traffic to your website from Pinterest is to find the content that's already being pinned from your site.

To find content pinned from your site, go to `www.Pinterest.com/source/` *YourDomainName.com* (substitute your domain name in italics). You can also view content that's pinned from any other domain by using the same website address. A sample is shown in Figure 10-14.

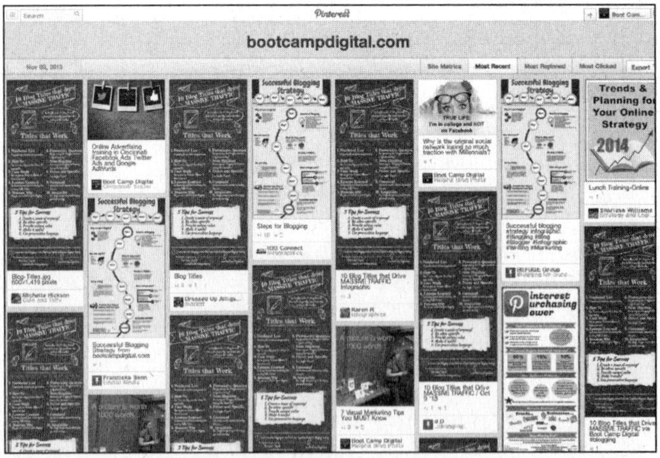

Figure 10-14: Viewing content that's pinned from a website on Pinterest.

Viewing the content that's already pinned from your website can give you insight into the kind of content that people are interested in sharing from your site.

Making your website Pinterest-friendly

Pinterest can generate huge amounts of traffic to your website, and making your site easy to pin means that more content from your site will be pinned.

Adding pinnable images to your site

Make sure that every page on your site has at least one *pinnable* image — one that, by itself, describes what the page is about.

I discovered the importance of having pinnable images on my site a few years ago. I was looking at `www.pinterest.com/source/BootCampDigital.com` and found a photo of me pinned there. I wasn't sure why someone would pin my picture, so when I looked at it in more detail, I found that the person was pinning a *report* from my site on Google+. The page that was being pinned included a copy of the report. Because the report was on the page, there was no need to include an image of the report from a website design perspective. The picture of me was an image from the sidebar. Because the web page contained no images, when pinning the page the pinner had to select an image from the sidebar, and she selected the image of me.

Upon discovering this, I realized the need for our site to contain pinnable images to drive more traffic. I created a picture to represent the report. The before-and-after pins are shown in Figure 10-15.

Figure 10-15: Boot Camp Digital, pinned before and after pinnable images were added.

The second picture shows an image of the report. After the image on the page was replaced by a picture of the report, I found that it generated more pins and traffic.

Assess your website, especially the pages that you want people to share on Pinterest.

Adding the Pin It button to your site

To encourage people to pin your website, add the Pin It button to content that people may want to share on Pinterest. Many sites have already done this on their product pages, blog posts, and resource pages.

Your webmaster should be able to add this button to your site. Alternatively, if you use a website platform that supports plug-ins, such as WordPress, you should be able to find a Pinterest plug-in.

Pinterest website analytics

If you have verified your website with Pinterest (as discussed in the "Exploring Pinterest" section, earlier in this chapter), you can access analytics for your site. You can see analytics for your own website only if you have verified it; you can't see other sites.

Analytics let you see how content from your site is performing. To access analytics, click on your user icon in the upper-right corner of the screen and select Analytics from the drop-down list.

Pinterest initially shows you site metrics. When viewing analytics, you can change the date range by clicking on the Date button in the upper-left corner. From there, you can Quick-Select (to use the site's term) predetermined date ranges or choose the dates yourself by clicking on the calendar. Analytics reports can also be exported by clicking the Export button in the upper-right corner.

Analytics are broken down into four categories:

- **Site Metrics:** Site metrics includes eight different metrics, based on the selected date range. All the metrics shown are daily averages; for example, the pins number is the daily average number of pins from your website. The left side also displays +/− percentages that show the increase or decrease from the current date range you're viewing compared to the previous date range. Analytics provided in site metrics include

  - *Pins:* The average number of pins per day from your website

  - *Pinners:* The daily average number of pinners who pinned content from your website

- *Repins:* The daily average number of times that pins from your site were repinned

- *Repinners:* The daily average number of unique pinners who repinned your pins

- *Impressions:* The daily average number of times that your pins were viewed in a newsfeed, in search results, or on a board

- *Reach:* The daily average number of unique people who saw your pins on Pinterest

- *Clicks:* The average daily number of clicks to your site from Pinterest

- *Visitors:* The average daily number of unique people who visited your site from Pinterest

✔ **Most Recent:** The Most Recent Content tab shows the most recent pins created by any user of content from your website. This tab doesn't let you choose a date range, because it's a feed of the most recent pins.

✔ **Most Repinned:** The Most Repinned tab displays the 100 most repinned pins as of the date you selected. In this view, you can choose only an individual date, yesterday, past 7 days, or past 14 days.

✔ **Most Clicked:** This option displays the most-often-clicked-on pins from your site. These pins are the pins that are driving the most traffic to your site. You can also select date options here.

Analytics help you to understand how content from your website is performing. Use analytics to your benefit to optimize and adjust your Pinterest marketing strategy.

Chapter 11

Instagramming Your Way to Success in Visual Marketing

In This Chapter

▶ Generating meaningful results for your business

▶ Exploring the vast functionality of Instagram for capturing and sharing photos and videos

▶ Maximizing the exposure of your Instagram photos with captions and hashtags

▶ Participating in the Instagram community to grow your presence

▶ Optimizing your photos with creative Instagram strategies

*I*nstagram is an emerging social network that allows users to take photos or videos from their mobile devices to share with the Instagram community or on Facebook, Twitter or other social networks. Photos and videos taken with Instagram can be edited by applying a number of different filters that make Instagram photos look more interesting.

This large social network consists of more than 150 million active users who have shared more than 16 billion photos. Instagram users are highly active and engaged on the site, with users liking more than 1.2 billion photos on Instagram every day.

Instagram (www.instagram.com) was purchased by Facebook in April of 2013 for a billion dollars, which shows that the giant of social networking sees potential in Instagram. Instagram now also allows users to take and share short videos in addition to photos.

The site is a powerful part of a visual social marketing toolbox because it's a simple and effective way to create and share visual content on the go from a smartphone or tablet.

Throughout this chapter, I show you a variety of screen shots and examples from Instagram. Depending on the device you're using and the version of the application you have downloaded, your screen may look slightly different. The functionality of Instagram (how it works) is the same; however, its appearance may be different on different devices.

Exploring Instagram

Instagram is a mobile application that works on smartphones and tablets. To use Instagram, therefore, you must be using a smartphone or tablet. Though you can view certain Instagram content on a computer and access your profile, you can't take full advantage of Instagram without a mobile device.

The Instagram application can be downloaded from the app store that your mobile device uses — for example, iTunes or Google Play. From a computer, you can access only limited amounts of Instagram features for now (though additional features are added regularly). From a computer, you can log in to your Instagram account and view your newsfeed or update your profile information.

Instagram, which is a mobile application, lets users take, edit, and share photos or short videos with the Instagram community or on other social networks. Using the Instagram application, users can take photos or videos on their mobile phones and apply a number of filters to change the way the image or video looks. Then they can share the photos with the Instagram community or on other social networks. This section explains how these features work.

Similar to the way other social networks work, to get started on Instagram you create an account with a username (which is how people find you and refer to you), a profile picture, and additional information about yourself. When choosing your username on Instagram, choose a name that's consistent with your username on other social networks.

You can create an Instagram account only from a mobile device (smartphone or tablet) that's compatible with Instagram.

After you've set up your account, you're ready to get started.

Benefitting from using Instagram

Using Instagram has a number of advantages, many of which are more fully explained throughout this chapter. People use Instagram because of its photo editing options, to participate in the Instagram community, and to experience the ease of sharing Instagram photos on other social networks.

Instagram has a number of unique photo editing capabilities that are extremely simple to use. Instagram has customized photo editing functionality that might be found in traditional photo editing software. Instead, it has a limited number of functions that change the look of the photo, which makes Instagram photos extremely easy to edit, even with no photo editing experience.

Instagram also has an active photography community: Its 150 million active users share 55 million photos on Instagram every day. People on Instagram (known as Instagrammers) also view, like, and comment on billions of photos every a day. Instagram is a social network in that people follow and connect with other photographers they like. Instagram tends to be a more open social network, where you can view and follow most users' photos.

Though users can keep their photos on Instagram private (which would mean that only their followers can view the photos), most Instagram accounts are public.

Finally, Instagram makes it quite easy for users to share photos to other social networks such as Facebook, Twitter, Tumblr, Foursquare, and Flickr. With only the click of a few buttons on your part, a photo can simultaneously be shared on all these social networks.

Evaluating how businesses use Instagram

A business account on Instagram is treated no differently from an individual account. To create your business account, simply create a new account and use business information instead of personal information. There's no verification process, and you don't need a personal account to access your business account.

Using Instagram has a number of benefits for businesses. They can

- ✔ **Take photos to share on other social networks:** Some businesses use Instagram primarily as a way to take great-looking photos to share on Facebook, Twitter, or other social networks. Because Instagram makes it easy to take and edit interesting photos, some businesses use it simply as a tool for taking and sharing photos.

- ✔ **Grow brand awareness:** With more than 150 million active users, Instagram is a powerful way to connect with customers and build awareness for your business.

- ✔ **Share products or services:** Some businesses use Instagram to share new products or services. A local restaurant near me shares photos of its daily special. An interior designer in my neighborhood uses Instagram to share samples of her work.

- ✔ **Build brand equity:** Brand equity is how people perceive your business. Instagram can help you to position your business and change how people think about it. For example, at Boot Camp Digital, I want to build brand equity as being on the cutting edge of social media. The company uses Instagram to share the latest tips and statistics on social media. In this way, Instagram is helping to build my company's brand equity.

✔ **Generate sales:** Instagram can be a tool to generate sales; however, this is quite difficult to measure. Photos shared on Instagram can't include clickable links to websites, which means that directly driving sales or tracking sales is difficult. Regardless, some businesses are generating sales by way of Instagram. A local restaurant Instagrammed a photo of its specialty cocktail, and the next night I stopped by to try it.

These are only a few of the primary benefits that businesses are generating from Instagram. Evaluate your own marketing goals to see how Instagram might fit into your marketing strategies.

Every business can take advantage of Instagram — it isn't only for restaurants or companies with visually oriented products. Even large, industrial companies such as General Electric are using Instagram. With its large, highly engaged, and growing community, Instagram can be a powerful way to grow your business.

Navigating Instagram

After creating your Instagram account, you return to the Home screen on Instagram, as shown in Figure 11-1.

Figure 11-1:
The
Instagram
home
screen.

At the bottom of this screen, you see the navigation menu that lets you move between the different functions of Instagram. I explain why and how you use these screens in the rest of this chapter. For now. I help you explore what each button does. The navigation buttons (which are highlighted on the Home screen — refer to Figure 11-1) are described in this list:

- ✔ **Home:** The first button on the left; opens the home page. It's where you see the Instagram photos of other users you follow (similar to the Newsfeed screen in Facebook).

- ✔ **Explore:** The compass icon, where you can explore Instagram by searching for photos or viewing popular photos and videos.

- ✔ **Camera:** The middle icon; takes you to the screen where you can take photos or videos.

- ✔ **Notifications:** A callout box with a heart in the middle that shows notifications about your friends' activity on Instagram. It's where you see activity related to your posts — for example, people who have liked or commented on your photos. You can also choose to view the activities of the people you're following.

- ✔ **Profile:** Looks like a card; how you access your profile to view or edit any profile information.

A small, blue circle appears at the bottom of an icon image if you have new updates. For example, you see the blue circle at the bottom of the notifications image if you have new notifications. You see a circle at the bottom of the profile icon if there are new photos taken of you or other updates related to your profile.

Breaking down your profile on Instagram

In your profile (the card icon in the navigation menu), you can view your profile and other information about you. Clicking on the icon opens the screen shown in Figure 11-2.

Figure 11-2:
Instagram
profile.

The information in the profile can be broken down this way:

✔ **Profile picture and description:** Your profile picture appears in the upper-left corner of the profile screen. Below it is your description. To edit or change your profile picture, simply click on the picture, and you receive a number of options for changing your profile photo. You can edit your description in the Edit Your Profile section. In this short section, you can describe yourself or your business. Your website appears below the description. You can edit the websites in the Edit Your Profile section.

✔ **Usage statistics:** The usage stats are composed of:

   • *Posts:* The number of photos or videos you've posted.

   • *Followers:* The number of people who are following your account. Your followers see your updates in their newsfeeds. Instagram allows any user to follow you (unless your profile is set to private), so you don't have to approve followers.

   • *Following:* The number of accounts you're following. The number of accounts you're following appear on the Home screen when you log in to Instagram.

✔ **Edit Your Profile:** Clicking on this button lets you edit your profile information. From there, you can change your real name, username, website, description, password. and privacy settings. Changing your privacy settings can make your posts visible only to your followers.

✔ **Image Icons:** The bottom section of your profile contains four icons that you can use to view information related to your profile. The first icon, which looks like a grid, displays a small grid of all your Instagram photos. The second icon, represented by four lines, shows your newsfeed — it's a stream of all photos you have uploaded, along with any comments they generated. The next icon is the photo map which shows the locations where you have taken different photos. (To see this one, photo maps must be turned on in your privacy settings.) The last icon, which displays a person in a callout box, shows photos or videos of you. These photos are taken by you or other Instagram users that you have been *tagged* in, which signifies that you're in the post.

Taking and Editing Photos and Videos with Instagram

Taking photos is one of the primary functions of Instagram. To take a photo or a video using Instagram, click on the camera icon. It should be in the lower center of your screen when you log on to Instagram.

After you click on the camera icon, your camera is activated and you see a number of additional options, as shown in Figure 11-3.

Figure 11-3:
The Camera
screen on
Instagram.

The contents on the screen are described in this list:

- ✔ **X:** This button, in the upper-left corner, lets you cancel out of the camera function if you want to return to the previous screen you were viewing.

- ✔ **Switch Camera:** This icon is a camera with an arrow around it. Many smartphones and tablets now have two cameras — one on the front and one on the back. Clicking this button lets you switch between the front and back cameras.

- ✔ **Flash:** This button lets you choose between using flash, no flash, or automatic flash, where the sensors in your phone determine whether flash is needed for a particular photo or video. The current mode for flash is displayed as a small letter or icon beside the lightning bolt. A small *A* below the flash button indicates that it's set to automatic; a small circle with a line through it appears if flash is turned off; and no icon appears if flash is turned on. To change the flash mode, simply click on the lightning bolt. The options then rotate.

- ✔ **Grid:** This small grid lets you display or remove a grid from the camera display. Some users like to use a grid when taking photos to ensure that the image is centered. Pressing the grid button makes a grid appear or disappear from your camera screen. If you choose to use the grid. the gridlines don't display in your final photo — they're simply there as a guide when taking photos.

✔ **Gallery:** The button in the lower-left corner is the Gallery button. Rather than take a photo or video, you can use this button to select a photo that's already on your mobile device. For example, you may have already taken a picture with your mobile phone that you now want to share on Instagram. The Gallery lets you view photos that are already on your phone and choose one to import into Instagram.

✔ **Camera:** This icon in the lower middle area of the screen captures the photo. You click on this button to take your picture.

✔ **Video:** The lower-right button lets you capture video instead of photos. I describe how to capture video later in this chapter, in the section "Capturing Instagram videos."

In the center of the screen, you see the feed from your camera, which is what your camera is capturing at the moment.

Editing your Instagram photos

After you successfully capture a photo, editing it is the next step.

One reason that Instagram is so popular is the many editing features that make photos from Instagram look unique.

The editing options appear after you take a photo, as shown in Figure 11-4.

Figure 11-4:
The photo-editing screen on Instagram.

Framing

The first editing option, framing, is located on the icon on the upper-left corner. Clicking the Frame button adds a frame to the photo or removes a frame from it. The frame that's applied to the image is predefined based on the filter you choose. (I cover filters in the later section "Filters.") If you haven't selected a filter yet, clicking on the Frame button has no effect because the Normal setting has no frame. However, as you apply filters to the image, the frame that matches a specific filter is applied to the image.

Focus

This icon, which looks like a teardrop, lets you change the focus of your photo. After you click on the teardrop, you see three options: a circle, a line, and the letter *x*. Clicking on the *x* removes any focus that you have applied to the photo.

The line and circle let you change the focus of your photo, and they blur the part of the image outside the focus zone. For example, choosing the circle creates a circular zone of the image, which continues to be clear, but the rest of the image becomes blurry. This lets you create a focus center for the image.

After you click on the circle, an overlay appears on the image with a clear center (the focus area). The remainder of the image shows a white overlay (the section that will be blurry). You can move the focus section around the image by touching and dragging the clear circle around the image to the section that you want to see in focus. You can make the focus area larger or smaller by moving two fingers apart from each other or toward each other, to stretch or shrink the focus area, respectively.

The line image does the same thing as the circle; however, the area remaining in focus is a horizontal line instead of a circle.

 Instagram lets you experiment and remove editing options later. You can experiment with the focus of the image and if you aren't happy with the result, click on the X button, under the Eyedrop menu item, to remove the focus you applied.

AutoEnhance

The third button along the top, which looks like a sun, is the auto-enhance button. Pressing this button "automatically enhances" the photo, by analyzing the photo and adjusting its color, contrast, sharpness, and brightness to improve the appeal of it.

Rotate

The Rotate button lets you rotate an image. Every click of the Rotate button turns the image 90 degrees.

Straighten

The Straighten button is a "crooked" square with a dotted line through it. Click the Straighten button to straighten a photo.

Filters

The Instagram filters appear at the bottom of the photo editing screen. A filter may change the contrast, color, or saturation of a photo, which is what gives Instagram photos their unique look. In Figure 11-5, you can see an image taken with Instagram and how it looks with various filters applied.

Figure 11-5:
Applying various filters on Instagram.

You can apply an filter by clicking on the Filter icon along the bottom of the screen. Scrolling to the left reveals additional filters. You can apply only one filter to each photo; however, you can experiment with different filters until you find the one that works best for your photo. When you click on a filter, it's applied to your photo, and the previous filter is removed.

You can add a border to, or remove it from, any photo (some filters have preset borders) after you have applied a filter.

Next button

The green arrow button in the upper-right corner of the screen is the Next/Finished button. Click on it to indicate that you've finished editing the image and you're ready to share it. This action finalizes the enhancements you have made to the image and processes it so that it can be shared.

Capturing Instagram videos

Instagram recently added video capabilities to its application. You can now take videos that are as long as 15 seconds, using Instagram. To get to the Video Capture section of Instagram, click on the camera icon in the primary navigation menu and then click the video camera icon.

To record video, press and hold the red video camera icon at the lower-center of the screen, as shown in Figure 11-6. When you remove your finger from the button, the camera stops recording. You can create your video in segments if you start and stop and restart the camera recording multiple times.

Figure 11-6:
Instagram
video-
capture
screen.

You can also delete segments from your video. The lower-left button, which looks like an arrow with an x in it, is the Delete button. It lets you delete an individual segment from your video. You can delete all segments if you want to start over.

After you finish recording the video, the green arrow button in the upper-right corner of the screen brings you to the video editing page. Editing the video lets you change the look of the video, though you cannot change the contents of the video after you advance to the next screen.

Enhancing Instagram videos

The editing options for videos on Instagram are now fairly limited. You can apply filters to the video to enhance the look of the video, as shown in Figure 11-7. Similar to editing photos, the filters for videos appear along the bottom of the video editing screen. Scrolling to the left reveals additional filters. Only one filter can be applied to a video, so you can click on different filters to see how they look before finalizing the video.

Figure 11-7:
The video
editing
screen.

If you decide that the video doesn't look right at this point, you can also return to the video capture screen by clicking on the x in the upper-left corner.

If you're satisfied with you video and filter, you can click the green Next button in the upper-right corner of the screen to finalize the video.

Choosing the cover frame

The *cover frame* is the snapshot or frame of your video that's displayed before the Play button is pressed.

This screen displays your video in the center; at the bottom is a line with a picture in it, as shown in Figure 11-8. The line represents the timeline of your video, and the small image is the frame that will become the cover frame. You can drag the picture along the line to choose a different frame from your video. The cover frame selection is displayed in the large display in the middle.

Figure 11-8:
The cover
frame selec-
tion screen.

After the cover frame has been selected, proceed to the sharing screen by pressing the green Next button in the upper-right corner of the screen.

Sharing Instagram Photos and Videos

Whether you're sharing photos or videos from Instagram, the process is the same. After you have finalized the photo or video, you see the Share screen, as shown in Figure 11-9.

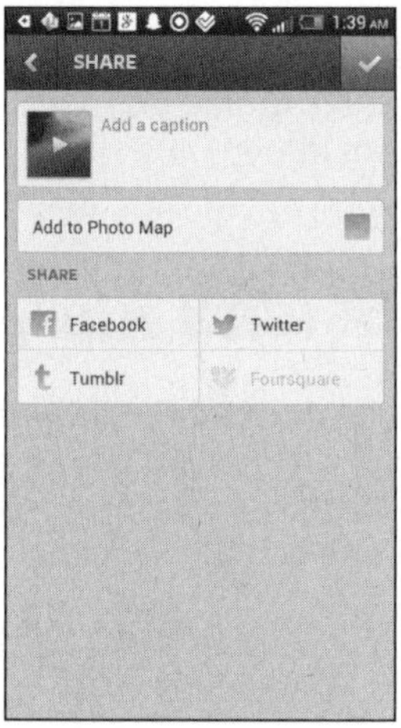

Figure 11-9:
The
Instagram
sharing
screen.

The sharing screen lets you add a description to your post and determine where you want to share it. After you add an optimized caption to the post (see the following section), you can also choose to share it on other social networks you're connected to. For example, you can connect your Facebook, Flickr, Foursquare, Tumblr, and Twitter accounts to Instagram and immediately share your Instagram posts to these social networks.

You can also choose to add your photos to a map. When you add a photo to the photo map, the location of the photo is visible to everyone who visits your map. Instagram uses the location of your mobile device to automatically determine the location of your photos. To add an image to the map, turn the Add to Map switch to On.

Optimizing the caption on your post

After you shoot a photo or video and open the Share screen, the upper-left corner of the screen displays a small *thumbnail* (miniature image) of the image or the cover frame of the video you're sharing. Beside the image is a section where you can include a caption, which should describe the content you're sharing.

You can fully complete the caption to maximize your visibility on Instagram. Many Instagram photos generate more views and visibility based on being found by people who are searching for specific content on Instagram. For example, an Instagram user may search for images of a city, a favorite bar, or an active hobby. For example, I ride a motorcycle, so I may search for photos of motorcycles on Instagram.

The challenge is that if you post a photo of a motorcycle, for example, Instagram has no way of knowing that a motorcycle is in your photo unless you use the word *motorcycle* in the caption or comments. That's why the caption is vital — it tells Instagram what is in your photo or video so that it can be found by others.

To maximize the exposure of your photos, include as many words as possible in the caption. The words should describe what's in the photo or video and use words or phrases that people might search for.

Maximizing your exposure with hashtags

A *hashtag* is a word or phrase, preceded by the pound (#) symbol, that describes or labels a topic (in this case, the photo). The hashtag, which is a powerful way to increase the exposure and reach of your Instagram photos, originated on Twitter and is now used across a variety of social networks such as Facebook and Pinterest.

Though the caption can contain a number of descriptive words, words with hashtags refer specifically to the overall theme of the post. For example, I may share a picture of me riding my motorcycle in Cincinnati and add the description "Me on my #motorcycle in #Cincinnati." By using the hashtag in front of the words that describe the image, I'm drawing attention to *motorcycle* and *Cincinnati* and signifying that my photo is about *motorcycle* and *Cincinnati*.

Use hashtags in the description in addition to text. The reason that hashtags are used in addition to text is that a caption can include a number of words that aren't relevant to the theme of the photo. For example, I may caption my photo this way: "I had an amazing ride around the city today." But then I might add #motorcycle #Cincinnati to tag the image based on the general theme.

People often search Instagram for specific hashtags. For example, a motorcycle enthusiast may want to find pictures of motorcycles. Using hashtags helps your photos be found by people who are interested in the subject.

I recently posted two similar photos on Instagram from an event I attended. Both images were slides from a presentation, as shown in Figure 11-10. In the first image, I included a general description of the photo, with no hashtags: "Great advice at @thecircuit_ event: fail fast & cheap, plan for mistakes, be scalable @hcbctr." This photo generated one comment and two likes, from people who already follow me on Instagram. The second description included hashtags: "More #entrepreneur #success tips: work hard, be vision driven and have unwavering confidence @thecircuit_ @hcbctr." This image generated 23 likes, mostly from people who aren't already following me. Both images were similar in content and were posted at the same time of day.

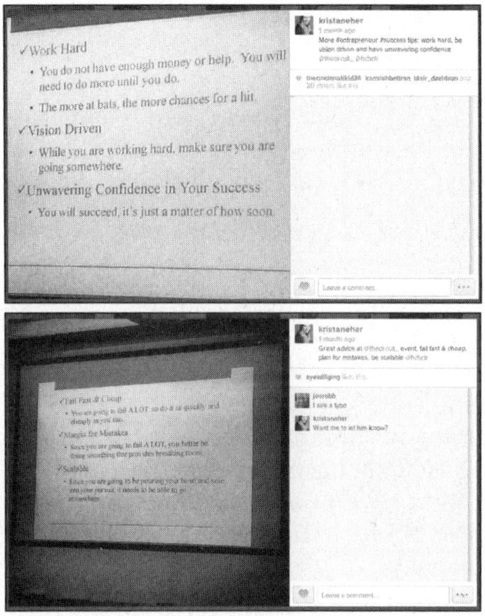

Figure 11-10: Two Instagram photos, with and without hashtags.

This example shows that adding hashtags to a description can increase the views and likes on your photos. Because people specifically search for hashtags, including them on your images invites more exposure.

Building an Audience on Instagram

Taking and sharing photos with optimized captions and hashtags is the first step in creating your presence on Instagram, but building an audience of people who follow you takes more effort than simply posting photos. I've interviewed many people from companies that have been successful on Instagram, and one characteristic that they have in common is that they don't post only photos — they interact and engage with other Instagram users in their target audience.

Building an audience on Instagram helps you generate more visibility of your posts. On Instagram, similar to other social networks, users may choose to follow you. Then your posts appear in their newsfeeds whenever they log on to Instagram, and they then see your photos. That's why generating followers is valuable — it increases the number of views your photos generate.

Finding relevant Instagram users

A *relevant* user on Instagram is someone who may be interested in your photos, business, product, or service. The first step in finding relevant users is to find the users on Instagram whom you want to connect with. The starting point for this task is knowing the target audience you want to reach. Then follow these steps to find them on Instagram:

1. **Write down the types of photos that your target audience is sharing or interested in.**

   Consider your target audience. What types of photos are they sharing? What types of photos are they interested in? The answers to these questions can help you search for your target audience on Instagram.

2. **Brainstorm the hashtags your target audience may be using.**

   Evaluate the hashtags that your audience might be using in their posts. Make a list of the hashtags that describe the images your target audience may be sharing or interested in.

3. **Search Instagram.**

   Spend some time searching Instagram for users who are taking, sharing, and liking images. Search for the hashtags identified in Step 2. Note the users who are sharing photos with these hashtags and the users liking and commenting on these photos. These Instagram users might be interested in *your* photos as well.

4. **Note the types of images that are shared and popular.**

   As you explore hashtags and search for Instagram users, notice the types of photos they're interested in. Pay attention to the pictures that generate a lot of likes and comments, because they can inspire ideas for posting on your own Instagram account. Also note their captions and hashtags — they can give you ideas for additional searches as well as for hashtags and captions for your own photos.

5. **Interact with these users.**

   After you identify the users who might be interested in connecting with you, the next step is to interact with them, as covered in the later section "Interacting with users on Instagram."

You can either search Instagram on your mobile device with the Instagram application or search Instagram from a computer by using the Statigram website (www.Statigr.am).

Interacting with users on Instagram

Interacting with users on Instagram is one of the best ways to get noticed and to build an audience for your Instagram account. People are more likely to follow you, like your photos, and comment on your photos when you're following them and liking and commenting on their photos.

Use these methods to interact with other Instagram users:

✔ **Follow other users.** When you follow a user on Instagram, her posts are displayed in your newsfeed on Instagram and (this is important) the user is notified. People often note who is following them, and if the follower is also posting interesting photos, they follow the user back. In this way, by following people on Instagram, you can increase the number of people following you. Follow the steps for finding relevant Instagram users to find users who are likely to be interested in your content. To follow a user, simply click on the Follow button beside the user's profile image.

Don't simply follow any random user on Instagram; connect with users with whom you share an interest or a common bond.

✔ **Like images.** Liking photos on Instagram is a helpful way to get noticed and build awareness for your account. Instagram notifies a user whenever another user likes his photos, and most users enjoy drawing more likes of their photos. Like images that are relevant based on your target audience and not too personal in nature. Some Instagram users don't realize that all their images are public, and liking images that are private in nature, especially with a business account, many seem aggressive. To like an image, click on the heart button that's displayed with the image.

✔ **Comment on images.** Similar to liking an image, commenting on an image can increase your visibility on Instagram, because the user is notified of your comment. Plus, your comment is displayed whenever other users view the photo, so you generate visibility for your account with everyone who views the photo.

Make your comments relevant and genuine — you don't want to seem insincere. Instagram users don't respond well to accounts whose owners leave meaningless comments to boost their visibility.

✔ **Share other images.** You can also share images from Instagram to your Facebook, Flickr, Foursquare, Twitter, or Tumblr account. If you find on Instagram a photo that you want to share on your social networks, you can easily do so. When viewing an Instagram photo, simply click on the Ellipsis (. . .) button in the lower-right corner, and you can then add a description and share the photo. You can also share via e-mail, which sends the Instagram photo to an e-mail address that you specify.

When you interact with other Instagram users, keep your contact relevant and natural. For example, don't follow too many users too quickly or like every photo you come across. This activity may make you appear too aggressive, and other users may assume that you're disingenuous or that you're simply trying to build a following. Be sure that you're interacting with users who share interests with you; if you leave a comment, be sure that it's relevant to the photo.

Creating great-looking content for Instagram

One of the most important ways to build an audience on Instagram is to post appealing content that your audience is interested in. People won't follow your account if you post boring images. For some businesses, finding appropriate photos is easy. For example, restaurants and retailers have no shortage of customer-oriented photos that they can take directly from their stores. Other businesses may find it more challenging to find items or scenes to take pictures of that are related to their businesses. Regardless of your type of business, taking appealing photos is a can't-miss strategy.

Follow these tips for posting interesting pictures on Instagram:

- ✔ **Start by searching.** Search Instagram for photos related to your business. Note the types of photos that are popular. Searching is a useful source of Inspiration.

- ✔ **Writing can make an appealing picture.** Many businesses struggle with Instagram when they have no visual products to take pictures of.

  For an easy way to add text to a photo, write a comment and take a picture of it. At Boot Camp Digital, employees have a white board on which they write social media tips each week. Someone then takes a picture of the white board to generate Instagram content from a more visual topic.

- ✔ **Keep your eyes open.** Form the mindset of creating images for Instagram, and you'll be amazed at the number of photo opportunities you can create. I often take photos of slides that I like during presentations, and I take pictures of interesting items around the office. I may also snap a photo of a headline from an article and share a few quick thoughts. I take pictures of the neighborhood where my business is located, to build goodwill. Start thinking about opportunities for great-looking photos in everything you do. Conferences and live events are especially powerful locations for photo opportunities.

- ✔ **Evaluate your current image library.** You can have photos in your current image library that you want to share on Instagram. Koyal Wholesale (www.Instagram.com/KoyalWholesale), an online wedding supply company, often shares photos of products that weren't originally taken with Instagram. Company employees aren't often able to shoot their own photos of products, so they use product pictures from their computers to populate the Instagram account. (Instagramming photos from your computer is covered in the later section "Viewing Instagram Photos on a Computer.")

✔ **Instagram contests.** An Instagram contest is becoming a popular way for businesses to engage their customers. An Instagram contest typically encourages users to take a photo and use a specific hashtag to enter the contest. Even large businesses have run contests. For example, in the contest that General Electric ran on Instagram, users shot photos and used the hashtag #GEInspiredMe to represent how GE had inspired them. More than 4,000 photos were submitted to the contest, and the winner received a tour of a jet engine plant (to photograph with Instagram). Regardless of the size of your business, an Instagram contest can be a helpful way to get your customers to take and share photos.

✔ **Use photos from other users.** Some Instagram accounts are composed of images taken by other Instagram users. For example, the Pure Michigan Instagram account (`www.Instagram.com/PureMichigan`) is composed of photos (see Figure 11-11), taken by other users, that are tagged #PureMichigan. The original photographer is credited in the image comments.

Have your legal team review this strategy to be sure that you have the rights to use other users' images in your Instagram account. You don't want to violate copyright laws or create other legal issues.

Figure 11-11: The Pure Michigan Instagram account.

A business can benefit more from Instagram when it engages its audience. Rather than simply post photos, use Instagram as a tool to interact with customers and encourage their feedback.

One company that engages its audience well is Koyal Wholesale. Koyal uses its Instagram account to encourage feedback (especially about new products) from its customers. As a wholesaler, it's always scouting for new products and trying to decide which products to add to its catalog.

As you can see in Figure 11-12, Koyal poses questions about new products, such as "Love it or leave it?" and "Hot or not?" In one instance, Koyal shared a new product idea on Instagram, and the Instagram community provided feedback about what it liked and didn't like. Koyal shared the feedback with the supplier, who then changed the product accordingly.

Figure 11-12:
Koyal
Wholesale
engages
customers on
Instagram.

Viewing Instagram Photos on a Computer

Because Instagram is primarily a mobile application, most of its functionality is available only via the mobile application. However, you can view certain Instagram features on a computer by way of Instagram and other websites that pull information from the site.

Instagram.com

At www.instagram.com, you can access Instagram from your computer, to complete a limited number of tasks:

✔ **Log on and access your account.** You can log on and access your account on Instagram; however, you'll have limited functionality. After you log on, you can view your newsfeed, which shows you the pictures that people you follow are sharing.

✔ **View your profile.** When you click on your profile picture in the upper-right corner, you can view your profile and see the images you've shared.

✔ **Edit your profile.** By clicking on your profile picture in the upper-right corner, you can choose to edit your profile. From there, you can manage your profile information, your password, the applications connected to your Instagram account, and the badges you can use to share your Instagram account on your website.

✔ **View other Instagram accounts.** You can't search for other users on Instagram, but if you know their usernames, you can view their profile. To view the profile of another Instagram user, add the username to the Instagram web address by typing `www.Instagram.com/`*`username`* into your browser. In Figure 11-13, you can see my Instagram profile, at `www.Instagram.com/KristaNeher`, as viewed on a computer.

Figure 11-13: My Instagram profile.

As you can see, the computer version of Instagram has a limited amount of functionality. You can't take or share photos or search for other images.

Statigr.am

An alternative way to access Instagram functionality from a computer is to use the Statigram website: `www.Statigr.am`. Statigram lets you search and view Instagram content from your computer.

Some of the more useful tasks that you can complete at Statigr.am that you can't do on Instagram are described in this list:

- **Search for users or hashtags.** On Statigram, you can search for users or hashtags and view the results. For example, I can search for #motorcycle to see other photos of motorcycles. I can also find users by searching for their usernames.

- **Interact with other users.** After you find images you like, you can like or comment on the photos directly from Statigram. (You must be logged in to your account, however.)

- **Follow new users.** From Statigram, you can also follow new users. After you click on a user's profile, you see a large Follow button, which you can click to begin following a user.

- **Click the links labeled My Following or My Followers.** After you're logged in to Statigram, you can also view the users who are following you (My Followers) and the ones you're following (My Followings).

- **Analyze statistics.** Statigram shows you basic statistics for your account, including the number of followers, likes, and comments on your account. You can also view your most popular posts and the Instagram users who most often interact with you.

This section describes only *some* of the functionality of Statigram. If you find that you would rather access Instagram from a computer, or if you want more advanced functionality such as statistics and reporting, spend some time exploring Statigram.

Instagram photos on a computer

There's no easy way to share on Instagram a photo that's now only on your computer. Instagram was designed primarily to take photos from your mobile device. Though the precise steps to share photos this way may differ slightly on your device, the general steps should be the same.

First, place the photo that you want to share on your mobile device. You can do this in a few different ways:

- **E-mail the photo to yourself.** E-mail the photo to an e-mail account that you access via your mobile device. Then open the message on your mobile device, and choose to download the image.

✔ **Copy the image over when you sync your device.** Most mobile devices can be synced with a computer to download photos, videos, and music from a computer. This process usually simply involves plugging your mobile device into your computer and choosing the image that you want to copy.

✔ **Upload the photo online, and save it from a web browser or application.** You may also be able to choose to download an image that's displayed in a web browser or application. For example, you may upload the picture to the Internet by way of a photo-sharing site and then access it from the Internet browser on your mobile phone. Depending on your device, you should be able to click and download to your phone the image that you're viewing. Similarly, some images that have been uploaded to Facebook can be downloaded to your mobile phone. Simply access them via your Facebook mobile application and choose to download them. The specific functionality and steps to do this will vary, depending on your mobile phone.

✔ **Upload the picture to a cloud-based drive.** If you use a cloud-based storage drive such as MobileMe or Google Drive, you may be able to upload the image to the virtual cloud drive and access it from your mobile phone. To do this, you need to have an account with a cloud-based storage service and download its application to your phone.

To share a photo on Instagram, the photo must be in your mobile device library. The steps for this action may differ, depending on the device, but, typically, you can see whether the photo is in your mobile device library by choosing the photo viewer on your device.

After the photo is on your mobile device, you can easily share it via Instagram. Simply open your Instagram account, and rather than shoot a new photo, click the button to use an image or a video clip from your library.

Chapter 12

Sharing Presentations on SlideShare

As you explore opportunities for sharing visual content online, you'll likely encounter SlideShare (www.slideshare.net), which is "the world's largest community for sharing presentations." On SlideShare, users upload presentations to share with the SlideShare community or to post on other social networks.

Marketers and business professionals use SlideShare to share presentations and build exposure and visibility for themselves and their businesses. In this chapter, I show you the inner workings of SlideShare works and the business benefits of sharing presentations online. You can see how to optimize presentations to maximize your reach and exposure and how to share your presentations across social networks and on your blog or website.

Recognizing the Benefits of Using SlideShare

SlideShare, a large and quickly growing social network, has more than 60 million monthly visitors and 159 million page views per month, making it among the 200 most often visited websites in the world (www.slideshare.net).

SlideShare is a community where users view, like, comment on, and share presentations that they find interesting. Marketers flock to SlideShare because of the tremendous reach of the site. Many presentations shared on SlideShare generate hundreds, if not thousands, of views — considerably more views than most marketers generate from their blog posts or websites. The bottom line is that SlideShare can generate significant reach and awareness for any visual social marketer.

For example, in 2009 I uploaded 11 presentations to SlideShare and generated more than 10,000 views, which was more views than my blog generated that year. I continue to generate between 500 and 5,000 views on many of my SlideShare presentations, which is significantly more reach versus a blog post or a Facebook status update.

Though some marketers may not regularly create or give presentations, SlideShare can still be a component of a marketing strategy. Think of the site as another visual marketing opportunity, and create presentations for SlideShare as a part of your visual content strategy regardless of whether you give the presentations that you upload. Many marketers are creating presentations specifically for SlideShare.

In addition to sharing presentations, SlideShare supports the sharing of documents, PDF files, videos, and webinars. The focus of this chapter is on presentations, which is the primary content shared on the site.

With both free and paid (pro) accounts, SlideShare offers a wide variety of ways for businesses to promote themselves by using the site and to increase their visibility. Presentations on SlideShare generate a lot of views — for a number of reasons:

- **Search engine optimization (SEO):** SlideShare presentations often rank well in search engines such as Google. For example, a presentation on SlideShare specifying how to use visual social media marketing is likely to show up when someone uses a search engine to find the phrase *visual social media marketing*. Because many presentations on SlideShare are optimized for search engines, search engine traffic can be a major contributor to views on SlideShare.

- **Community:** Like many other social networks, SlideShare has users who actively search, browse, and view presentations on SlideShare. SlideShare users can follow other users — a feature that's offered in other social networks, such as Twitter — and receive updates when new presentations are uploaded. This strategy provides additional views for presentations.

- **Sharing:** One of the best aspects of SlideShare is that presentations can be shared on blog posts or on Facebook, LinkedIn, Twitter, Pinterest, Google+, and other sites. Social sharing also drives a significant number of views to presentations.

As demonstrated in Figure 12-1, a presentation on SlideShare allows for social sharing of the presentation. The presentation can be *embedded,* which means that it can be shared on a website or blog post or on social networks such as Facebook, Twitter, LinkedIn, Google+, and Pinterest. Additionally, SlideShare users can follow other users, so your followers are updated every time you upload a new presentation. These social sharing tools increase the visibility and reach of your presentations on SlideShare.

Figure 12-1:
Social
sharing
options for a
SlideShare
presentation.

Getting Started with SlideShare

SlideShare offers a free account, which is adequate for most users, as well as a variety of Pro (paid) accounts. Most users will find that a free account is all they need to generate results for their business. Users who are extremely active on the site may find that Pro accounts have a number of advantages. If you're just getting started with SlideShare, start with a Basic (free) account to get a feel for the site, and consider upgrading after you're already getting traction from the presentations you upload.

SlideShare offers these types of accounts (at the time of this publishing):

✔ **Basic (Free):** The free Basic account meets most users' needs. Users can

  • Create a standard profile

  • Upload an unlimited number of presentations (limited in size) to share publicly

  • Interact with other users

✔ **Silver ($19/month):** In addition to the functionality of the Basic account, users with the Silver account can

- Upload larger presentations

- Upload private presentations

- Upload ten videos per month

- Gain access to analytics for presentations

- Conduct private meetings

- Generate leads

- Track presentations

- Customize associated content that's displayed on a presentation page

- Customize the look of their profiles

At the Silver account level, many of these features are still limited.

✔ **Gold ($49/month) and Platinum (custom pricing):** Gold and Platinum accounts allow all the same features as Silver accounts; however, many features are unlimited or provide higher caps. For example, a Silver account allows for the capture of 30 leads to be captured, whereas a Gold or Platinum account allows for 75 leads. A Silver account allows for basic profile customization, whereas a Gold or Platinum account provides advanced customization or full branding.

You can find a complete list of the features and pricing of SlideShare accounts at www.slideshare.net/business/premium/plans. SlideShare also offers special pricing for nonprofits and educational institutions.

In the following overview of SlideShare, I focus on the features and functionality of the Basic account. I tell you how to create an account, customize your profile, and upload a presentation.

Creating a SlideShare account

Before you can upload and share presentations, you create an account and customize your profile.

First, go to www.slideshare.net and click the sign-up link in the upper-right corner. You're offered the option to connect via LinkedIn or Facebook, or to create a new account using an e-mail, username, and password. Choose the option that's easiest for you to get started, and complete the sign-up process.

After your account is created, the next step is to customize your profile information. The free account simply allows users to update basic profile information. Pro accounts allow users to customize the background and look and feel of their profiles.

You can see a Basic account profile in SlideShare, as shown in Figure 12-2. To see your profile, move the cursor over the arrow in the upper-right corner and choose View My Profile Page. If you signed in with an existing social media account, certain information, such as your profile photo or location, may already appear in your profile.

Figure 12-2: Profile page in a SlideShare Basic account.

To edit your profile, click the Edit Profile button. Then Click Upload a New Image to upload a profile image, and choose an image as you normally would do with any other social network. You can complete your profile by filling in the following:

✔ Location

✔ Workplace

✔ Occupation/role/activity

✔ Website/blog

✔ Phone number

✔ About section (700 characters limit)

✔ Links to social networks (Twitter, Facebook, LinkedIn, Google+)

You may notice an orange button labeled Style Your Profile beside your profile picture when viewing your profile. This feature is available only to Pro users, so if you've just created an basic account, you can't style your profile.

By contrast, Figure 12-3 shows a Pro profile, which offers these features:

✔ No display of ads

✔ Custom branding with an image at the top

✔ Customized color scheme

✔ More control over adjoining content, such as the other presentations displayed on the page

If you prefer a Pro account instead, click GoPro in the upper-right corner and sign up.

Figure 12-3: A customized profile page in a SlideShare Pro account.

After your profile is complete, you're ready to start uploading presentations. I cover this topic in the next section.

Uploading a presentation to SlideShare

Uploading presentations is relatively simple. SlideShare allows users to upload a variety of presentations including presentations, documents (such as Microsoft Word), PDF files, and videos (Pro accounts only). SlideShare doesn't support uploading KeyNote files from Mac computers, so these files must be converted to PowerPoint before uploading.

To upload a presentation to SlideShare, follow these steps:

1. **Click the Upload button.**

   It's the orange button at the top of the page.

2. **Choose the correct uploading option.**

   When you're uploading a presentation, SlideShare provides two buttons with different uploading options, as shown in Figure 12-4:

- *Upload (orange):* The basic uploader is available to all account types, which limits file sizes and makes all presentations public.

- *Upload+ (blue):* Pro users can benefit from larger file sizes and private file sharing.

- *Dropbox upload:* Below the orange Upload button is the Upload from Dropbox link. If you have your file on Dropbox, you can upload this way.

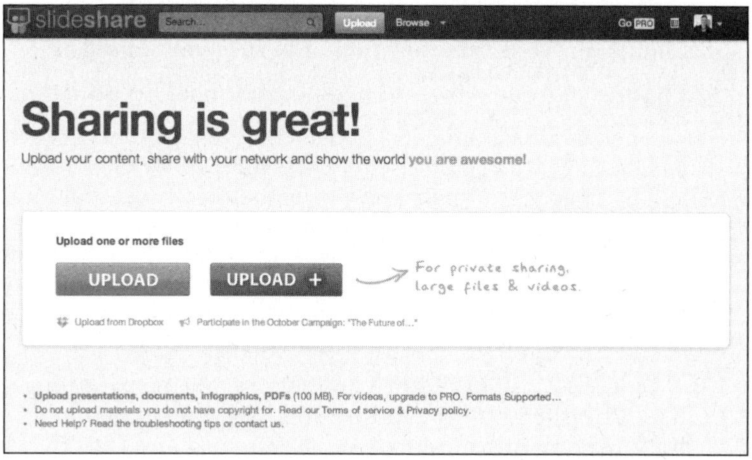

Figure 12-4: SlideShare uploading options.

After the presentation type has been selected, SlideShare uploads the presentation and provides a number of fields to complete, (I discuss these next), as shown in Figure 12-5.

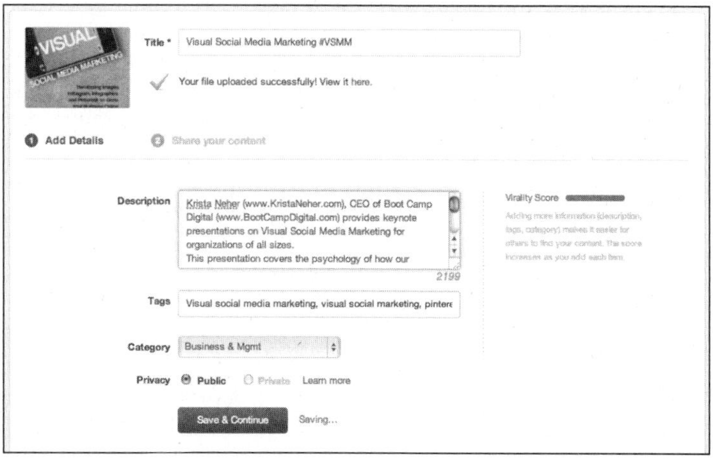

Figure 12-5: Fields to complete when uploading a SlideShare presentation.

3. **Add basic information about the presentation.**

   The fields you complete for your presentation are Title, Description, Tags, and Category. (You might notice that you can't change the Privacy setting with a Basic account.) This information about the presentation helps make your presentation discoverable on SlideShare and in search engines, and it's discussed in more detail in the later section "Optimizing SlideShare Presentations." All these fields can be accessed and edited at any time. You can also upload the presentation again, if needed; for example, you might notice an error on a slide or want to make another change.

4. **Click the Save & Continue button to save your changes.**

5. **Click Advanced Settings to update additional presentation settings.**

   When you initially upload a SlideShare presentation, not all the advanced customization fields are displayed. By clicking on the Info and Settings text, which is displayed below the presentation when you view your presentation, you can see all settings that can be customized. On this screen, you see a number of tabs, including Edit Details, Privacy Settings, Re-upload, Add Audio and Add YouTube Video. (see Figure 12-6). Here are two of the most important settings, which you may want to update:

   - *Allow Download:* You can find the download settings on the Privacy Settings tab. Consider this option carefully because it pertains to your intellectual property and the content you're sharing. Do you really and truly want people to be able to download, edit, and reuse your presentation? Remember that competitors, customers, or others in your industry may fall into this category. By default, most presentations are set to allow downloading, so if you don't want to allow it, be sure to update this setting.

   - *Choose a License:* **You can choose the license for your presentation on the Edit Details tab.** By default, you retain all rights to the files you upload. Though others can view your presentation on SlideShare, they cannot reuse any of your content. You can also choose to apply Creative Commons licensing to your file, allowing others to reuse your work. A variety of Creative Commons licenses are available. You can find out more about these licenses at www.creativecommons.org.

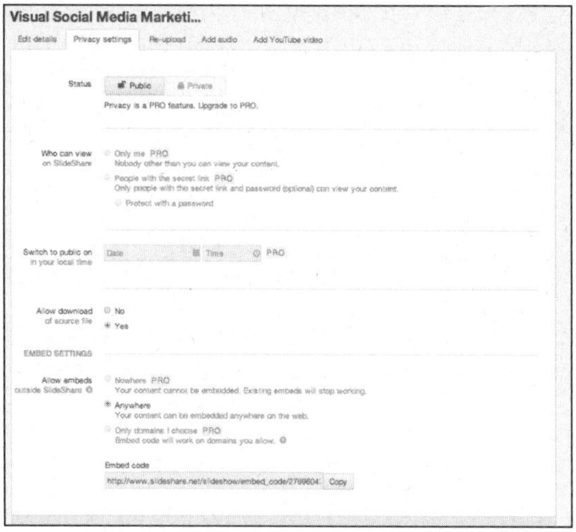

Figure 12-6:
Advanced
presentation
settings in
SlideShare.

6. **Click the Updates button and review the presentation, description, and transcription.**

After the presentation has been uploaded, you may view it to check for accuracy and any display issues. Below the presentation and comments is a transcription of the presentation. The transcription is automatically generated based on the words on the slides of your presentation, as shown in Figure 12-7.

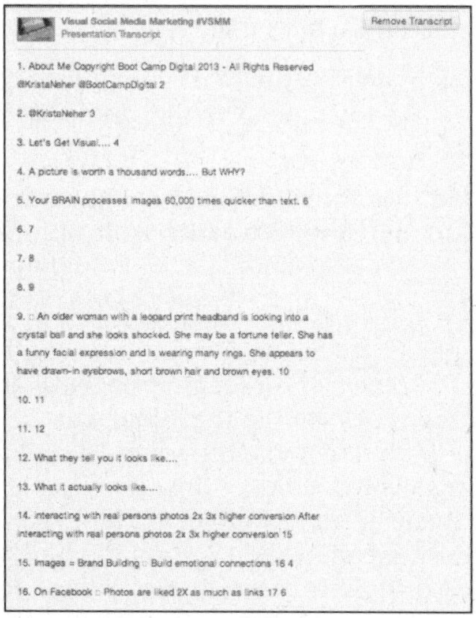

Figure 12-7:
Transcription
of a
SlideShare
presentation.

Depending on how you create your presentation, the transcription may or may not be relevant. SlideShare doesn't allow you to edit the transcription, but you can remove it. Keep the transcription active because the additional words used in it can help the discoverability of the presentation. If it's irrelevant or misleading, however, you may choose to remove it.

Exploring Advanced Upload Options

After you upload a basic presentation, two additional advanced options — adding audio and video — can make the presentation even more robust.

Access the advanced upload options by clicking on the Info and Settings button located below a presentation when viewing a presentation.

Uploading audio

To make your presentation stand out and truly tell your story, you may also add audio to it. You can then verbally give your presentation. Viewers will have the option to simply view the slides or to play the presentation with your audio. Audio can be added only after the presentation has been uploaded, and your audio file must be in MP3 format.

To add audio to a presentation you've already uploaded, follow these steps:

1. **Click the Add Audio tab when editing the presentation or during the upload process to upload an audio MP3 file.**

    You may also choose to link to an MP3 file that's already uploaded online by clicking on the link to an already uploaded MP3 audio file. SlideShare doesn't allow you to upload music.

2. **After the audio is uploaded, use the SlideShare synchronization tool (as shown in Figure 12-8) to match up the audio with the slides in the presentation.**

    In Figure 12-8, the slides are shown at the top of the screen, and the audio timeline is below them. Blue line markers indicate the beginning or end of each slide. Moving the blue marker forward or backward moves the slide transition forward or backward in the audio. For example, if you want Slide 1 to end earlier in the audio recording, drag the first blue line to the left. After you're satisfied with the positioning of the end of Slide 1, click on Slide 2 in the slide show (above the blue marker lines) to activate the blue marker for the end of Slide 2. Drag the blue marker for the end of Slide 2 to the left or right to move it forward or backward in the audio. Continue this process for each slide until the ending of each slide matches the correct position in the audio.

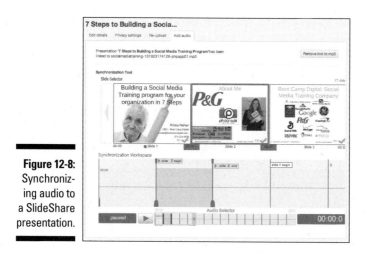

Figure 12-8:
Synchroniz-
ing audio to
a SlideShare
presentation.

3. **Review the presentation by moving the red marker to the beginning of the presentation.**

   After adding audio, presentation viewers can play the presentation with the audio, and the slides automatically advance at the correct time. You can test this process in the audio synchronization tool by moving the red marker in the audio editing portion to the beginning of the presentation and pressing the red Play button at the bottom of the editor. A flashing red dot appears under the slide that's now matched to the audio that's playing. After you finish testing the audio, test that the audio and synchronization work correctly by viewing your presentation with the audio from your profile.

Adding YouTube videos

Videos can make your presentation more engaging and compelling, so SlideShare has a tool that allows you to add any YouTube video to a presentation. Upload the presentation using the steps covered earlier in this chapter. Follow these steps:

1. **Find the YouTube video to include in the presentation and copy the URL.**

   SlideShare allows only videos from YouTube to be displayed — you cannot upload a video to be included or use one from another video sharing site. First be sure that the video you want to use is available on YouTube. (If it isn't, you may need to upload your video.) After you have found the YouTube video that you want to include in the presentation, copy the URL from your browser when you're on the page at YouTube that hosts the video.

2. **Click the arrow beside the profile button in the upper-right corner of the top navigation of SlideShare and click My Uploads.**

3. **Find the presentation that you want to add a YouTube video to. Click the Edit button below the presentation and choose Add Video from the drop-down list.**

4. **Paste the URL of the YouTube video (from Step 1) into the Enter Video URL box.**

5. **Choose where to position the video by selecting the appropriate slide from the Insert This Video At drop-down list box.**

   Then you can click the button to add additional YouTube videos and repeat Steps 1–4.

6. **Click the orange Insert and Publish button to publish the video in your presentation.**

7. **Review the presentation for errors.**

   Ensure that the video is playing at the correct slide in your presentation by viewing the presentation.

Optimizing SlideShare Presentations

As you upload presentations to SlideShare, you can maximize the value by optimizing the presentation to generate more visibility.

People may search for your presentations on SlideShare or via Google or another search engine, so optimizing the presentation can generate more traffic and views to your presentation.

To optimize your SlideShare presentation, follow these steps:

1. **Create a title based on search by typing a name for your presentation in the Title field.**

   When creating a presentation, you may have a catchy, unique, or provocative title; however, the best title for optimization is one that uses the words people search for and that clearly describes the presentation. For example, a presentation named Real World Advice to Use Online may generate more search traffic if it's named Social Media Privacy for College Students.

2. **Create a complete description in the Description field.**

   SlideShare provides 3,000 characters for the description, which is a lot of space, and probably more than you need. Use this space to your advantage. Consider adding the following items to the description:

- *Synonyms:* Include a variety of words and phrases that accurately describe your presentation. Don't be afraid to restate the title or parts of the description with different words. For example, a presentation to doctors may include the words *doctors, physicians,* and *surgeons* to maximize the reach in searches.

- *Details:* Elaborate on key points in your presentation by describing them in detail. When people search for presentations on SlideShare, words and phrases that are found in the Details section of your presentation are scanned to find a match for the search phrase. Using more words to describe your presentation increases the probability that your presentation will be displayed in search results. Longer descriptions with more words make your presentation show up more often in search results and generates more views.

- *Web addresses:* Include a link to your website with a description of your business, products, or services.

The bottom line is to use as much of the space as possible to your advantage, to increase the probability that your presentation will show up in searches.

3. **Add tags to your presentation in the Tags field.**

   A *tag* is a word or phrase that generally describes what a presentation is all about. Unlike the description, which uses complete sentences or bullet points, tags are simply words. According to SlideShare, tags can increase the searchability of your presentation by up to 30 percent. You can add a maximum of 20 tags to describe any presentation. Use as many of the tags as you reasonably can — it's a useful way to be sure that your presentation is found on SlideShare when people search.

Building an Audience on SlideShare

One of the best ways to generate traffic and views to SlideShare presentations is to take advantage of the SlideShare community. Many SlideShare users regularly look to the site to find and follow people who share interesting content.

A *follower* is simply another SlideShare user who chooses to follow your content. The follower receives updates whenever you post new content on SlideShare. If you can generate more followers for your SlideShare account, more people will see your presentations.

Because SlideShare is a community, like any other social network, participating in the community (in this case, SlideShare) can increase the number of people who follow you and view your content.

I tell you how to follow, and interact with, other users in the next couple of sections. On SlideShare, you can interact with other users by liking and commenting on content and sending private messages.

Following other users

Following other users on SlideShare generates visibility because SlideShare notifies the users that you're now following them. Users who receive this notification can click on your profile to check out your presentation or even follow you back. If they follow you back, they receive updates of your new presentations. Following relevant users can generate more views for your presentations.

Additionally, by following other users in your industry, you're notified whenever they add a new presentation, which may give you inspiration for new presentations to upload.

The key isn't simply to follow any user on SlideShare — find people in your industry or target market with whom you share something in common.

For example, if I'm a home builder and I want to generate awareness with realtors (my target audience), I may choose to follow other home builders who aren't direct competitors for inspiration as well as realtors with whom I want to build awareness.

Finding relevant users on SlideShare is easy. As shown in Figure 12-9, SlideShare includes robust search options. After you type a search word or phrase (such as a phrase related to your industry or your presentation topic or to whoever you want to reach), press Enter and you see search results along with filtering options.

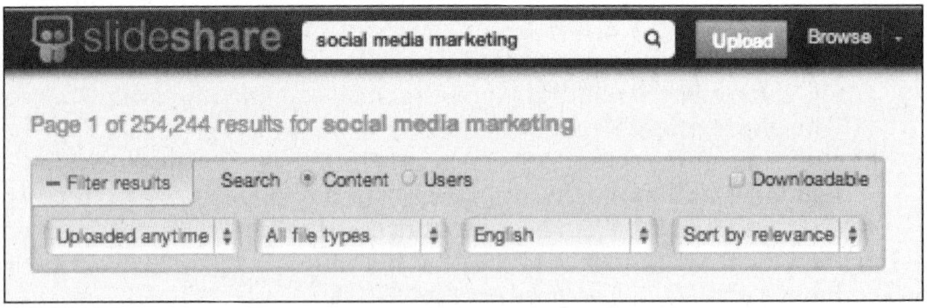

Figure 12-9: SlideShare search functionality.

| slideshare | social media marketing | Q | Upload | Browse |

Page 1 of 254,244 results for **social media marketing**

| — Filter results | Search ● Content ○ Users | | ☐ Downloadable |
| Uploaded anytime ⇕ | All file types ⇕ | English ⇕ | Sort by relevance ⇕ |

You can select one of these two radio buttons:

- ✔ **Content:** Search for presentations that include the phrase in their titles, tags, or descriptions.
- ✔ **Users:** Search for SlideShare users who include the specific phrase in their profile descriptions — a helpful way to discover people to connect with.

In addition to the basic search options, you can further filter your search results to specify how the results are sorted, how recent the results are, the file type, and the language. Click the arrow next to the appropriate drop-down list to make your selections.

Conduct a number of searches to find users who are interesting and relevant for you to follow. To follow a user, simply click the Follow button, which is usually displayed below the user profile image.

You can follow any user who interests you on SlideShare. The person doesn't have to accept your following request. When you follow a user, that person simply receives a notification and you begin to receive updates whenever she uploads new presentations.

Interacting with other users

Following users that you're interested in or want to reach is a good first step to interacting on SlideShare, but you can take other actions to increase your visibility.

When you find a presentation you like, you can like it or leave a comment. Commenting on and liking presentations are valuable activities because your action (the like or the comment) is displayed below the presentation. You then generate visibility for your profile with everyone who views the presentation you liked.

Liking a presentation

You can like a presentation by clicking on the heart or Like button displayed above a presentation. Liking a presentation sends a notification to the user that you have liked his presentation, and it may encourage him to check out your profile or to like one of your presentations.

Commenting on presentations

Commenting on presentations is a helpful way to grow your credibility and visibility on SlideShare. You can leave a comment at the end of any presentation. When you leave a comment, the user receives a notification that you commented on her presentation, similar to liking a presentation.

In addition to the user being notified, your comment is publicly displayed below the presentation, which can increase your visibility. Now everyone who views the presentation also sees your profile image, username, and comment, as shown in Figure 12-10.

Figure 12-10:
A comment on a SlideShare presentation.

Commenting on presentations is a powerful way to showcase your knowledge and expertise while gaining visibility with potentially large audiences. For example, if you leave a comment on a presentation that generates 10,000 views, you're gaining exposure of your profile and your comment with those 10,000 viewers.

Leave comments that are thoughtful and insightful to maximize the impression you generate by commenting. Saying simply, "Great presentation" is acceptable, but a comment that showcases your unique knowledge of the subject area, such as a detailed question or observation is more powerful in building a strong brand online.

Sending private messages

SlideShare also allows users to communicate privately with one another. After you're following a user, you can send a private message by clicking on the Mail button beside the user profile image from the profile page. Messages are similar to e-mails, and are sent directly to the user's inbox on SlideShare.

Don't abuse private messages and send spam or sales messages to other users. Any private message you send should be relevant and useful to the recipient.

Sharing SlideShare Presentations

One thing that makes SlideShare extremely powerful is that presentations on SlideShare can be shared and displayed on other social networks or websites online. SlideShare integrates with a number of social networks in addition to allowing you to simply share a link to a presentation.

SlideShare makes it easy to share presentations across social networks with the social sharing buttons that appear to the left of the presentation. Using these buttons to share a presentation displays a link to the presentation on the social network you select.

You can also integrate SlideShare with select social media accounts and embed SlideShare presentations in your blog. I explain how to do those tasks in the next two sections.

Integrating SlideShare into LinkedIn, Facebook, and Google+

SlideShare also offers integration with Facebook, Google+, and LinkedIn. The integration with these social networks allows SlideShare to post status updates based on your activity on SlideShare. For example, SlideShare may post a status update on Facebook when you upload a presentation, save a presentation, make a comment, like a presentation, or follow a new user.

You can customize which updates you want to share on each social network. Depending on how active you are on SlideShare, you may want to turn off some notifications.

To access the Integration tab, log in to SlideShare, hover the cursor over the arrow in the upper-right corner, and choose the Account Settings option. On the General Settings page, click Sharing. This screen shows which social accounts are integrated with SlideShare (simply click Connect to integrate an account), and you can adjust the settings by clicking on the Settings button, as shown in Figure 12-11.

Figure 12-11:
SlideShare
integra-
tions with
other social
networks.

Embedding presentations into your blog or website

SlideShare presentations can be embedded directly into a blog or website so that a website or blog visitor can view your presentation without having to leave your site. Figure 12-12 shows how a SlideShare presentation may be displayed in a blog. A blog visitor can simply click on the arrow buttons to scroll through the slides in the presentation, without leaving the web page.

Figure 12-12:
A SlideShare
presentation,
embedded in
a blog post.

You can embed any presentation on SlideShare into your blog or website — not only the presentations you create.

1. **When viewing a presentation on SlideShare that you want to embed, click the Embed button.**

   The button is at the top of a presentation display.

2. **Click the Customize button below the code to customize the display of the embedded presentation.**

   From there, you can choose customization options:

   a. *Without related content:* Clicking this button displays the presentation without related content. Related content is typically displayed at the end of viewing a presentation, and it directs the viewer to view other similar presentations.

   b. *Start from slide number:* When embedding a presentation, you can select the starting slide number. Select the slide number from the drop-down list.

   c. *Size:* You can select from four predetermined sizes to embed the presentation into your blog or website. Click on the size that you want to use.

3. **Copy the embed code.**

   Copy the code that is generated after you have selected the customization options.

4. **Paste the code into your website to display the presentation.**

Sharing SlideShare presentations on your blog or website is a useful way to add visual content to your site. Your website visitors can view the entire presentation directly from your site, without having to click a Download button. Presentations also make inviting blog posts because they can tell a story visually and get readers even more engaged.

Chapter 13

Using Infographics to Share Your Story

*I*nfographics have been used to clearly convey information since the 1600s, but in the past few years they have taken the social media marketing world by storm, recently emerging as a popular way to share a story visually. You've probably spotted infographics on the Internet as they have become quite popular on blogs and many news sites.

An *infographic* is a visual representation of data. It's typically a longer-format graphic that includes pictures, illustrations, charts, or graphs to explain information. An infographic is a powerful communications tool because it can make complex information easier to consume and understand.

Marketers are turning to the use of infographics as a part of their visual social marketing strategies because this element can be a powerful tool to share information and generate attention on social media sites. Infographics are popular across social networks and can especially generate interest on Pinterest and Facebook.

Organizations of all types are using infographics creatively to communicate information. Politicians are using them to share their points of view on complex issues. Companies have used infographics to share their annual reports. Organizations have created infographics to share their press releases. Infographics are also used to share data from studies or the results that nonprofits have achieved.

In this chapter, I delve into the details of infographics to explain how to create them and show why they're valuable marketing tools. Creating infographics involves much more than simply hiring a designer — this chapter shares the steps to building an infographic, from brainstorming its content to promoting the completed infographic.

Introducing Infographics

An *infographic* is a graphical element that tells a story visually. The sample infographic shown in Figure 13-1 was created by my company, Boot Camp Digital, to share information in a more interesting and relevant way. The infographic, which is based on a blog post I wrote, has generated more than 20 times more traffic to the company's website than did a blog post containing the same information. In addition, the infographic generated significant number of social media mentions, likes, and comments.

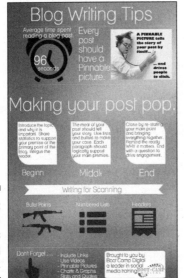

Figure 13-1:
Infographic that gives blog writing tips.

Infographics have become popular in the marketing world because people like to read and share them. My company has created a number of infographics, on different social media topics, all of which can be found by looking at the board titled Our Infographics on our Pinterest board (www.Pinterest.com/BootCampDigital).

Creating an interesting infographic isn't simply a matter of adding data to an image and sharing it online. An appealing infographic tells a story in a logical and interesting way.

Recognizing the Value of Infographics

Infographics are popular with marketers because of not only their appeal as social media content but also their ability to provide a lot of different types of value to an online marketing strategy. Most infographics generate value in more than one of the ways described in the following five sections. Creating an infographic is a time-consuming and potentially expensive task — undertaking it shouldn't be taken lightly. Because of the investment of resources, time, and money in creating an infographic, you should have a clear idea of what you want the infographic to achieve. Different types of infographics may be more appropriate, depending on your marketing objectives. In the following sections, I share with you some of the most common benefits of infographics.

Driving traffic

One major reason for a business to create an infographic is to drive traffic to its website. Typically, whenever a business creates an infographic, it's shared in a blog post or on another page on the site. Because infographics files are large, they're often difficult to view on social networks, so most users click on them to view the original large file infographic on the website instead. That's how infographics drive traffic.

The more interesting and unique the topic of your infographic is, the more likely it is to drive traffic.

My company's infographics have been quite effective at driving traffic to its website, even drawing hundreds of visitors a month. In Figure 13-2, you can see the content from `www.bootcampdigital.com` that was pinned on Pinterest. As you can see, infographics from the company's site are frequently pinned on Pinterest.

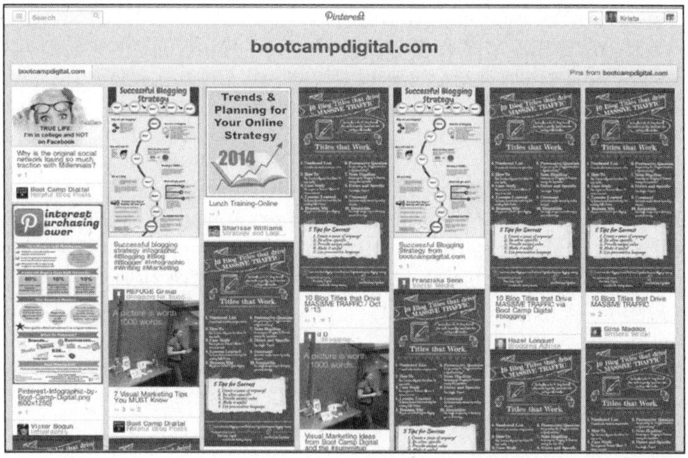

Figure 13-2: Content shared from my company's website.

An infographic created with the objective of driving traffic should be based on a concept that's highly sharable via social media. The infographic should be thought-provoking, interesting, or entertaining in a way that makes people want to share it.

Generating links

A *link* (or *hyperlink,* originally) is a word or picture on a web page that you click to visit another page or website. Infographics are popular partly because of their ability to generate links back to websites.

Infographics generate links because bloggers and new sites often discuss and share infographics. Whenever they discuss an infographic, they usually include a link back to the organization that created it.

Links are powerful tools for search engine optimization (SEO), a process for moving your website nearer to the top of search engine results. Links from other websites help with your SEO because they indicate to search engines that your website is important.

My company's infographics are often covered by social media bloggers. An average infographic generates five to ten links back to the website, which helps with our SEO efforts.

If you're creating infographics to generate links, the infographic should contain newsworthy content for bloggers or media in your industry to talk about. Additionally, if links are your goal, plan to spend time promoting your blog posts and building relationships with bloggers.

Content for social networks

Infographics make for appealing content on social networks because people enjoy liking, sharing, and commenting on them. Because infographics provide quick ways for people to access information, they're ideal for social networks where people don't have a lot of time to spend looking at every individual status update.

Infographics provide useful content to share across social networks, including blogs, Pinterest, Facebook, Twitter, Instagram, LinkedIn, SlideShare, and Scribd. A short infographic on a relevant topic makes for an inviting social network post.

You may need to customize how you share your infographic on social networks. For example, viewing an entire infographic in the photo viewer on Facebook is difficult. At my company, we share a portion of an infographic on Facebook and add a link to the entire infographic on the website. Spending a little time customizing the way we share on Facebook dramatically increases the results.

If you're creating infographics for social network content, think about creating infographics that are highly sharable. Consider topics that people are already talking about in social media or linking to pop culture or another type of popular content.

Create an infographic based on content that has already been popular in social media. An infographic can be a way to benefit from an already established idea. For example, my company created the infographic Hygiene vs. Social Media based on the popularity of a tweet about how more people own cell phones than toothbrushes.

One of our most popular infographics is (still) "37 Ways to Thrive on LinkedIn," which you can see in Figure 13-3. It was one of our most popular blog posts that we turned into an infographic. Because the infographic was created based on a blog post that was already popular, it had a high probability of success.

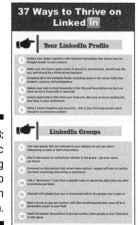

Figure 13-3: Infographic showing 37 ways to thrive on LinkedIn.

Start with content that you already know is popular on social media to maximize the probability of success.

Exposure

Infographics can translate into exposure for your organization. Exposure is a measure of the number of people who are seeing your organization, business, or product and talking about you. By packaging your story in a more user-friendly way, infographics can generate exposure for your company.

As your infographic is shared around the web (and your brand is attached to the infographic), you're driving awareness of your business or organization.

 If the goal of your infographic is general exposure, create one based on proprietary data or a unique aspect of your business. Be sure that the infographic includes branding, such as your logo, but don't overwhelm it with your brand and products — or else it will look more like an advertisement. Adding your logo, a brief description, and your website's URL at the bottom of the infographic ensures that its exposure translates into exposure for you and your business.

Sales

Infographics can drive sales for a business in a few different ways, though it isn't always easy.

Unmetric, a social media benchmarking company, created an infographic to generate exposure and drive sales. As a data company, it had interesting information that it could share in an infographic that also linked back to its business services. For example, Unmetric created an infographic about the social media marketing of luxury brands that led to several inquiries from luxury brands. Unmetric also landed an energy supply client that had initially heard about Unmetric from its infographics.

Another example is a ski resort that creates an infographic about snowfall and temperatures to show that it's the ideal place to ski. As long as the data is new and interesting, the infographic can be relevant *and* sell the resort. The challenge of this approach is that driving people to take a specific action directly from the infographic typically doesn't work well. Because the entire infographic is a single image, people can't click on its individual components to move to a different web page or sales offer.

Infographics can also be used strategically to support the sales process. Businesses are creating infographics to tell their sales stories rather than creating standard brochures or sales tools. For example, you can see in Figure 13-4 that the owner of Girlfriendology created an infographic to convince brands to market on her website. The infographic tells the story in a much more interesting way than a traditional PowerPoint presentation.

Figure 13-4:
Girl-
friendology
uses
infographics
to sell.

Don't let your infographic focus too much on selling. Readers who are simply looking for interesting information often don't want to feel like they're "being sold to." An infographic works only if people actually look at it, so balance your desire to sell with creating one that's interesting to your target audience.

Options for Designing an Infographic

When you begin creating infographics, you have three main options:

- Create it yourself.
- Hire a designer.
- Hire an infographics firm.

As with many things in life, you get what you pay for — the lower-cost options typically don't generate the same quality as the more expensive ones.

The lowest-cost option is to do it yourself. Hiring a designer should be relatively cost effective, but you still have to create the idea and the story yourself. Finally, if you hire an infographics firm, you're hiring experienced professionals who can handle your infographic from start to finish.

When determining which method you want to use to create an infographic, start by evaluating how much time, money, and effort you're willing to invest in the infographic.

Creating it yourself

The do-it-yourself (DIY) approach to creating an infographic is a low-cost way to get started. All infographics created by Boot Camp Digital are created this way, without hiring a designer. (I created many of them myself.) The design portion of the infographic usually takes between two and six hours, depending on the complexity of the infographic and the number of changes we make while designing.

This approach takes the longest length of time, but costs the least amount of money. Depending on your skill level, doing it yourself can create a fairly high-quality infographic that meets your marketing objectives. The downside is that you're using an infographic tool, so you'll have less flexibility in the final design, including the look and feel of the infographic.

The key to this approach is to use an infographic building tool so that you don't have to try to learn to use a design tool such as Photoshop or Illustrator. Even if you're comfortable with design tools, using an infographic creator gives you a template to start with, which can save a lot of time.

The Piktochart (www.Piktochart.com) infographic building tool lets you easily create your own infographic with no design knowledge or software experience. You can test Piktochart for free (with limited themes) or upgrade to a paid account, which now costs $29 per month or $14 per month with an annual plan.

What makes Piktochart easy to use is that you start with a theme you can customize. When choosing a theme, be sure to select one that matches the way your data is organized. After you select a theme, it's time to start designing. As you can see in Figure 13-5, Piktochart uses simple drag-and-drop technology for you to create the infographic. You can choose elements from the left side of the screen such as text, illustrations, designs, and images and then drop them into the infographic, where you can customize them.

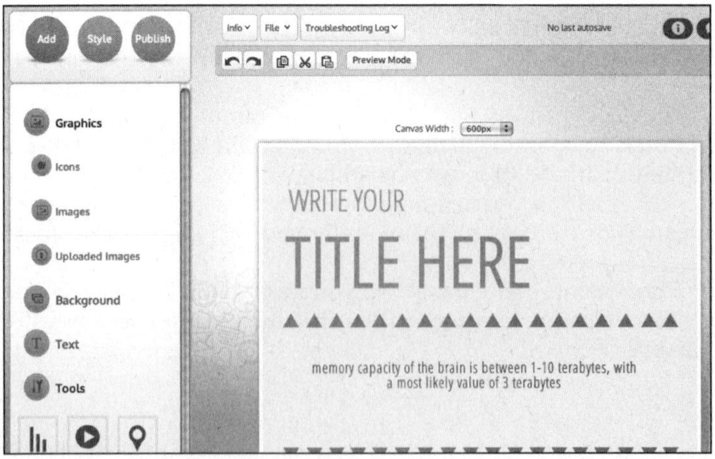

Figure 13-5: Piktochart drag-and-drop infographic creation.

Using an infographic design tool such as Piktochart makes it easy for you to get started, but you need to invest time in learning to use the software. Also, if you create your own infographic and you aren't a designer, ask for feedback from friends or coworkers before you publish.

Hiring a designer

Another option for creating an infographic is to hire a designer to design it. Though the task can be difficult, try to find a designer or design firm that's experienced with infographics. Hiring a designer is the medium-cost way to get started — it's usually less expensive than hiring an infographics company.

The cost of hiring a designer for your infographic depends on a number of factors:

- The experience level and hourly rate of the designer
- The complexity of the infographic
- The number of revisions included in the project

Hiring a designer to create an infographic may cost as little as $500 to as much as $3,000. (This is only an estimated range.) The turnaround time for an infographic created by a designer will likely vary depending on the designer, but should take one to three weeks, including revisions.

When hiring a designer, find one that's experienced in creating infographics. Also, be sure to clearly communicate your timeline upfront, and make sure that you account for revisions or changes in the scope of the project.

Though the next section of this chapter covers the steps to creating infographics, note that design is only one step — you still have some work to do in finding the idea, researching data, and outlining the story.

Hiring an infographics company

Some companies specialize in creating infographics. They're experts at the entire process of infographics, from brainstorming the initial idea o promotion of the completed product.

You gain certain benefits when you hire an infographics company:

- **Experience:** You work with people who specialize in infographics (and who probably have a track record of success). They know the types of infographics that are likely to achieve results and automatically incorporate best practices.
- **Coverage from start to finish:** A company that specializes in infographics can handle everything from the brainstorming stage to the execution.

✔ **Minimum time investment:** Hiring an infographics company takes the least amount of time because it can handle every aspect of your infographic.

✔ **Optimum timeframe:** The timeframe when working with an infographics company is typically two to four weeks; however, it includes the entire process, not just the design.

The downside of hiring an infographics company is the cost. Hiring an infographics company typically costs between $5,000 and $10,000 per infographic.

When deciding which option is best for you, consider the potential benefit and exposure you expect to gain from the infographic. For example, a small company with limited reach may expect only 100 people to see its infographic. In this case, it may not make sense to spend thousands of dollars. A larger organization with hundreds of thousands of social media connections will likely generate tens of thousands of views, so investing in the infographic may be more worthwhile.

Creating an Infographic

Creating an infographic is a process — it isn't as simple as designing a pretty chart that's derived from statistics. A solid infographic must be built on an interesting idea that meets your marketing or business objectives. It must contain interesting information that tells a story in a logical way. It should be brought to life in a visually entertaining way that's easy for readers to consume. Finally, it must be promoted, or else no one will ever see it.

In this section, I show you the steps to creating an infographic that gets results. To bring this section to life, I use the example of the first infographic that Boot Camp Digital created, *Cincinnati is Social,* as shown in Figure 13-6.

Figure 13-6: Cincinnati is Social.

Brainstorming and defining the topic

The first step in creating an infographic is deciding what the infographic intends to convey. The creative concept is the foundation of the infographic, and it can make or break its success.

The topic of the infographic should be original and interesting. Regurgitating industry data that's broadly known won't cut it. You need a new angle, an interesting take, some fresh data, or a noteworthy concept to "break through the noise."

The brainstorming process should include these key components:

✔ **Marketing objectives:** Start with your marketing objectives clearly outlined upfront so that you can determine whether your infographic meets these goals. Also decide upfront how the infographic will be used: For example, Is it for marketing purposes, or will it be used for a specific communications purpose?

✔ **Brainstorm topics:** Brainstorm ideas or topics about interesting subject areas that relate to your business and marketing objectives. Get creative. In this stage, there are no bad ideas. Evaluate everything, no matter how strange. (Stranger topics are often more interesting.) If you're having trouble, link your infographic to popular culture or a seasonal element. Or imagine an outrageous or interesting claim that you can make. Spent time on this stage and invite people from inside and outside your organization into the process (if possible). During the brainstorming phase, do research and look online for inspiration. Also, looking at popular content in your industry and other industries can provide insights into the kind of content that people are interested in. Pay attention to the kind of content that's trending on YouTube, Reddit, Pinterest, humor sites, and other social media sites.

✔ **Evaluate the ideas:** When you have come up with some ideas, evaluate them and choose the best one. Evaluate ideas based on the marketing objectives that you set upfront. Also, assess how likely people are to share or write about your infographic based on how interesting, entertaining, and unique it is. Be sure that your idea matches the identity and feel of your brand or business. Determine whether sufficient data is available to support the idea you have for the infographic.

When my company created *Cincinnati is Social,* we started with our business objectives. We wanted to raise awareness within our local market (Cincinnati) and reach social media marketers who could recommend our training to their clients. After we brainstormed the topics, we had a long list of ideas ranging from boring to outrageous. We had links to random days (Talk-Like-a-Pirate Day) and pop culture trends.

One primary goal was to drive social sharing — when we evaluated the ideas, it seemed that people in Cincinnati would be motivated to share an infographic about how Cincinnati's sociability. We didn't pick the most interesting or outrageous topic, but we chose the one that we thought would best meet our marketing objectives.

The topic for the infographic should also match, and deliver on, your marketing objectives.

Researching and finding data points

After the idea for an infographic is clear, the next step is to research and find the data and information that will be a part of the infographic. Depending on the topic, the process may be relatively easy or involve a lot of work.

Start by looking for studies or research in your field. Don't be afraid to ask around. Even seasoned researchers can't find everything — ask your contacts whether they know of any data or studies that can support your idea.

You may also choose to conduct your own research. More and more organizations are taking their own surveys and doing their own research to support the necessary data for infographics.

For the *Cincinnati is Social* infographic, we had a difficult time finding data. We found one study about how businesses in Cincinnati are using social media, but we didn't have enough data to create a story. We then got creative about the definition of data. Rather than include only statistics from a study, we included items such as a quote from an executive at Procter & Gamble (a Fortune 500 company that's headquartered in Cincinnati). We also included headlines from newspapers and blogs.

When we were truly stuck, we found ways to create data. For example, to demonstrate that people in Cincinnati are active on social media, we simply quoted the number of Facebook, LinkedIn, and Twitter accounts that listed Cincinnati as their location.

Finding data might be difficult — be prepared to get creative about your data, and don't be afraid to include nontraditional sources. Think "outside the box" to find data that can be reinterpreted.

Building the story

After you know the general premise of the infographic and you've done your research, the next step is to build the data into a story. Your infographic should have a logical flow to it that leads to a natural conclusion.

Start by looking at all the data you've collected, and determine how it can be grouped. An infographic doesn't simply place data on the page — it is about sharing information with visual content.

Building the story combines the idea for the infographic with data to tell the story. If you don't already have the data to support the story you want to tell, you may need to loop back and conduct additional research.

When my company created *Cincinnati is Social,* we had a bunch of statistics and no clear story. We started grouping the statistics into business, professional, and personal categories, to help us create the story we wanted to tell:

- ✔ Show how Cincinnati is a highly social city
- ✔ Indicate how Cincinnati brands are digital
- ✔ Close by specifying how Cincinnati stays ahead of the curve. The closing section also linked to what we do by talking about social media training.

Before you start the design stage (as described in the following section, outline a clear story with data and key points, and specify how they contribute to telling a story. A strong story should relate to the original concept and link back to your business and marketing objectives.

Designing the infographic

After you define the story and gather the data and information to support the story, the next step is to design the infographic. In the previous section, I cover the options for creating an infographic — doing it yourself, hiring a designer, or hiring an infographic company.

Regardless of your choice, following a number of best practices for infographic design can make your infographics truly stand out. Incorporate these design principles into your infographic:

- ✔ **Place graphs and charts liberally.** Graphs and charts make data stand out and help to tell the story visually. When comparing data points, capitalize on graphs and charts to highlight the most relevant data in your story.

✔ **Avoid overbranding.** Some businesses want to create infographics that are branded with their company design themes and logos. Most of the best infographics aren't visually branded to match a company design or logo, however. Resist the urge to make the infographic look like an ad, and use a color scheme and visual content that will interest the reader.

✔ **The visual content should enhance your story.** Avoid simply adding random images or visual elements to your infographic. The visual content you use should support your story and its data and help make your point.

✔ **Organize the data with the layout.** The general layout of the infographic should reflect the logical flow of the story you're telling. For example, if your infographic is a comparison, you may lay it out as a side-by-side comparison. Alternatively, if your story is about steps or a journey, lay it out as a document that flows continuously.

✔ **Make the key points stand out.** The most important data or points should truly stand out with the visual design of the infographic. Make the most shocking or informative points stand out.

✔ **Limit the amount of text you use.** Text-heavy infographics are difficult to read, especially when they're shared on social networks in smaller image sizes. Try to reduce the amount of text you're using, and don't worry about creating sentences; bullet points and short descriptions are fine.

✔ **Include sources at the bottom.** People often ask about the sources of the data from an infographic. Either add the individual sources for data points to the bottom of the infographic, or include them on a page on your website and add a link to the Resources page at the bottom. To follow the best practice, cite your sources.

Most infographics cite the sources of any statistics or data that they use. Failure to do this may leave your viewers with questions about the legitimacy of your data.

✔ **Include your business name and logo at the bottom.** Most infographics include the business name, logo, and URL at the bottom, where you can let people know that you made the infographic and can drive business value back to your brand.

The visual design stage is where you visually bring data to life. The objective is to create a visual that is interesting and that uses illustrations and charts to support your points.

Promoting your infographic

Creating a useful infographic is only the first step in promoting it. If you don't promote it, chances are good that no one will ever see it. Even the best infographics usually have a promotion planned, to spread the word initially.

This list describes some of the best ways to promote your infographic:

- ✔ **Write a blog post about it.** Most infographics start with a blog post, so the infographic is posted on the blog on the company website. This is then the central place that all the promotional efforts tie back to. You don't want to share a downloadable version of the infographic — you want the infographic to drive traffic back to your website.

- ✔ **Promote it on your social networks.** Start by using your social networks to promote your infographic. Share it on Facebook, Twitter, LinkedIn, Pinterest, and other sites. Infographics also tend to have longer lives on social networks, which means that you can continue to share and promote them beyond the initial launch. Some of my company's infographics are more than a year old and are still generating new tweets, shares, and pins.

- ✔ **Include it in your e-mail.** If you regularly send out an e-mail newsletter, add a link to the blog post in your infographic. Online readers love infographics, and you might be surprised to find that promoting an infographic via e-mail can generate more clicks than other content does. When sharing your infographic by e-mail, don't add it as an attachment — just include a link to the blog post or web page where people can view it. From the blog post, they can easily share the infographic on social networks.

- ✔ **Write a press release.** If your infographic is particularly interesting or engaging, a press release can draw additional attention to it. Announce the infographic and include a link to the blog post as well as some of the most interesting and relevant data points.

- ✔ **Reach out to bloggers or journalists.** Having other people share your infographic can generate more views, awareness, and links to your website. Look for blogs or online news sites in your industry that might be interested in sharing your infographic. At Boot Camp Digital, we have a list of bloggers who cover social media and often share infographics. We e-mail them every time we have a new infographic, and many of them promote the infographic on their sites.

- ✔ **Promote it on your website.** Depending on your website's design, you can promote the infographic directly on your home page or on other heavily trafficked pages of your website, to drive your existing website visitors to your infographic and inspire them to view and share it.

- ✔ **Promote it with ads.** Some of the most effective social media campaigns include advertising as an element. Depending on your marketing budget and target audience, you might run Google ads, online display ads, Facebook ads, Twitter ads, or LinkedIn ads to promote your infographic. If you have a useful infographic, spending a small amount of money to initially spread the word can pay off with more views, shares, and traffic.

You should have a promotion plan for your infographic before it's even complete. Creating an infographic is a fairly sizable investment in social content, so be sure that you have a promotion plan that will maximize the exposure you can generate.

After you have the promotion plan in place, be ready to get started on the launch date of your infographic to attract as much interest as possible right out of the gate.

You can periodically promote the infographic, even after the initial launch. Most infographics don't go stale or seem out of date until years after their initial publication. Every few months, go back and reignite interest for the infographic by repromoting it.

Part V

Launching into Video Social Media Marketing

Find out why businesses are using Vine at www.dummies.com/
extras/visualsocialmarketing.

In this part . . .

- ✔ Incorporating videos into your marketing strategy
- ✔ Using YouTube to grow your business
- ✔ Creating and sharing videos on Vine

Chapter 14

The Big Picture: Marketing with Videos

In This Chapter

▶ Making video marketing part of your marketing strategy

▶ Crafting a video marketing plan that gets results

▶ Optimizing your videos to maximize their impact

▶ Incorporating best practices into your video marketing strategy

▶ Knowing the reality of viral videos, driving views, and promoting your videos

*V*ideo is an important part of your visual social marketing strategy. Videos can communicate a business, a product, an idea or a value proposition quickly and effectively. If a picture is truly worth a thousand words, a video is worth 100,000 words. Using motion, images, and sound can communicate information, feelings, and emotions. According to Dr. James McQuivey of Forrester Research, a single minute of online video is the equivalent of 1.8 million written words.

Video marketing isn't just about being seen on YouTube, in case that's what you think. Though YouTube is the most popular video network (Chapter 15 is dedicated to YouTube), it isn't the only opportunity to harness the power of video for your business. In addition to YouTube videos, videos should be a part of your social network marketing strategies. *Microvideo* sites, which are sites where users share short videos with their followers, such as Instagram and Vine are emerging as new, short-format, video communications tools. (Instagram is covered in Chapter 11; Vine is covered in Chapter 16.)

Video is also a powerful tool for websites, according to Marketing Profs, users spend 88 percent more time at websites that include videos. More and more home pages are adding video as a quick way to engage users.

Video can also increase interest in a product, with 46 percent of people saying they would be more likely to seek out information about a product or service after seeing it in a video online according to a study by BrainShark. Video doesn't simply make for appealing social content — it can also drive sales to your business.

Understanding the Importance of Video

Video is an important marketing communications tool. Regardless of whether your business is targeting consumers or other businesses, sharing your story via video can communicate a lot of information and help drive visitors to your website to take action.

In addition to the communication benefits, video can be a powerful tool to increase your business's online *footprint,* which is the content that people can find about your brand. Videos from video sharing sites, in particular, often show up in search engine results, so adding them to your visual social marketing content helps people see them when searching for your business.

For example, when I search for the phrase *how to change a faucet,* the top results in the search engine are videos created by businesses and hosted on YouTube, as shown in Figure 14-1.

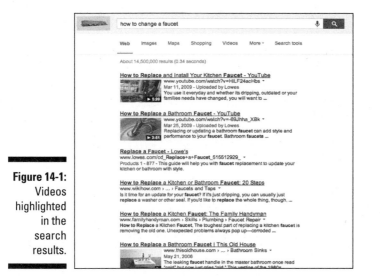

Figure 14-1:
Videos highlighted in the search results.

Enhancing your website with videos

Creating videos for your website is an important part of your online marketing strategy. Most digital marketing efforts center around sending traffic to your website and generating new customers over time.

Video has been shown to be a powerful tool to engage website visitors and generate new customers for your business. Video is especially powerful for businesses with complex products or services, or on websites where customers may want to see videos in action.

Consider adding a video to these areas on your website:

✔ **Home page:** The home page is often the first point of entry that people have with your business. Highlighting videos on the home page is becoming more and more popular across many types of businesses — even businesses with products or services that aren't highly visual. According to a study by FindLaw study of websites of lawyers and attorneys found that consumers are more likely to choose attorney if they feature videos on their websites. Consumers typically visit 4.8 websites before choosing a lawyer; however, when video is added to a website, the number drops to 1.8, showing that (depending on the product or service) adding video to the home page can increase sales and the amount of time people spend on the site.

✔ **Pages featuring products and services:** Videos are increasingly showing up on product pages to show visitors how the product looks. I recently shopped online for custom-printed mugs at `www.discountmugs.com`. Though the site showed pictures of the product, I found it difficult to imagine the size of the glass and how it would look. Toward the bottom of the page was a video of the product, as shown in Figure 14-2. Viewing the video made it easier for me to visualize how the product would look. (And I did purchase from the site.)

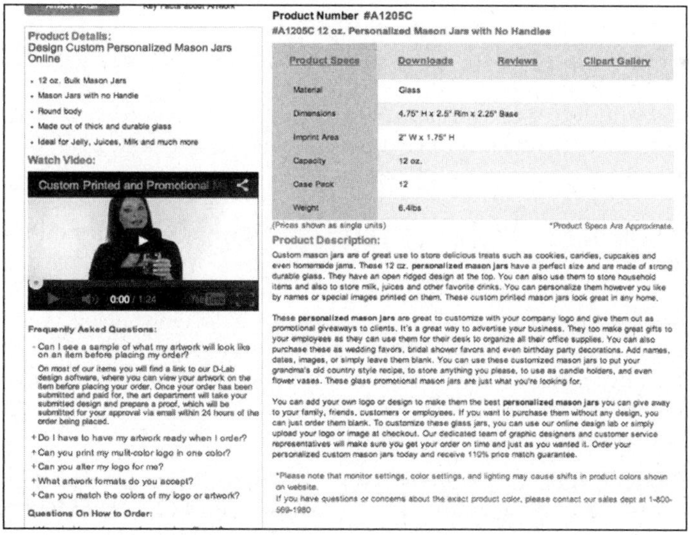

Figure 14-2: Discount Mugs uses videos on its product pages.

✔ **Testimonials:** Videos can become powerful and believable testimonials. Request video testimonials to bring your testimonials to life and increase their believability.

✔ **Blog posts:** Videos are also sometimes shared in blog posts. For example, rather than type your thoughts on a specific topic, you can create a short video about them.

When sharing video on your website, you have to decide how to display it there: You can upload the video to a video sharing site such as YouTube or Vimeo or use a customized player to play the video on your site.

A customized video player allows you to customize the look and feel of the viewer and the viewing experience. You can customize its frame, buttons, and controls. Additionally, some video players let you create clickable sections where you can direct users to other areas on your site from inside the video.

A video from a video sharing site is shown in a standard video player that doesn't have a lot of customization options. Regardless, these video players usually have standard controls that customers are accustomed to, making them easier to navigate. Video sharing sites also usually have social sharing built in so that users can easily share on Facebook, Twitter, Pinterest, and other social networks.

When choosing between using your own video player and embedding a video from a video sharing site, no single best option exists. The best choice depends on how the video is being used and on your objectives. Weigh the pros and cons of each option relative to your objectives for the video, and choose the option that makes the most sense for you.

Building your brand on video sharing sites

Video sharing sites are powerful ways to grow awareness for your product and generate new customers. Video sharing websites such as YouTube and Vimeo let you share your video online.

You should post your videos on video sharing sites for a number of reasons, as described in this list:

✔ **You can generate more views via search.** Video sharing sites can generate more views of your video because consumers search video sharing sites for interesting or useful videos. YouTube (see Chapter 15) is the second-largest search engine online. (Google is the largest.) Posting on a video sharing site draws more visibility for your content.

✔ **Sharing sites may suggest your videos as related content.** After you finish watching a video, many video sharing sites show links to related videos. If you share your videos on video sharing sites, you can increase their number of views by periodically being recommended in the Related Videos list. Being recommended as a related video is based on the words used in the title and description of your video when you upload videos to video sharing sites such as YouTube (a topic I cover in more detail in Chapter 15).

✔ **They have user-friendly controls.** Most people are used to watching videos on sites such as YouTube, and they know where to find the controls on the video players. When you share your videos on YouTube, your customers can easily control the videos.

✔ **You can share on social networks.** Video sharing sites have social media sharing built-in, making it easy for customers to quickly share your videos with their friends and generating more views of your videos.

✔ **You benefit from social network integration.** Video sharing sites are also often integrated directly into social networks. For example, when a video from YouTube is shared on Twitter, the video can be played directly inside the tweet, making it easier for people on social networks to view your videos. Pinterest, for example, doesn't allow users to upload videos, and it allows pinning only from YouTube and Vimeo.

Based on these benefits, it's no wonder that many businesses use video sharing sites for their videos. If your goal is to generate views of your videos, posting on a video sharing site increases your views because these sites already have an audience built-in.

Businesses use YouTube to share their videos because it has the largest viewership and can generate the most views. Vimeo is popular because its video players can be customized and because users can upgrade to professional accounts to share larger video files. For this reason, the site is heavily used by designers and creative professionals.

Sharing videos on other social networks

Videos are also popular content on other social networks. Videos are often shared on Facebook, Twitter, LinkedIn, and Pinterest. Even business-to-business marketers are harnessing video as a part of their social media content strategies, with video ranking the seventh most popular type of content that's created to share on social networks, according to a study by the Content Marketing Institute and Marketing Profs. Other popular content (ranked in order) is social media, articles on your website, e-newsletters, blogs, in-person events, and case studies.

When it comes to sharing videos on social networks, only Facebook allows users to upload their videos directly to the site. A video can be uploaded directly to Facebook in the same way as a photo.

All social networks, including Facebook, allow users to share videos from video sharing sites.

Video should be a part of your content marketing strategy for the social networks you participate on, so add video to your blog posts, Facebook status updates, Pinterest pins, Twitter posts, LinkedIn updates, Google+ posts, and more. Across most of these sites, videos have been shown to generate more engagements and interest.

Harnessing user-generated videos

In addition to creating your own videos, assess the power of leveraging user-generated videos. This type of video talks about your business or product and is created by your customers or someone from the general public.

One of the most famous uses of user-generated video is Frito-Lay's decision to let its customers create Super Bowl commercials about Doritos. Its Crash the Super Bowl contest invites fans to create their own Doritos commercials and submit them via Facebook or other social networks. The winning commercial is displayed during the Super Bowl, and the winner also receives a cash prize.

The contest started in 2006, and more than 1,000 videos were submitted that year. In 2013, more than 3,500 commercials were submitted.

You don't have to be a big-name brand, such as Doritos, to ask your customers to create and share videos about your product. Typically, the best way to encourage user-generated videos is to run a contest with a prize. Often, these contests involve voting to "amp up" the social reach and excitement as finalists ask their friends and family to vote for them.

If video is important to your strategy and you have a highly visual product or service, run a video contest or encourage customers to create and share videos about your business. These days, most people can record video directly from their smartphones and post them to YouTube in only a few minutes, making it easy to capture and share videos.

Building a Video Plan

When it comes to crafting your video marketing strategy, think through the purpose and execution of your video. Having an idea for your video is only a small part of the process. To build a video plan, follow these steps:

1. **Determine the purpose of your video.**

   The first step is to clearly define why you're creating the video. The purpose of your video dictates every aspect of how you approach creating the video. Many businesses start with the statement, "I think we need a video," though they aren't sure why. Start with defining why, and clearly define what you want your video to do for you.

2. **Craft the concept of the video.**

   The concept is the "big idea" on which your video is based. The concept is a description, a few paragraphs long, of what the video is generally about. The concept should also include the general look and feel that the video should portray. As you build the concept, be sure to ask, "Why would someone want to watch this video?" If your video is an advertisement for your business, whom do you think would want to watch it? Evaluate the audience, and ask yourself, "What's in it for them?"

3. **Script the video.**

   After you have the concept, the next step is to script the video. The *script* consists of the words that will be used in the video. Depending on the type of video you're creating, you may not write a specific script — for example if you're generating testimonials or interviewing employees. Regardless, you should still have an idea of what you want them to talk about.

4. **Determine the format of the video.**

   Videos can be live action (shot with a camera, for example) or animated. Choose the video format that best brings your video concept to life. More and more home page videos are animated videos that explain the concept of the business.

5. **Develop a storyboard for the video.**

   The storyboard portion of the video brings the script to life by adding visual cues. A typical storyboard has the words matched up to the images or visual elements that will be used to describe them. You can complete this step in a Microsoft Word document, with presentation software, by using a storyboarding software program or even with pen and paper.

   Storyboard software can help you draft a script and match it up with visual elements to plan your video. Check out Atomic Learning StoryBoard Pro (www.atomiclearning.com/storyboardpro), Storyboard That (www.storyboardthat.com/), or PowerProduction Software (www.powerproduction.com/index.php).

6. **Shoot the video.**

   In this step, the footage is shot or the animations are created. You should have a clear idea, based on your storyboard, of the shots that are needed to execute your video strategy. Shoot the footage needed for your final video, and then shoot some extra footage (in case the video script is modified in the editing stage).

7. **Edit the video.**

   Cut the videos you recorded to the sections that you want to include in the final video, and combine them. In the editing stage, you use the video elements you recorded in addition to elements from video editing software to create the video. (Chapter 5 has tips, tricks, and tools for video editing.)

8. **Finalize the video.**

   Make sure that the video matches your marketing objectives and represents your business well. When you're satisfied with the result, export the video so that it can be uploaded to a video sharing site or to your website. Depending on how you plan to use your video, different video export formats may be needed. Check the video site that you want to use for accepted formats, and be sure to export your video into a format that's compatible with your video sharing site. The export options depend on the video editing software you use.

9. **Post and promote the video.**

   Post the video on your website or a video sharing site, and promote it. Many businesses post their videos on YouTube and simply hope that it generates views. Attracting viewers to your videos takes effort, and a promotion strategy is vital. (The last section of this chapter provides more detail about how to promote your video.)

Creating videos

When it's time to create the video (either by yourself or by hiring someone), assess the type of video that's needed, based on how you anticipate that the video will be used. Evaluate these factors when you're deciding on an option:

- ✔ **Quality level:** Assess the quality level you need for your video. The higher the quality level you want, the more you should consider investing in professional video creation.

- ✔ **Perception of your business:** If you work for a large, respected, multinational company, you may need to invest more in your videos than does a small business. Consumers expect different quality levels from different types of organizations. The larger and more serious and professional your businesses, the more you should plan to invest in your video.

- ✔ **Number of views:** Estimate the number of people that you expect to see your video. For example, a video on your home page may generate more views than a video on a blog post. For this reason, you may choose to invest in more professional-looking video for your home page in place of blog posts, based on the number of views that each video is likely to receive.

- ✔ **Importance of the video:** Important videos should have a higher production quality. For example, a $5,000 product should have a better video than one selling a $10 product. A video aimed at attracting investors (which is important) may warrant more investment than a video that explains how to navigate your website.

✔ **Where the video will be used:** The quality level of your video may also depend on where the video will be used. For example, a blog post with a video can be created quickly and use a do-it-yourself approach. A home page video that creates the first impression of your business may be professionally created.

Use the five criteria in this list to determine whether you need to hire a professional for your video or you can do it yourself (DIY). When hiring professionals, the cost of your video can vary dramatically, depending on the amount of production required. No single answer exists to the quality level you need for your videos. Assess these factors and determine what quality level best represents your brand and budget.

Many videos that are successful aren't overproduced. Consumers on social channels are showing an appetite for content that looks more realistic than professional. Again, assess your marketing objectives when choosing your approach.

If you choose to do it yourself, consider a few factors in how you approach your video:

✔ **Sound:** Videos can be distracting if they have poor audio quality with lots of background noise. If you're creating your own videos, invest in an external microphone that can capture higher-quality audio than the built-in microphones supplied with most cameras. The main benefit of an external microphone is that the microphone can be placed closer to the source of the audio, which eliminates background noise. You can purchase an entry-level microphone for as little as $20 on sites such as Amazon.com.

✔ **Video quality:** If the objective of your video is to share it online, you don't need a high-quality video. Most videos are compressed to view online, and even videos recorded from smartphones have a quality level high enough for online viewing.

✔ **Shot composition:** Determine what items you specifically want in each shot and the angles and framing of each shot. Look at other videos for inspiration. For example, testimonials and interviews are often filmed as straight-on shots in front of a white wall, which doesn't make for an interesting video. Evaluate the angle, frame, and background of your video, and aim for interesting but not distracting.

✔ **Video format:** Before recording, be sure that you're recording in a format that's compatible with the video sharing site you're using. For example, if you plan to share your video on YouTube, check the video formats that the site accepts, and be sure to record in those formats.

✔ **Lighting:** Shadows and poor lighting can make your video distracting to watch. When creating your video, pay attention to your lighting, and avoid shadows or distracting bright lights. If necessary, you can invest in a basic lighting kit for about $150.

Following video best practices

Based on the videos that are frequently shared on social networks and frequently viewed on video sharing sites, a number of best practices can increase the success rate of your video. These are only guidelines, however. Based on your unique objectives, you may violate these best practices, and a number of videos have been wildly successful despite not following them.

Use this list as a guide for your video strategy:

✔ **Length:** Start with short, 1- to 3-minute videos. After you've mastered video marketing and you have an audience, you can consider increasing their length. Most YouTube videos that generate a lot of views fall into this range. Experiment with deleting slower parts of your video or any dialogue that doesn't support your main communications objective.

✔ **Post regularly:** Creating one video for your website is a useful way to start. If you want to grow an active audience for your videos on social networks or video sharing sites, create a regular posting schedule. If you create a video that people love, they'll want more.

✔ **Talk naturally, and avoid overscripting:** Some videos sound like the person talking is reading a script. Though having a plan in mind is important, script reading takes away from the authenticity and genuine appeal that can make a video powerful. Unless you have hired actors for your video, ditch the script and try to capture the passion.

✔ **Apply branding intelligently into your video:** Your video should have some branding that links back to your business, but don't overbrand and distract from your video. Evaluate the best way to add branding to your videos without distracting from the content or storyline.

✔ **Include a call-to-action:** If appropriate, include on your video a call to action that directs people where to find more information and resources. If you have a video that talks about your product, make a special offer at the end and include a link to your website. Don't hesitate to drive people to act from your videos.

✔ **Specific topics work better:** The more specific the topic, the more likely it is to generate views. For example, a video labeled "Video Marketing" is vague and fails to give you a good idea of what specifically you'll learn. Instead, a video titled "Ten Ways to Maximize Views on YouTube" is more specific and can generate more views. Don't make your videos to fit into too much of a niche, but choose topics that communicate clear value to the viewer.

✔ **Optimize the video's title and description for searchers:** YouTube is the number-two search engine by volume of searches, and videos are often displayed in regular Google search engine results. If you optimize your videos, therefore, they'll be found by searchers. When uploading your video online, whether it's to your website or to a video sharing site, choose a title that represents the content of the video while also using words or phrases that people might search for. Also, add a description that clearly shares what the video is about. Search engines such as Google don't understand what your video is about unless you tell them in the description, so make your description count.

Finding video inspiration

You may be starting without a clear idea of what subject areas your videos should cover. You can find inspiration for video topics in a few ways. In Chapter 18, I tell you the ten types of videos to include in your video strategy. Even when you know the type of video you're creating, determining the concept of format can be challenging.

The following two sections describe some ways to find inspiration for your video marketing strategy.

Start with search

Start by searching for videos on similar topics to the topics you have in mind. Check out the videos and note the video topics and types of videos that generate a lot of views and engagements.

When deciding what to search for, choose a variety of different terms, phrases, and how-to type content. Look for content that's related to what you do, and evaluate your competitors' postings to see how many views they're generating.

Search in a few different places:

✔ **YouTube:** Start with a YouTube search to specifically find videos that have been uploaded to the site. (It *is* the number-one video sharing site, after all.)

✔ **Vimeo:** Do a search on Vimeo, which tends to contain more professional and creative content

✔ **Google video search:** To search for videos via Google, go to www.google.com and enter your search term. The Google search engine results page opens. At the top of the page, you see different ways to further refine your search, such as Web or Images. Click on the More button to open the drop-down menu. Choose Videos, and you see video search results, as shown in Figure 14-3. Video search results in Google include videos shared on websites that aren't on YouTube.

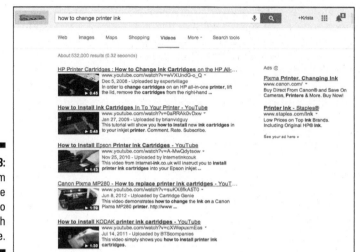

Look at YouTube suggested search

Another option for finding video inspiration is to look at YouTube suggested search results. When you start typing a search term into the YouTube search box, YouTube begins to display, beneath the input box, suggestions for what you may be searching for. These suggestions are based on terms that other people on YouTube searched for. A sample of YouTube suggested search terms is shown in Figure 14-4.

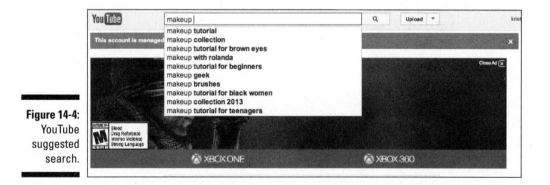

The YouTube suggested search feature gives you an idea about the content that people are searching for on YouTube, which can be a helpful way to narrow down a content idea while still choosing a popular topic.

For example, I may want to create a video about social media training, but I'm looking to be a little more specific. The YouTube suggested search shows me that people also search for *social media training for employees* and *social media training video*. I can explore the videos under these categories and also generate ideas for new videos from the suggested search.

Getting Realistic about Your Video Marketing Strategy

Many businesses follow this approach to video marketing: If you build it, they will come. Though they believe that by creating a video and posting it on YouTube, they'll automatically generate views, that simply isn't the reality. Video marketing is more challenging now than ever before, simply because of the number of videos that are created every single day.

One hundred hours of video are uploaded to YouTube every single minute.

With video creation becoming easier and easier, more and more people and businesses are creating and uploading videos to the Internet. If you want to generate views of your videos, you therefore need appealing videos (mediocre video doesn't cut it), and you have to plan to promote your video to generate awareness and views.

Recognizing the reality of viral videos

A *viral* video is one that becomes popular by being shared on the Internet. Viral videos are usually shared via websites, social media, and e-mail. Most viral videos are humorous and are shared, and reshared, repeatedly online.

One example of a viral video is the "Gangnam Style" music video, by Psy, which has generated more than 1.8 billion views. The video that now holds the record for the most viral video in history is "Kony 2012," by Invisible Children. (You can find it on YouTube by searching for the phrase *Kony 2012*). This video generated more than 24 million views on the first day it was uploaded.

Businesses have also created viral videos. For example, one of the first viral videos was "Will It Blend?," by Blendtec. (You can view all Blendtec videos at www.willitblend.com.) The Will It Blend videos show Blendtec using its extremely powerful blenders to blend objects such as an iPad and a Justin Bieber doll. The first video, which was recorded for less than $100, generated millions of views. As a result of its videos, Blendtec has increased sales and even launched a consumer line of its products.

Creating a video that will go viral is challenging because lots of funny and interesting videos are online. Competing with talking cats, dancing comedians, and popular culture is challenging for many businesses. Your video has to be truly noteworthy and interesting. I meet with businesses all the time that have a viral video concept, and usually they are, at best, mildly entertaining.

The concept behind a viral video must be highly entertaining, and its execution must also be strong. An advertisement for your business, or your product being used in an unusual way, isn't usually a strong concept for a viral video. Viral videos usually appeal to the humor or emotions of the viewer, and they must "nail it."

Even if you create an amazing video, it's difficult to predict whether it will go viral. Most viral video successes include big budgets to create and promote the videos. (Promotion is covered in the later section "Promoting your videos.") For example, one of the most popular early viral videos was "The Evolution of Dance," by Judson Laipply, which generated millions of views in only a few months. The interesting thing about the video is that it was recorded as part of Laipply's longstanding stand-up comedy routine, and he had no idea that it would become so popular online.

Another example is the Old Spice Guy video campaign from 2010. Old Spice launched an online video series centered around its commercials with a "manly man" talking about Old Spice. The award-winning campaign generated significant "buzz" and reignited an interest in creating viral videos. This same concept had been tried many times over the history of Old Spice advertising, and none of the other concepts had hit the mark. It took years of trial and error (and a significant investment) to hit viral video success.

If you've created a video that you believe can go viral, send it to 100 people in your target audience to see how many of them forward it or post it to social media. If people don't share it, it can't go viral.

The bar has been set high for the quality of videos that go viral. To view some recent viral videos, search YouTube for these:

- ✓ **"Kony 2012:"** The Kony 2012 video is referenced earlier in this section.
- ✓ **"The Man Your Man Could Smell Like:"** The original Old Spice commercial generated more than 50 million views.
- ✓ **"Dove Evolution of Beauty:"** The commercial generated millions of views for the Dove brand by repositioning beauty.
- ✓ **The Evolution of Dance:"** This stand-up bit became one of the earliest viral videos.
- ✓ **"eHarmony Bio:"** An actress pretends to create a bio video for her eHarmony account about her love of cats.

Promoting your videos

After you've created an amazing video, the next step is promoting it. Even many viral video success stories included deliberate promotion and, sometimes, even an advertising budget to get them off the ground.

The Old Spice video that I mention in the preceding section, for example, launched by harnessing the existing social media audiences that the brand had already built. When the video was posted online, Old Spice already had thousands of fans to share the video with. It also ran paid advertisements to seed the video and generate initial views and interest. Finally, Old Spice built in a plan to get even more people talking: It created a response campaign in which it recorded videos of the Old Spice Guy responding to celebrities and other people on the Internet. Knowing that the Old Spice Guy might personally respond to a tweet spurred many people to tweet.

You must have a plan to promote your video, even if the video is *amazing*. You can use these three types of media to promote your videos:

- ✔ **Paid:** You pay to run ads to drive initial views of your videos. YouTube has an advertising platform where you can pay to have your video displayed as a featured or suggested video. YouTube ads tend to be more cost-effective ways to generate views, because you can sometimes pay only pennies per click. You can also run ads on social networks, search engines, or other media networks to drive people to view your YouTube video.

- ✔ **Owned:** You use assets that you own to spread the word, including your e-mail list, your website, your social media accounts, and signage at your place of business. Owned media generates views from marketing channels that you have already established, or *own*. Your owned media channels typically reach existing customers or fans, which is a receptive audience to share and spread your video.

- ✔ **Earned:** You generate attention and mentions because your video is engaging. Earned media may consist of a newspaper or blog in which you write an article about your video. People share your video because they loved seeing it. It's earned media because you earn the attention (and mentions) with your outstanding content. Don't rely only on earned media, however: Build a plan to reach out to people with large social media followings or influencers, and remember to ask people to share your content.

If you don't promote your videos, few people are likely to see them. Whether your plan is to go viral or to simply maximize the exposure you generate from your videos, be sure to have a promotion plan.

Chapter 15

Video Marketing on YouTube

*Y*ouTube is the largest video sharing website on the Internet, with the highest number of videos uploaded and views of videos. Most businesses that share videos post them on YouTube if their goal is to generate views of the video, because YouTube has a large and active user base.

More than a billion people across the world visit YouTube every month, and they watch more than 6 billion hours of video. YouTube reaches more adults ages 18 to 34 than any cable network. If your marketing goal involves putting your message in front of people's eyeballs, you can't afford to ignore YouTube.

In addition to the large number of users and video views, YouTube is the second largest search engine online (after Google) — people are searching YouTube for relevant, useful, and inspiring content.

If you want to grow your business with visual social marketing, YouTube is a huge opportunity. It has even more functionality than ever, allowing you to not only share videos but also create and edit them, making it easier to take advantage of this marketing opportunity.

In this chapter, I show you how and why businesses are using YouTube. I describe how YouTube works, including unique features such as channels and playlists. I also show you the core functionality of YouTube so that you're ready to hit the ground running. Finally, I share additional tips for making the most of your efforts on YouTube. To find out more about YouTube in detail, check out *Video Marketing For Dummies,* written by Kevin Daum, Bettina Hein, Matt Scott, and Andreas Goeldi, or *YouTube* For Dummies, by Doug Sahlin and Chris Botello (both from Wiley Publishing).

Growing Your Business with YouTube

YouTube is a huge opportunity for any business because it can generate a large number of views of your videos. If you create a video for marketing purposes, always be sure to post it on YouTube, the number-one video sharing site. Millions of consumers go to YouTube when they're looking for information, entertainment, or instruction.

Businesses are benefiting from YouTube in a number of ways, such as the ones described in the following list. Businesses can

- **Build awareness with interesting videos:** Many businesses use YouTube to build awareness for their products or services. Because millions of people are on YouTube, it's a natural fit to get your business in front of people's eyeballs.

- **Showcase products:** Businesses can use YouTube videos to show employees behind the scenes or to demonstrate what they can truly expect when they buy their products or services. Consider YouTube videos a part of your strategy to showcase your products in a relevant way.

- **Educate customers or prospects:** YouTube is full of educational videos about products and services. After recently using a new application, I was struggling to figure out how to do something. A quick search on YouTube generated hundreds of videos that showed me exactly how to do what I was looking for. Educational and how-to videos are absorbing ways to educate your customers or prospects.

- **Share commercials and other video footage:** YouTube is a good place to share video content because it's easy to search. Many businesses share their commercials on YouTube — not because they think that people want to watch them, but as a resource for those who want to reference or share them.

- **Host to share videos on other websites or social networks:** YouTube is a helpful source for uploading videos because they're easy to share and embed on social networks. If you want to share your video on sites such as Pinterest, Twitter, and LinkedIn, you first have to upload videos to YouTube because none of these social networks lets you upload videos directly to their sites. Even if you don't think that people on YouTube will want to watch your videos, hosting the video on YouTube makes it easier for people to post and share them.

YouTube can even generate sales and leads for your business, even if it markets primarily to other businesses. Employees at my company, Boot Camp Digital, upload videos about social media training topics. The videos, which are optimized for searches on YouTube, often appear in recommended searches. Though we don't yet have professional equipment, we use a lighting kit and green screen. (Each item costs about $100.)

I recently received a call from a large, multinational corporation looking to create a social media training program for its employees. While someone from the company looked at videos about organizational social media training programs, one of my videos showed up as a recommended video. After watching the video and then searching for my company's website, to learn more about our business, someone contacted me and I sent out a proposal.

Share videos related to what you do — you may be surprised at who is searching and browsing on YouTube. By sharing good videos about what you do in a way that presents your business well, you can generate a new, high-quality lead for your business.

Getting Started on YouTube

Creating an account on YouTube is relatively straightforward, though some aspects of your YouTube account are unique to the site.

When you create an account on YouTube, you're creating a *channel*. Because YouTube is a video sharing site, you're creating a channel composed of the videos you upload, similarly to a television channel. You can view a sample YouTube channel page from the SES Conference & Expo in Figure 15-1.

Figure 15-1:
A YouTube channel page.

After you create a YouTube channel, you can edit and optimize it. To edit the channel settings, click on Channel in the navigation menu on the left, Or, if you don't see the button the left, click on the down arrow in the upper-right corner of the screen, and then select Video Manager and then Channel Settings and then Defaults.

Navigating YouTube

You can navigate YouTube by using the navigation menu on the left side of the screen. It can help you explore the functionality and customization options in YouTube. The YouTube navigation has seven main sections: Dashboard, Video Manager, Community, Channel Settings, Analytics, Inbox, and Creation Tools. Each of these menus also contains subnavigation options with even more details.

This type of navigation is the best way to find and edit content on YouTube. It's also your guide to exploring more in-depth features that YouTube offers.

The first tab is the dashboard, as shown in Figure 15-2. The dashboard includes lots of valuable information about key statistics related to your account. From this page, your notifications, statistics, videos, what's new, comments, and more are visible onscreen.

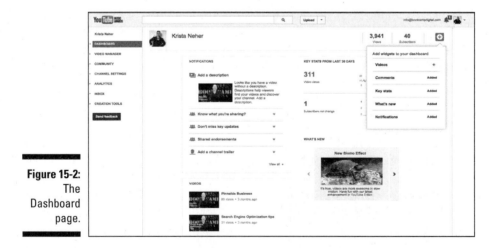

Figure 15-2:
The
Dashboard
page.

You can customize the information shown on the dashboard by clicking on the plus button in the upper-right corner of the screen. Create a custom dashboard that's helpful to you so that you can track the success of your YouTube marketing efforts and quickly view the content that's most relevant to you.

When you're viewing content on YouTube, you don't see this navigation — you see navigation options on the left side that are more appropriate to viewing videos. To navigate back to this menu, click on your user photo and select My Channel. This action opens your channel, and the navigation options appear on the left navigation menu.

Setting the upload default settings

From the Default Settings tab, you can edit the default settings that apply to all your videos. You can change these settings when you upload individual videos. The default section includes the settings described in this list:

- ✔ **Privacy:** You can make your videos public or private.

- ✔ **Category:** The overall category that your channel fits into.

- ✔ **License:** The standard YouTube license or a Creative Commons license.

- ✔ **Title:** A default title for your videos. Use keywords in your channel that your customers may be searching for.

- ✔ **Description:** You can create a standard default description. Use as many characters as possible to build a description that your audience may be searching for. Take the time to completely fill out the description, to optimize your profile for searchers — it can lead to more views of your profile.

- ✔ **Tags:** Add tags to your profile that describe what your videos are about.

- ✔ **Comments and responses:** Choose how other users are allowed to comment on, or interact with, your videos. Allowing comments, votes, and ratings on your content increases the interactivity of the content and can lead to more views. Unless you have a problem with displaying negative comments, keep them turned on.

- ✔ **Caption certification:** This option is related to posting content on your channel that has aired on television. Unless you're a television station or posting content from a public television statement, select from the drop-down the item titled This Content Hever Aired on Television in the U.S.

- ✔ **Suggest video improvements:** To show suggestions, choose between Show Edit Suggestions and Never Show Edit Suggestions.

- ✔ **Video location:** You can tag a default location for your videos.

- ✔ **Video stats:** If you select the check box, your video statistics are publicly visible on the page where people watch your video. To keep your statistics private, deselect the check box.

Optimizing your InVideo programming

The InVideo Programming tab allows users to further customize the way their videos are displayed. You can customize the following settings:

- ✔ **Add a Watermark:** Lets you add a watermark to videos. After you click on this option, you're prompted to select an image to use to watermark your videos. This image is placed in all your videos, so carefully select an appropriate watermark for creating videos.

- ✔ **Feature a Video:** Lets you select one video to feature across other videos. After clicking on the Feature a Video button, you're prompted to select a video from your existing uploads to feature across all your other videos. Alternatively, you can set this option to be the most recent video you have uploaded.

Editing the advanced settings

Advanced settings let you customize your channel. In this section, you can change the items in this list:

- ✔ **Your Image:** By clicking on the Change button under your profile photo, you can change your profile picture.

- ✔ **Your Name:** Click the Change button to the right of your name to change the name associated with your YouTube channel.

- ✔ **Country:** Select your country.

- ✔ **Channel Keywords:** To optimize your channel keywords for searches, select keywords that your customers or other people who are interested in your content will search for. Choosing relevant keywords can attract more views to your channel and videos.

- ✔ **Advertisements:** You can choose whether ads are displayed around your videos, and you can disallow advertisements only while uploading the content that you have no rights to.

- ✔ **Associated Website:** Add a website (especially your business's website) to associate with your YouTube account, to help YouTube verify your site and increase your visibility in searches.

- ✔ **Channel Recommendations:** You can choose whether your channel appears as a recommended channel on other channels.

- ✔ **Subscriber Counts:** You can choose whether to display the number of subscribers to your channel. If this number is low, you may want to hide this statistic.

✔ **Google Analytics Account ID:** To track your YouTube channel views and analytics, you can connect your YouTube account to your Google Analytics. Access Google Analytics and generate a new account for YouTube, and then copy the account ID into this field.

Updating other fields on your channel

To customize the look of information displayed with your channel, you can update a few other fields in your profile. To access additional fields, click on your user image in the upper-right corner of the screen and click the My Channel link. Then you can view your channel, as shown in Figure 15-3, and update a number of items on the screen.

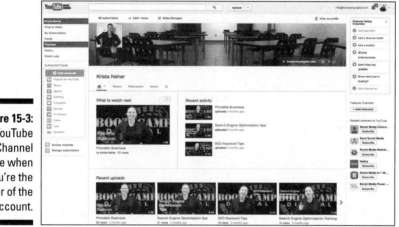

Figure 15-3:
A YouTube Channel page when you're the owner of the account.

A checklist on the right shows your status in setting up and customizing your channel for reference.

While viewing your Channel page, click on the pencil icon to edit the following additional settings and to further customize your channel (the icon appears whenever you hover the cursor over the section you want to edit):

✔ **Add or Edit Channel Art:** You can edit channel art by clicking on the pencil icon in the upper-right corner of the large image that appears at the top of your profile. The recommended size of an image for channel art is 2560 by 1440 pixels, with a minimum of 2048 pixels wide and 1152 pixels tall.

✔ **Add or Edit Links:** Editing links can also be found by clicking on the pencil icon in the upper-right corner of the channel art. After clicking on Edit Links, you can edit certain details of your profile. Clicking on Edit Links lets you edit a number of different pieces of information in your YouTube channel, as shown in Figure 15-4.

The About description of your channel can also be edited on the Edit Links page. Click on the About tab, below your name. As you hover the cursor over the About description, you see a pencil button displayed in the upper-right corner. Click this button to edit the channel description.

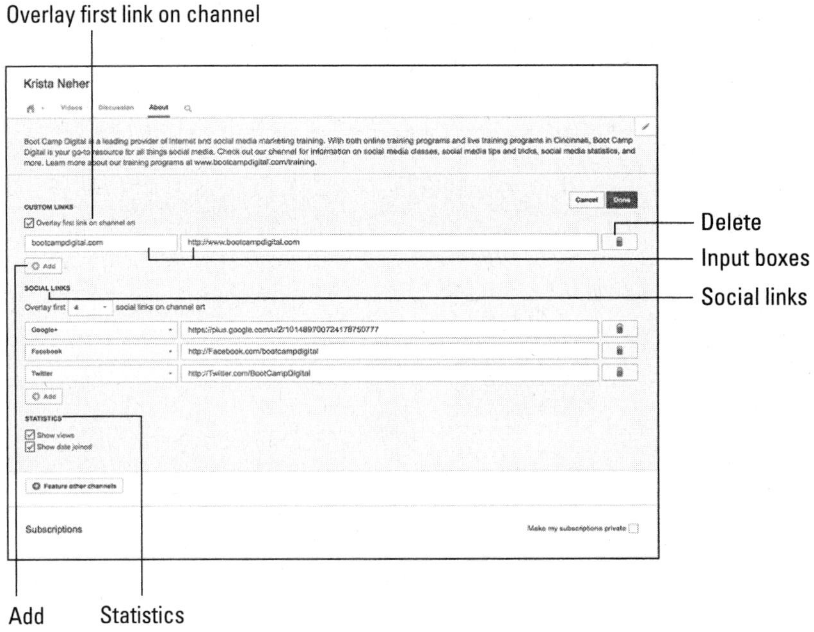

Overlay first link on channel

Delete
Input boxes
Social links

Figure 15-4:
Editing
channel
links.

Add   Statistics

YouTube lets users add a number of links to their websites and social networks to customize the Channel page. Here are the options:

✔ *Overlay First Link on Channel Art:* When you overlay the first link on channel art, the first website you enter is displayed in your channel profile, on top of the cover photo. (You can see it on the lower-right side of the channel art in your profile.)

✔ *Input boxes:* Below the check box, you see two input boxes where you can enter the title of the link (a maximum of 30 characters). This text is displayed in the profile, and users can click it to visit your website. In the second box, enter the URL of the website you want to direct people to.

✔ *Delete:* Click on the garbage can to the right of the link to delete the link.

✔ *Add:* Click the Add button below the link to add another website, though only the first website is displayed at the top of your profile page.

✔ *Social Links:* Include links to your social media profiles on your YouTube channel page. You can choose to display as many as four links to social networks on your profile page, over the channel art. To add a social channel, select it from the drop-down list on the left, and add the URL for your profile on the social channel on the right.

✔ *Statistics:* Choose to display or hide statistics from your profile. Deselecting the box hides the statistic. When you're deciding whether to display statistics, determine whether they add credibility to your profiles. Typically, only larger numbers or older dates add to your credibility.

Uploading Videos for YouTube

YouTube offers four different ways to add videos to a channel. To access the YouTube video upload page, as shown in Figure 15-5, click the Upload button that appears in the middle of the screen on YouTube. (You must be logged in to access the Upload page.)

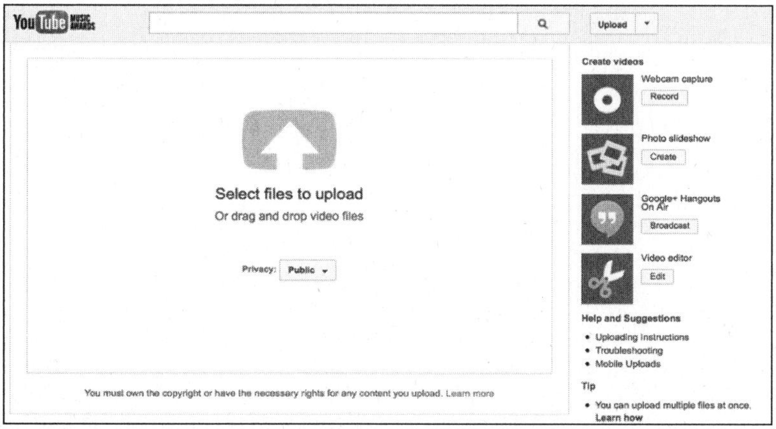

Figure 15-5:
YouTube
Upload
page.

You can upload a video to YouTube by clicking the Upload button in the top navigation menu. If you have already created a video and you're ready to upload it and share it, this option lets you easily do so.

YouTube also has a variety of ways create videos directly (and easily) in YouTube. These options, as described in the following list, are worth exploring if you haven't yet created a video — look for them on the right side of the screen:

- **Webcam Capture:** YouTube makes it extremely easy for you to record from your webcam and instantly upload to YouTube. This is the easiest and fastest way to create a YouTube video. To access the webcam capture, you must be using a computer that has a webcam. Using this option, you can record via your webcam, and the video is simultaneously recorded on YouTube. After recording the video, click the Upload button, to automatically upload it to YouTube, ready for you to customize and share.

- **Photo Slideshow:** This option makes it easy to create a video made up of photos or images. To create a photo slideshow, you must first upload your photos to your Google+ account. (And the Google+ account e-mail address must match the one for your YouTube e-mail account.) After selecting your photos from your Google+ account, you can customize the slide duration, effect, and transition as well as upload music (or add music from the YouTube library) to accompany the slideshow. This makes it extremely quick and easy to turn pictures into a video.

- **Google+ Hangouts On Air:** Google+, a social network launched by Google, allows users to host live video chats called *Hangouts.* A hangout can involve one or more Google+ users. Google+ On Air Hangouts allow you to broadcast a hangout by way of Google+ while simultaneously recording the hangout as a YouTube video. Unless you want to share your video recording on Google+, this option has the same effect as capturing video from your webcam.

- **Video Editor:** YouTube now includes basic video editing functionality so that you can edit your video directly in YouTube. The YouTube video editor has these four tabs:

  - *Quick Fixes:* Includes contrast, brightness, speed, rotation, pan and zoom, and stabilization

  - *Filters:* Lets you change the look of the video

  - *Text:* Lets you insert text over the video

  - *Audio:* Lets you change the volume level of the video

    On this screen, you can also choose Cut The Video (in the large, gray box at the bottom of the screen). This option lets you cut the video and delete segments. After you cut your video, you can add other elements to it, such as video clips, images, music, transitions. and header text.

The video editor that's built into YouTube has a lot of the basic functionality that most video editors need. If you're creating your own videos and don't yet have any video editing software on your computer, give it a try to see whether it can meet your needs.

Optimizing your videos

After your video has been uploaded. you can customize the settings for the video. After the video is uploaded, you can add it to a playlist, as shown in Figure 15-6.

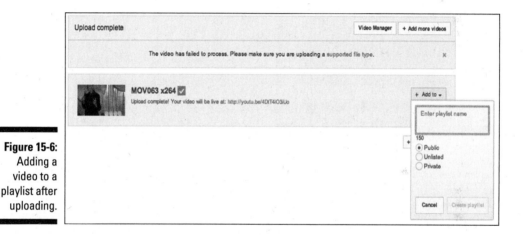

Figure 15-6:
Adding a
video to a
playlist after
uploading.

A *playlist* on YouTube is a way to group similar videos. The Boot Camp Digital channel includes all the videos we upload. Within the channel, my employees can create playlists to organize our company's videos. For example, I may have a playlist for social media tips, another for promotional videos, and one for customer testimonials. The idea behind playlists is that a user may be interested in viewing everything in a playlist, so you should create playlists that are populated with similar videos.

You don't have to add a video to a playlist. YouTube videos aren't required to be organized into playlists. If you haven't created a playlist yet, you can create a new one by clicking the Add To button on the right side and selecting Add a New Playlist.

Completing the basic information about your video

To edit the other information about your video, click the down arrow below the Add To button, or you may find that these options appear as your video is still uploading. This action brings up basic information that you can edit for the video, as shown in Figure 15-7.

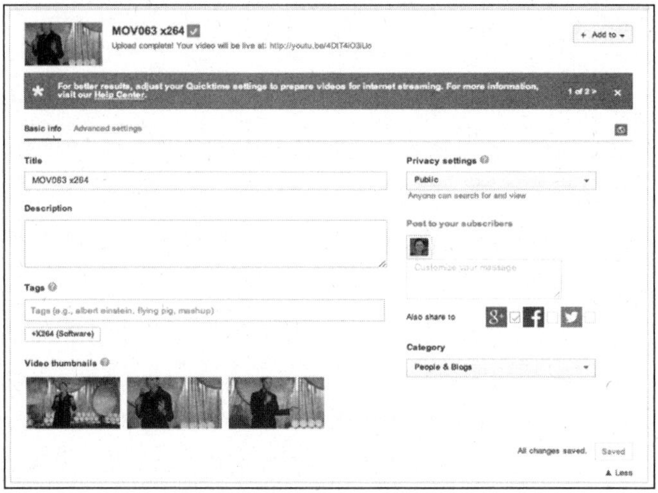

Figure 15-7: Basic information for a video.

You can edit these key fields in the basic settings:

- ✔ **Title:** The title of the video should be descriptive and catchy, and it should include words that your customers might be searching for. A default title may be based on the information that you uploaded with your video. Add a title that's specific and that will interest your audience. This primary headline on your video should entice people to watch.

- ✔ **Description:** Remember that people (and search engines) don't know what your video is about if you don't tell them. That's why the description is vital. Use as many words as possible in the description to maximize the possibility that your videos will show up when people are searching. You can also include links back to your website or specific products to increase the likelihood that people will visit your site after watching your video. As you craft its description, think about which words and phrases people may be searching for on YouTube to maximize the probability of your video showing up in search results or recommended videos.

✔ **Tags:** These words or phrases represent the theme of your video. Though the description includes longer sentences, tags are simply words. As you start typing, keyword suggestions show up underneath the input box, and you can click on these to add them. Below the Tags text box, you may also notice words that are suggested tags from YouTube. To add these tags to your video, simply click on them.

✔ **Video thumbnails:** The thumbnail is the screen shot from the video that someone clicks to play the video. By default, YouTube selects three thumbnails from the video to choose from. Click on the shot to select the image for your thumbnail.

✔ **Privacy:** You can set the privacy settings for your video. You have these three options:

- *Public:* Anyone can see your videos.

- *Unlisted:* The video doesn't display in your profile, but anyone with the specific link to the video can choose it.

- *Private:* Only the people you choose can see the video. If you select Private, a box appears below the privacy settings where you can enter the names, circles, or e-mail addresses of people who can view your video. *Circles* refers to people in the Google+ circles that you specify.

✔ **Post to Your Subscribers:** You can choose to customize a message for subscribers to see when you share the video (as long as the privacy setting is Public). The video with your message appears in the feeds of your subscribers. You can also share your video (with the same message) on social networks (including Google+, Facebook, and Twitter) by selecting the check box beside the social network.

✔ **Category:** Select the category in which your video fits. You must select a video from the category options that are provided — you can't create your own.

Making the most of advanced settings for videos

After editing and optimizing the basic settings, you can also edit the advanced settings. To do so, click on the Advanced Settings tab at the top of the editing page.

I describe some advanced settings in the earlier section "Setting the upload default settings." In addition to those settings, you can edit a number of new ones:

- **Distribution Options:** Lets you further customize how people find and share your videos. If you pick the first option, Allow Embedding, other users can embed your video to display on their websites. If you want your videos displayed only on your site and YouTube, do not select this option. Selecting the second option, Notify Subscribers, notifies people who subscribe to your channel of your new video.

- **Age Restrictions:** If your content isn't appropriate for viewers of all ages, you may choose to select the Enable Age Restrictions box. Doing so disallows underage users from viewing your video.

- **Recording Date:** Set this option to the date that the video was recorded, if you want to share the date of the video with the video information.

- **3D Video:** You can choose the 3D video option that's appropriate for your video. Most videos have the default setting, No Preference.

- **Video Statistics:** Selecting this check box makes the statistics about views of your video publicly viewable.

After you customize the advanced settings, you can click the blue Save and Share button in the lower-left corner to post the video on your channel and share it with subscribers.

Editing videos after uploading

Any of your video settings can still be edited after they're uploaded. To edit a video, navigate to it. The easiest way to find the video is to view your channel and then click on the video you want to edit.

Editing buttons are displayed below your video, as shown in Figure 15-8.

You can see editing buttons only for the videos you have uploaded to your account. After you click on an editing button, you're directed to a new page, where you can edit all settings by selecting the tabs along the top, as shown in Figure 15-9.

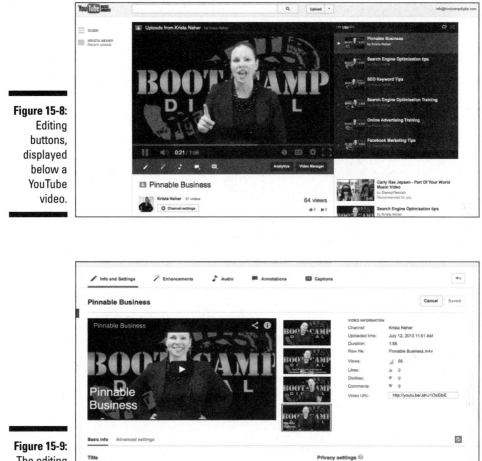

Figure 15-8: Editing buttons, displayed below a YouTube video.

Figure 15-9: The editing page.

This list describes the editing buttons:

✔ **Video Information:** The top portion of the screen shows the video as well as some basic video information about the video: the channel, time of upload, duration of video, raw filename, and number of likes, dislikes, and comments. You can also see the URL to share the video.

✔ **Edit Info and Settings:** Clicking on this button lets you edit the basic and advanced information related to the video.

✓ **Enhancements:** Enhancements are composed of three sections: Quick Fixes, Filters, and Special Effects. if you make changes while enhancing the video that you don't want to keep, you can click the Revert to Original button in the upper-right corner of the screen to return the video to the original view. The first Quick Fixes screen is shown in Figure 15-10.

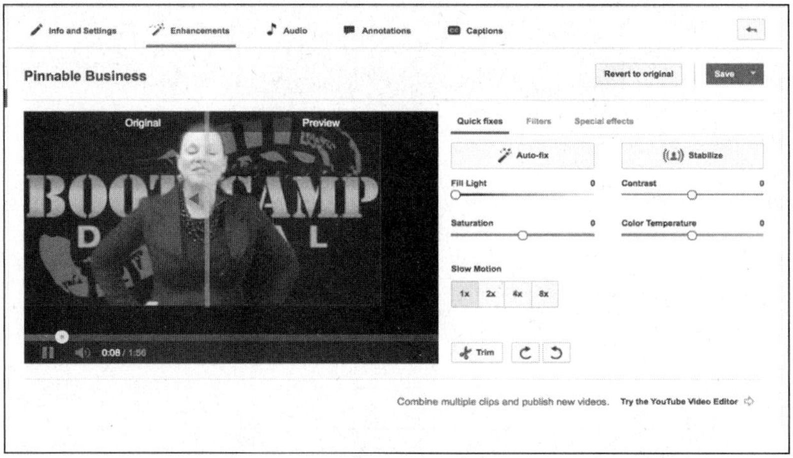

Figure 15-10:
The
Enhance-
ments
editing
page.

✓ **Quick Fixes:** The quick fixes include *auto-fix,* which automatically enhances certain features of your video. *Stabilize* stabilizes shaky videos. The next four lines allow you to adjust aspects of the video display, including Fill Light, Contrast, Saturation, and Color Temperature. These settings affect the look of the video. You can slow the video to be played in slow motion or click the Trim button at the bottom to cut and remove parts of the video.

✓ **Filters:** Filters — which change the overall look of the video — include Black and White, Old Fashioned, Cartoon, and more. To select a filter, click on it. You can preview how the filter will make the video look by playing the video in the video player on the left side after you've applied the filter.

✓ **Special Effects:** The only special effect now allows you to blur all faces in your video. It may not blur 100 percent of the faces, but if you don't want the people in your video to be identifiable, this is an easy way to blur them.

✓ **Audio:** From the Audio tab, you can add or change the music in your video. To add music from the YouTube library, click on the track you want to add. After you select a track, it's displayed below the video player, as shown in Figure 15-11. Beside the song title is a slider bar that can slide between Music, Favorite Music, and Favorite Original Audio. The slider dictates how the music and original audio are balanced. Beside the slider, you can click on the Position Audio button to make an audio editor appear below the video. You can position the audio to the correct section of your video.

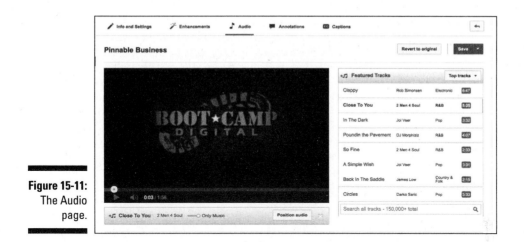

Figure 15-11:
The Audio
page.

✔ **Annotations:** Add annotations to your video. An *annotation* is a text box or bubble that appears in your video for a set period. An annotation is a useful way to add interest to your video and engage viewers. If you don't have video editing software but you want to add text to your video, this is an easy way to add it. You can choose from these five types:

- Speech bubble
- Note
- Title
- Spotlight
- Label

After you select the type of annotation you want, as shown in Figure 15-12, you can customize it. Complete the text box with the text you want displayed in the annotation.

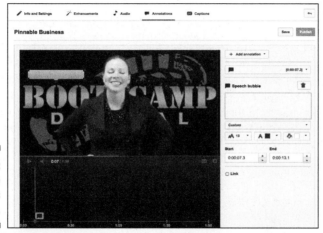

Figure 15-12:
The
Annotations
page.

✔ **Captions:** Captions can make your video more accessible, because people can read the text in your video rather than have to listen to it. To edit captions, click the blue Add Captions button. Then you can upload your captions or select the Transcribe and Sync menu option. Both methods require you to manually create or add a transcription for the video. You may also choose to have YouTube automatically transcribe the video by clicking on the language and the Automatic Captions button. Next, you see a page with the timing of the video and the transcribed text that will accompany it. You can click on any of the text to edit it. As you can see in Figure 15-13, the captions are easy to edit. However, they aren't accurate in some cases, so be prepared to view your video and edit it.

Figure 15-13:
The
Captions
page.

Getting More from YouTube

You can get more benefit from YouTube by fully taking advantage of all the features and functions it has to offer. YouTube is an extremely robust video sharing and editing tool, and this chapter hands you the most important and useful information. For the details of marketing your business on YouTube, check out the Video Marketing For Dummies, written by x (and published by John Wiley & Sons, Inc.)

In the remainder of this chapter I share some additional thoughts to help you get more out of YouTube.

Connecting with the YouTube community

YouTube is a social network, in addition to a site to post and share videos. It's a network where you can connect with other users and their content. Though many people use YouTube only to view videos, the site also has an active community of participants who subscribe to channels and interact with videos. Connecting with the YouTube community is an important way to generate traction for your videos.

To connect with the YouTube community, you can

✔ **Subscribe to other relevant channels:** Find other relevant channels to subscribe to. Users receive a notification whenever you subscribe to their channels, and they may be interested in subscribing to your channel, if it's interesting to them.

✔ **Interact with other videos:** Grow exposure for your channel by liking and commenting on other videos. When you interact with other relevant videos and people view that video, they see your profile photo and your comment, which can increase the exposure of your account.

If your goal is to build a community of people on YouTube who are interested in seeing your videos, don't forget to connect with the community.

Sharing YouTube videos

You can share any video on YouTube, whether it's one you create or any other video. YouTube videos make appealing content for other social networks.

To share a YouTube video, navigate to the video you want to share. YouTube videos have sharing features built-in to them, which is the easiest way to share.

To share a YouTube video, follow these steps:

1. **Click on the Share tab below the video.** You then receive sharing buttons in Video view, as shown in Figure 15-14.

2. **Click to select the social network you want to share on.** You see, with only the click of a button, the social networks on which you can share the video. Click on the social network that you want to share on.

Figure 15-14:
The Share
tab on a
YouTube
video.

3. **Customize the text that you want to accompany the link.** Customize the text that you want to accompany the link to the YouTube video. Then click the button labeled Share or Post (depending on which network you're sharing to).

4. **Alternatively, copy the web address.** If you would prefer to copy the web address of the video to share, you can copy the URL that's displayed below the Sharing buttons. The advantage of sharing the web address with the link on the sharing page versus the link in your web browser is that you can customize the part of the video where you want to start playing.

In addition to sharing to social networks, you can embed a video by clicking on the Embed tab. Clicking this tab generates code you can use to embed the video into your website or blog. Finally, you can select the third tab and e-mail the video. From there, you can enter the e-mail addresses that you want to send the video to and customize the message.

Chapter 16

Creating and Sharing Videos via Vine

....

....

*V*ine was launched in late January of 2013 as a microvideo sharing site from Twitter. Vine, a mobile application, allows users to share short videos (a maximum of 6 seconds) from their mobile devices. In this sense, it's similar to the video version of Twitter, where users share short-format content. When Twitter was launched, it seemed impossible to communicate *anything* in 140 or fewer characters, yet it's now the norm for many people. Twitter is hoping that Vine will have the same impact, by making 6-second videos the new standard of efficient video communication.

Since Vine was launched, a number of other short-format video formats have emerged. Instagram launched Instagram Video, allowing users to record, edit, and share 15-second videos (as covered in Chapter 11).

Snapchat, a similar application that's known for protecting the privacy of its users, lets users share photos and videos that auto-delete after a set period. Snapchat is still emerging as a possible marketing platform for brands. Given the highly private nature of Snapchat and the fact that videos are deleted after someone views them, Snapchat is more challenging for marketers. The majority of Snapchat users (72 percent) are under the age of 29, making the service appealing for brands targeting younger audiences.

This chapter focuses on Vine video because a number of major brands have already adopted it as their *micro* (short-format) video sharing platform. Additionally, the lessons learned from Vine videos can be adapted and applied to other video sharing sites such as Snapchat and Instagram.

Top brands such as McDonalds, General Electric, Lowes, Taco Bell, and Xbox, as well as a variety of small- and medium-size businesses, are already using Vine.

Vine has a natural advantage over other microvideo sharing sites because of its integration with Twitter. Every second, five tweets are posted that contain a Vine video, and a branded Vine video is five times more likely to be seen than a regular branded video.

In this chapter, I show you how Vine works, how businesses are using Vine, and success factors for generating results on Vine. Because I can't show you actual Vine videos in this book, I highly recommend downloading the application and looking at a few videos. If you don't have a smartphone handy, you can instead see Vine videos shared on the Internet. To get a feel for how they look, search YouTube for the phrase *Vine videos,* or look for blog posts with Vine videos embedded.

The screen shots and navigations of the application in this chapter are based on the Android version. The Apple version is similar, though you may notice that it isn't identical.

Marketing Your Business with Vine

Vine is emerging as an interesting new marketing application that many businesses have embraced. Though six seconds hardly seems like enough time to communicate a topic, creative marketers are harnessing the power of Vine and challenging themselves to rethink video marketing and communications.

Here a few businesses that have embraced Vine:

- ✔ **Lowe's Fix in Six:** This is probably the best-known use of Vine by a large organization. Lowe's has created a number of vines showing, in only six seconds, how to fix items around your house. The vines, which are useful, cover topics such as how to unscrew a stripped screw, remove stubborn stickers, and clean a dirty cookie sheet. The videos have hundreds of likes, comments, and revines.

- ✔ **General Electric:** General Electric uses Vine to inspire and build its brand. GE films short videos for topics such as Gravity Day and Thomas Edison's birthday. It has also created the concept of 6 Second Science Fair Vine, in which it shares the marvels of science in only six seconds.

- ✔ **Honda #WantNewCar:** Honda has launched a Vine campaign in which it asks users to add the hashtag #WantNewCar to tweets on Twitter to share why they need a new car. Honda selected the best tweets and responded with customized Vine videos. The effort led to an increase in Vine followers and mentions of the brand.

In addition to these large brands using Vine in innovative ways, countless businesses have turned to Vine to make their marketing more visually oriented. Businesses are "vining" a wide variety of content, including holiday greetings, useful tips, product demos, behind-the-scenes, office humor, trade show booths, contest promotions, brand history sharing, random entertainment, and more.

As you evaluate whether Vine is right for your business, remember that in addition to generating views on Vine, you can use your videos on your website. For example, the Lowes Fix in Six videos can be found on a Pinterest board and the company's Tumblr site, in addition to other social networks.

Exploring Vine

Because Vine is a mobile application, Vine videos are recorded via the Vine application on smartphones and tablets. Vine accounts can be accessed, and video created, only on applications on mobile devices that are compatible with Apple or Android. No computer-accessible version of Vine is available, though Vine videos can be shared and viewed on computers. (I explain this topic later in this chapter, in the section "Share vines online".)

To get started, go to the app store for your mobile device, download the application, and create an account.

Because Vine was created by Twitter, you can use your Twitter account to sign in to Vine. The benefit of using Twitter to sign in is that your profile information is automatically transported from Twitter to Vine, making setup much quicker.

The term *Vine* is used both to describe the application (Vine) and the video that's created (a vine). A *vine* is a 6-second video that's shown on a loop, which means that it automatically repeats itself. Vine videos have sound; however, the default is for them to play without sound. Because the video is shown on a repeating loop, the sound can quickly become annoying.

Start by experimenting with creating different types of Vine videos. Vines range from short, amateur-looking videos to professional-quality, stop-motion animations captured and shared by using Vine.

Vine Feed

After you log in to Vine, you see your feed (also known as your home page), as shown in Figure 16-1, which is a view of the vines that are shared by the users you follow. You also see vines that are Editors Picks, which are vines selected by the application. You can navigate to the feed by clicking the icon that looks like a house.

Figure 16-1:
Vine home
feed.

As you scroll down the screen, vines automatically begin to play whenever you can see them on the screen — the app has no Play or Stop buttons. To pause (or unpause) a vine, simply tap the video.

Activity

The Activity tab shows activity and interactions with you. On this tab, you can find notifications about new followers and interactions with your vines. On an Android device, you access the Activity tab by clicking the icon that looks like an eye. On an Apple device, you can find the tab by clicking the Home button and then clicking the Activity button.

Explore

The Explore tab, as shown in Figure 16-2, lets you explore and discover new vines. You can search by Popular Now or On the Rise, or by Channels or by the trending tag. This is an excellent place to discover the different types of vines, and to find inspiration for creating your own. Exploring Vine can be fun, because many Vine users are highly creative.

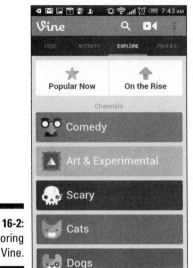

Figure 16-2:
Exploring
Vine.

On Android, you access the Explore tab by clicking the icon that looks like a bell. On an Apple device, you can find it by clicking the Home button and then clicking the Explore button.

Spend some time exploring vines before starting to make your own. It's a helpful way to get a feel for the types of videos you can create.

Profile

The Profile tab lets you view your profile information, find people to follow, and view your posts.

On an Android device, you access the Profile section by clicking the icon that looks like a person. On an Apple device, you can find it by clicking the Home button and then clicking the Profile button.

Search

Using this search feature, you can search for users or for videos based on tags in the video.

On an Android device, the magnifying glass in the top navigation menu of Vine lets you access the Search function. On an Apple device, you can find it by clicking the Home button and then clicking the Explore button. A search box is displayed at the top of the Explore screen.

Capture Video

The Capture Video button sits beside the Search button in the top navigation menu of Vine. Capturing video with Vine is covered in the later section "Creating a Vine Video."

More

The last button in the top navigation menu is an ellipsis, represented by three dots, that provides additional menu features. On an Apple device, the More features are found by clicking on the button on the Home screen that says "Want to see more? Tap to find friends."

The Find People option makes it easy to find users to follow. Vine can connect to the address book of your mobile phone or Twitter account to find users you can follow. This makes it easy to find and follow your friends on Vine. You can also search for, and invite, specific users to connect with you on Vine by clicking on the magnifying glass. The next option on the More menu is to mute or unmute the audio on your application. Finally, you can access the settings of your Vine account. From Settings, you can update your profile information, manage your password, manage privacy settings, change your notification preferences, find friends, connect with other social networks, and find support.

Creating a Vine Video

Creating Vine videos is easy to do, but it may take some getting used to. To create a video, open the application and click on the video camera icon in the top navigation menu. This action opens the Vine video recording screen, as shown in Figure 16-3. Vines are recorded in a square format.

Figure 16-3:
Vine recording screen.

The center of the recording screen shows a stream from your camera, which previews what you'll be recording.

To record a Vine video, tap and hold your finger on the camera viewer section of the screen. The video records for as long as you're touching the center of the screen. To stop recording, remove your finger from the screen. Because you have only six seconds of video footage to record in Vine, you can start and stop recording multiple times to capture footage. Your vine plays as a single continuous video.

A green progress bar on top of the camera shows how long you have recorded video. When the progress bar reaches the end, you have completed the six seconds, and the video is automatically processed. If you don't need the entire six seconds for your video, you can click on the right-arrow button at any time to finalize the video and move on to the sharing screens.

After the video is processed, you can still return to the editor by clicking on the arrow pointing to the left. When you're happy with the video, click the green button to process the video and move to the sharing screen.

Experiment with the stop-and-start video capture that Vine has to offer. It can take a while to get used to recording vines, so set aside some time to practice creating videos.

Additional camera features

On the bottom of the video capture screen are these additional features:

- ✔ **Switch Camera:** The first button on the bottom of the video capture screen is a circular button with two arrows on it. Tapping it lets you toggle between the front and back camera of your phone.

- ✔ **View Grid:** This button lets you view a grid that's superimposed on your video screen viewer. Tapping this button overlays a grid on your camera viewer. This grid is a guide to let you better manage the space in the video recording, and it can help you to position the camera better. The grid lines aren't included in the final video — they only serve as a guide for you while recording. To remove the grid lines, tap on the button again.

- ✔ **Focus:** Tapping this button, which looks like a bull's-eye, lets you adjust the focus. First tap on the Focus button. Then tap the area on the screen that you want to focus on. The bull's-eye is displayed in that area, indicating that the focus of the camera is shifting to the area you tapped. After you're satisfied with the focus, touch the Focus button at the bottom to turn off the focus feature.

✔ **Ghost:** The ghost feature lets you view and edit the individual frames that have already been recorded. Tap on the Ghost button to activate this editing feature. Then tap on the top part of the screen, where the recording progress is displayed. This action opens a new viewer, shown in Figure 16-4, where you can edit the video you have already recorded. Ghost view allows for frame-by-frame editing of a Vine video. You can tap on the center of the video to play or pause the video. To view or remove an individual frame, tap on the frame in the bottom section. When an individual frame is selected, it displays a white square around it. Tap on the garbage can button at the top to remove the selected frame from your Vine video. After you have finished ghost editing, tap the Save button to save your changes, or click Cancel to return to the original video capture screen.

Figure 16-4:
Vine ghost
editing.

✔ **Save:** The final button in the navigation, represented by a square, lets you save videos and access saved videos. To save the video and continue working on it later, tap the Save button. If you have saved videos, a number appears inside this icon, indicating the number of saved videos you can access. To access saved videos, tap on the Save icon and scroll the list of your saved videos to find the one you're looking for.

Vine video best practices and tips

Creating appealing vines can be simple or complicated. Some Vine users spend days creating complex, stop-motion animations, though other popular Vine videos take only seconds to create. The key to success on Vine is having a good video concept and a plan for how to bring it to life in a maximum of six seconds.

Creating an inviting video starts with a clear plan. Follow these steps:

1. **Determine the purpose and idea for the video.**

   Start by knowing why you're creating the video, and make sure that it's a topic that your audience will be interested in. The video concept should appeal to your audience and provide something valuable, useful, interesting, entertaining, educational, or noteworthy.

2. **Plan out your six seconds.**

   After you come up with the concept for the video, plan the frames for the six seconds. Because you have limited time, it's extremely important to know what shots you need to capture and plan out how long each one can last.

3. **Evaluate audio.**

   Vine records audio, too. Audio can be tricky with Vine, especially when a video is made up of many different shots. If you aren't planning any specific audio, try to shoot with a quiet background so that the noise doesn't become a distraction. Also, you can prevent Vine from accessing your camera's microphone if you want to omit audio.

4. **Gather all necessary materials.**

   If you need props, lighting, or a tripod, gather everything you need before you start shooting. Taking long breaks between shots can make the video look choppy, and the video can also be affected by lighting or other environmental changes.

5. **Shoot!**

   After you have planned your shots and assembled the props and actors (if you have them), start shooting!

In addition to planning your video, follow a few other helpful tips when creating fabulous vines:

- **Avoid camera shake by using a tripod.** Even engaging videos can be distracting because the camera is shaking. Invest in a small tripod for your mobile device to smooth out your video.

- **Prevent lighting from being a distraction.** Shadows or bright lights can become quite distracting. Pay attention to the lighting to ensure that you're capturing the best possible video.

- **Use a microphone for audio.** Nothing ruins a video like terrible audio. You can purchase a number of microphones for smartphones and tablets to improve the audio quality. Consider using a microphone if the video has lots of audio.

- **Keep it simple.** Keep your vine concept and video simple. You have only six seconds, so complex messages don't usually do well. Shorten your message to make it fit, and don't try to overcommunicate or make longer content fit into six seconds.

Sharing Vine Videos

After you have recorded your Vine video, you will arrive at the Share screen, as shown in Figure 16-5. On this screen, you can add information to your video and share it.

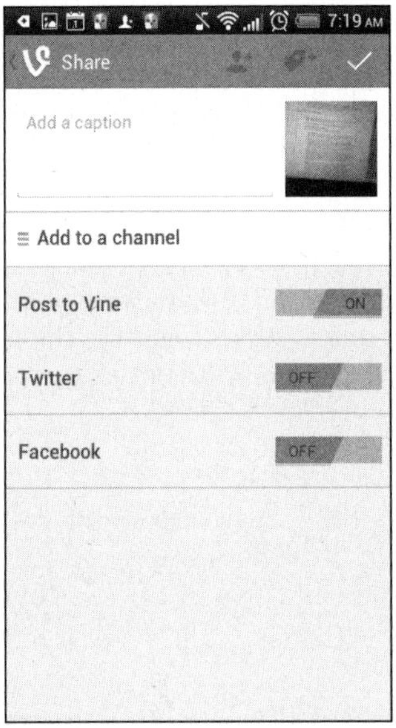

Figure 16-5:
Vine video
sharing
screen.

Add a caption

The first part of the Share screen invites you to add a caption to the video. The *caption,* the text below your Vine video, should describe your video in an interesting way. The caption should entice a viewer to want to watch your video.

Keep the caption short. If you choose to share your Vine video on Twitter or Facebook, the caption is shared with the link to the video.

The caption doesn't simply display below the video — it's also used to describe the video when it's shared on other social networks.

Add Location

This option is available only in the Apple version of Vine. Clicking the Add a Location option lets you add a location from Foursquare, a location-based social network.

Add to a channel

When users are exploring Vine and looking for new videos to watch, one way that they can browse is by channel. A channel includes Vine videos from multiple users and is basically a category that you can assign to your video. To increase the exposure of your Vine video, add it to a relevant channel so that it can be discovered by other Vine viewers.

Post to Vine

You can turn the Post to Vine option on or off. Turning it off hides your Vine video from other users on Vine. Also, if you choose not to post to Vine, you can't share your video on Facebook or Twitter.

Post to Twitter and Facebook

The Twitter and Facebook buttons let you share your vine immediately to Twitter or Facebook. To access this functionality, you must connect your Vine account to Twitter or Facebook. When the video is shared, it automatically includes the caption you created.

Add people

In the top navigation menu, an icon of a person with a plus sign (+) beside it lets you tag people (add them to your video). Clicking this button adds the at-sign (@) to the screen and provides a drop-down list of Vine users you may want to tag. You can either click on the user to add the username to your caption or use the at-sign to manually add someone. Using the at-sign and a username lets you tag people in your video. When you tag a user, that person is notified in their notifications on Vine.

Add tags

The Tag button, which is in the top navigation menu, looks like a tag with a plus sign (+) beside it. It lets you create tags to describe your video. Tags (also known as *hashtags*) describe what your video is about. Though your caption can include a number of words that describe your video, words with the hashtag (#) in front of them are indicating the general theme of your video.

On Vine, videos are explored with hashtags. When exploring and searching for new videos to view, Vine searches for hashtags, not just words in the caption of your video. For example, if I add the caption "The sunrise over Cincinnati" to my video, it doesn't show up in any searches on Vine, because the caption doesn't contain any hashtags. Instead, if the caption says, "The #sunrise over #Cincinnati," my Vine video may appear whenever users search for #sunrise and #Cincinnati.

On Apple devices, the last two options — Adding Tags and Adding People — appear only after you click to start adding information to the caption. These options aren't in the top navigation, but are in the center of the screen.

Add relevant hashtags to your captions. Using hashtags makes your Vine videos more discoverable and can lead to more views and exposure.

Share vines online

Though you can easily share vines to Facebook and Twitter, they can also be shared and viewed across the web in a number of other ways (which is part of what makes Vine a powerful platform). In addition to sharing vines on the Vine app, your vine videos can make useful content for other social networks and can even be embedded on websites.

When vines are shared online, the default setting has the volume muted. To turn on the volume, click on the sound icon in the upper-left corner of the Vine video.

Vines shared on Twitter

Because Vine was created by Twitter, Vine videos are integrated directly into the Twitter platform. When you view a Vine video on Twitter, you can watch the video directly from the tweet, without having to "click away" and leave Twitter. A tweet with a vine embedded is shown in Figure 16-6.

Figure 16-6:
Vine video that's viewable in a tweet.

Vines shared on Facebook

Though Facebook isn't directly integrated with Vine, you can still share a Vine video to Facebook with the click of a button. To view the video. you must click on the video and view it on the Vine website.

A sample Vine video that was shared on Facebook is shown in Figure 16-7. The thumbnail of the vine is displayed, though it can't be viewed in Facebook.

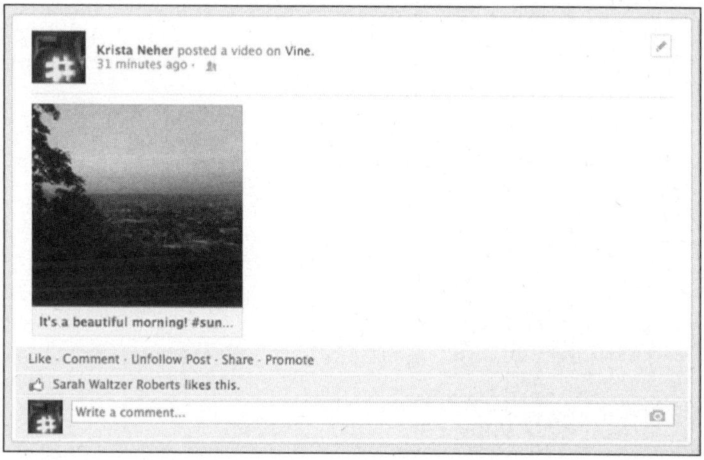

Figure 16-7: Vine video, shared on Facebook.

Clicking on the video thumbnail on Facebook opens a web page on Vine.co (the Vine website) where the video can be viewed, as shown in Figure 16-8.

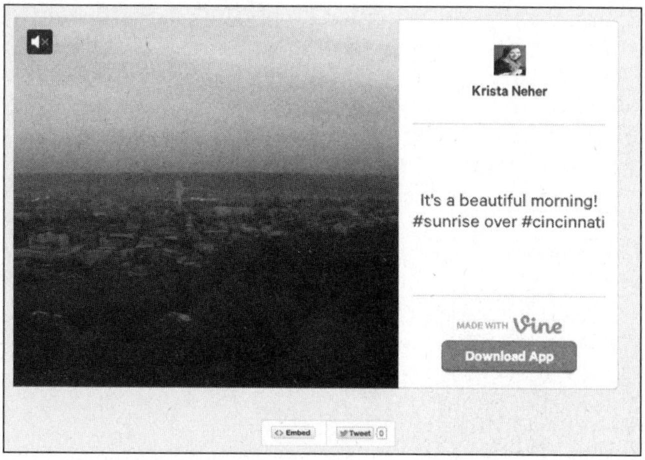

Figure 16-8: Vine video, displayed on Vine.co.

Vines embedded into blogs or websites

Vines can also be embedded into blogs or websites. When embedded into a website, the video can be played directly in the website. To embed a Vine video into a website, go to the web page on Vine.co with the vine in it. You can find this link by clicking on the Facebook Share button, or at the bottom of the tweet.

After you're on the Vine page, click the Embed button, displayed below the vine. This action opens a new page, with the embed options shown in Figure 16-9.

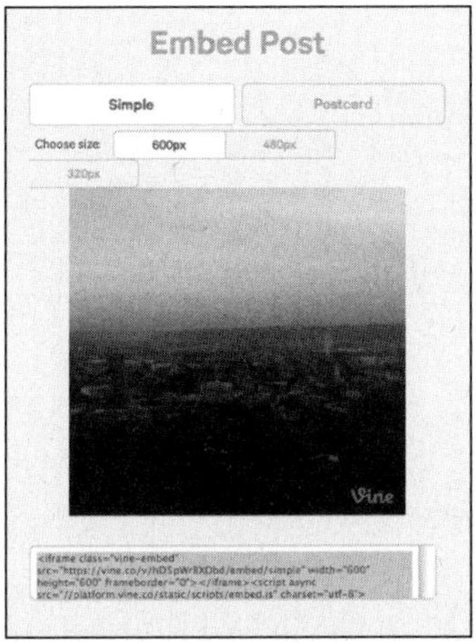

Figure 16-9:
The Vine embed page.

This page lets you customize the vine before embedding it. You can choose either the Simple or Postcard embed style. The postcard style adds a white border to the vine. You can also customize the size of the vine by select-ing 300, 480, or 600 pixels. After you're satisfied with the video, copy the embed code that's generated at the bottom of the page and insert it on your website or into your blog. This action displays the vine on your site and plays it directly on your site. An example of an embedded vine is shown in Figure 16-10, where it's shared on the Vine.co blog.

Figure 16-10:
Vine,
embedded
in a blog
post.

Building Community on Vine

As with any social network, simply posting content doesn't get you noticed on Vine. To build an audience for your Vine videos, you need to participate and connect with the community on Vine. Connecting with other Vine users can attract more exposure and views for your videos.

Finding and following users

The first step in growing your audience on Vine is to find other relevant users to follow. You can find Vine users to follow in a few different ways:

- ✔ **People you know:** Early in this chapter, in the section "Exploring Vine," under "More" I show you how to find, and connect with, contacts from your mobile phone or your Twitter followers who are already using Vine. Connecting to people you already know on Vine is a helpful first step.

- ✔ **Vine people search:** In the Find People section of Vine, you can add existing contacts or search for people. Searching for people can be a useful way to find people who share your interests. For example, I can search for people based on a city, such as Toronto, to find Vine users in Toronto, or who mention Toronto in their usernames or profiles. You can also search for people based on interests or other words that may be in their profiles. For example, if you want to search for motorcycle enthusiasts, you can search for *motorcycle* to find users who have *motorcycle* in their usernames or descriptions.

✓ **Search channels:** If the people you want to connect with are interested in a particular category of video, this is an appropriate place to start. Start by searching for vines in a category that's relevant to your business.

✓ **Search hashtags:** Search by hashtag for relevant hashtags that your audience might be using. The bottom of the Explore screen shows trending hashtags; however, you can choose to search specifically for tags that relate to your topic of interest.

You can follow any Vine user who has a public profile. Users don't have to approve you to follow them. When viewing a user profile, click the Follow button displayed below the profile, as shown in the Lowes profile in Figure 16-11. When you follow a user, her videos appear in your feed when you log on.

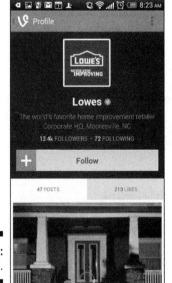

Figure 16-11: Vine profile.

As you search, you may come across users who share your interests. As you determine whom to follow on Vine, look beyond users creating videos, and connect with Vine users who are liking, commenting on, and revining videos as well. (I explain revines in the next section.) Many people in the Vine community don't create many of their own videos — they simply love to watch and look around.

Connecting with other Vine users can generate exposure for your account and views of your video. Often, users you follow will check out your profile and videos. If they like what they see, they may choose to follow you back.

Interacting with Vine videos

After you discover interesting or relevant Vine users, you can start to connect with them. Interacting with other users on Vine sends them notifications, and many users can check out your profile and watch your vines. In this way, interacting with others is a useful way to bring attention to your own account. You can interact with other users on Vine in a few different ways.

When viewing a video on Vine, the video is displayed, and below it you see information about the video, as well as options to interact with it (as shown in the General Electric profile in Figure 16-12).

Figure 16-12:
Comments
below a Vine
video.

You can interact with Vine videos in a variety of ways:

- **Like:** Liking a Vine simply means that you like it. To like a Vine, click the smiley face icon below the video.

- **Comment:** Clicking the callout box icon beside the smiley face lets you leave a comment on a video.

- **Revine:** Revining a post is similar to retweeting on Twitter or sharing a status update on Facebook. When you revine, you're resharing a video with your followers, and it appears on your profile. To revine a video, click on the button with two arrows forming a circle, and the video will be shared from your account.

- **Share:** The three dots to the right of the interaction buttons comprise the Share button. Click on this button to share the Vine video on other sites. You can share on Facebook or Twitter by way of the Vine application. Clicking on Share To lets you share with other applications that are connected to your mobile phone. From this screen, you can also report a post as inappropriate.

You can also share by embedding the link into an e-mail message. The link automatically opens when you tap the button. This option e-mails you a link to the vine that can be viewed from an Internet browser.

Interacting with other users increases your visibility because your likes, comments, and revines are displayed on the original post — exposing more people to your profile and videos. Users also receive notifications whenever someone interacts with their vines, which creates additional exposure for you.

Part VI
The Part of Tens

Find out ten sources of inspiration for your visual content at www.dummies.com/extras/visualsocialmarketing.

In this part . . .

✔ Ten types of images to create for your visual marketing

✔ Ten types of videos to create for your visual marketing

Chapter 17

Ten Types of Images to Create

. . . .

. . . .

Regardless of the type of business you're in, you can share a wide variety of images — of all types — to bring your message to life. The key to success is variety — mix up your pictures to appeal to different audiences.

Creating a visual element typically takes more effort than simply updating your status. For example, creating an image of a statistic can take longer than simply tweeting that statistic. To maximize the return on your time investment, focus on visual elements that are more likely to get the results you want. One way to do this is to create visuals of content that has already been popular on social media. For example, if you tweet a quote that generates a lot of comments, replies, or retweets, make it a visual post on Pinterest and Facebook. At my company, Boot Camp Digital, most of our infographics are based on content that has already been popular on our blog. We know that our audience already likes the content, so we're maximizing the probability that the infographic — which is more time consuming to create — will get results.

Statistics

Many businesses, especially those that market primarily to other businesses, struggle to come up with a creative image strategy. Statistics, especially those that surprise readers, can make useful content in your visual social marketing strategy.

Businesses of all types have interesting statistics that support their marketing and communications objectives. A restaurant might share how many potatoes it peels in a year. An IT company might share stats about how much productivity is lost from users experiencing computer problems. A manufacturer might share statistics about how much of its product is consumed every year, or how much of a specific material it uses. A lawyer might share statistics about settlement values.

Regardless of your type of business, you can share a variety of interesting statistics to make your message "pop." Look for internal *and* external industry statistics.

The key to sharing a good statistic is to make sure that it's interesting. As you can see in Figure 17-1, the more interesting the "stat," the more likely it is to be shared.

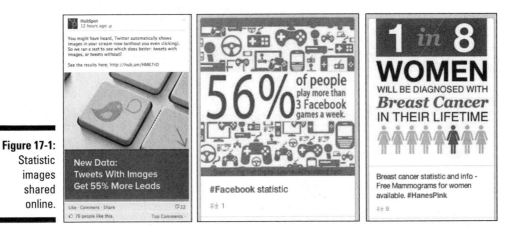

Figure 17-1:
Statistic images shared online.

Inspirational Quotes

Inspirational quotes are extremely popular on social networks such as Facebook, Instagram, and Pinterest. People often like, comment on, and share quotes that they think their friends might benefit from.

The trick to using inspirational quotes is to find quotes that are interesting and emotional — but not overused. These quotes are most likely to be shared by your fans.

To create an inspirational quote image, start with the quote. Be careful to avoid quotes that are very long, because they may be difficult to fit into a graphic that's viewable on social networks such as Facebook and Pinterest.

When sharing a quote graphic, you have a few options for picking the image underlying the quote. You can share the quote on an image or a photograph that represents the quote. Alternatively, you can share the quote on a plain background, to emphasize the words. Finally, the quote can be shared in an image that's branded with your business.

Often, the best image quotes have subtle branding. Consider the right way to share your quote as an image.

Inspirational quote images are shown in Figure 17-2.

Figure 17-2: Inspirational quote images.

Real-Life Images

Sometimes you can easily get so caught up in creating graphics for visual social marketing that you forget to use the visual content that's right in front of you. If you have a highly visual product, such as a retail store or restaurant or a physical product, this strategy works well. Even if you don't have a visual product, you can still use this strategy.

One image trend we see on social networks is that consumers have an appetite for real-life pictures of real-life objects taken by real people. People are skeptical of perfectly produced, professionally photographed products because they know that the product they buy might not actually look the same as the one in a photo.

For this reason, taking pictures on the go is a helpful way to increase the credibility of your visual marketing efforts. Take pictures of your products in action, such as a daily special or a new product coming off the production line. Snap a photo of a happy customer or a new promotional piece that you just created for your business. You can see in Figure 17-3 some examples of a variety of real-life businesses using real-life photos in their strategy.

Figure 17-3:
Real-life
pictures.

As you dig into visual social marketing and start thinking about how to share your story visually online via social media, you'll start to notice that more and more photo opportunities arise throughout the day. Keep your eyes open for the visually interesting events happening around your business, and start snapping photos of them.

Infographics

Infographics are visualizations of data — they're custom graphic images, in a longer format, that tell a story or share data or information. (Infographics are covered in detail in Chapter 13.)

The idea behind infographics is that the use of visual elements to support storytelling can give your story more impact and make it more memorable and relevant. Plus, infographics are quite popular on social networks, and they can provide a lot of traffic to your website.

Create infographics as a way to share a story or longer-format information with your audience. If you have a shorter story to share, or if you don't have enough information to create a full, long-format infographic, create a short-format infographic (no more than the height of a typical computer monitor) to visualize quick data points or a segment of the larger story. You can see some sample long- and short-format infographics in Figure 17-4. To view these infographics in a larger format, go to `www.pinterest.com/bootcampdigital/our-social-media-infographics`.

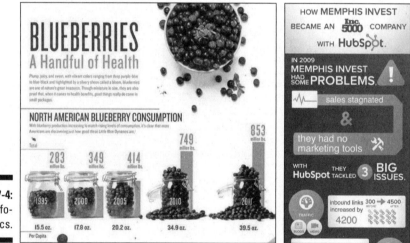

Figure 17-4: Info-graphics.

Stock Photos with Text

If you have no real-life images to use to tell your story, consider purchasing stock photos or selecting photos from free photography sites to create visual content from existing professional images. You can find lots of amazing, low-cost photos that are easy to buy online and that you can use to create visual content.

The advantage of using stock photos is that you don't have to worry about taking pictures or purchasing licensing rights that may arise from images you take yourself. A stock photo can also be a quick way to find a highly relevant image.

Chapter 4 gives you more details about purchasing stock photography, and it lists sites where you can get photos for free. Chapter 5 shares tips, tricks, and tools on how to create these types of images. When choosing stock photos to use, select photos that are interesting, eye-catching, stunning, or entertaining. Use photos that truly stand out from the others and that break through the "noise" on social media.

Figure 17-5 shows examples of how stock photos with text can be created and used in your visual social marketing efforts. These types of images are useful in blog posts and on Facebook and Pinterest.

Figure 17-5: Stock photos with text.

Customer Testimonials

Even customer testimonials can become visual marketing assets. By turning testimonials into visual content, you can make them stand out and become more memorable.

Turning a testimonial into something more visual by creating an image with the quote and the person who is leaving the testimonial is a great way to increase the appeal and effectiveness of the testimonial. Showing the person who is leaving the testimonial also makes it more personal and believable.

Figure 17-6 shows examples of how businesses, such as HubSpot, are creating visual content from their testimonials.

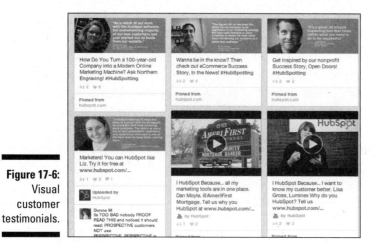

Figure 17-6:
Visual
customer
testimonials.

Cartoons

Cartoons can make eye-catching and interesting graphics, which is why they've been a staple of print newspapers for many years. Cartoons help brands create stories from visual content and share their personalities.

Though cartoons can seem difficult to create, you have a few options for creating appealing ones: You can hire a cartoon artist, use a cartoon application on a smartphone or tablet, or draw one by using the drawing software on your computer. If you need only one frame for the cartoon, you may even be able to purchase it from a stock photography site and add text to it yourself.

The key to success for most cartoons is humor. The distinguishing factor of most cartoons versus other types of graphics is that they're generally funny. If humor doesn't come naturally to you, you may want to skip this image strategy.

You can see how businesses are harnessing the power of cartoons in Figure 17-7.

Figure 17-7:
Cartoons.

Collages

If you have a number of photos of a single item, or from a single event, sharing them as a collage may be better than individually posting similar pictures.

The advantage of creating collages is that you can share many pictures at one time. Individually posting similar pictures to social networks can become redundant and burn out your audience. Instead, a collage creates a beautiful and interesting display of many of your photos at one time.

Collages can be created using photo editing software on your computer. The easiest way to create collages is to use photos from a smartphone or tablet. Many mobile applications for creating collages are available, and you can easily create one in only a few minutes using these apps.

One of the more popular collage apps is Instacollage. As its name suggests, it creates collages almost instantly. You can view some collages in Figure 17-8.

Figure 17-8:
Collages for
visual social
marketing.

Product Images

If you have a business that has a physical product, product images can be good assets for visual social marketing. Consider using images of your most popular, interesting, or unique products.

Rather than share only traditional, professional product photos, mix up your image strategy with images showing your product being used or taken in different settings.

You can view some product images that are shared on social networks in Figure 17-9.

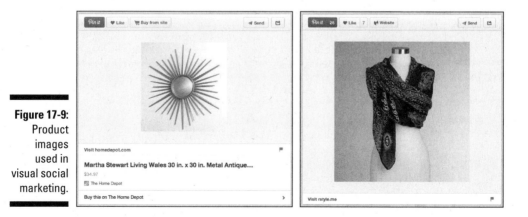

Figure 17-9:
Product
images
used in
visual social
marketing.

How-to Pictures

Using images to show how to complete a task can be a powerful way to share step-by-step instructions. One reason that how-to images are popular is that they're easy to follow and understand. Most are collages with images showing every step required to complete a task. How-to images are also popular for people to share, especially on Pinterest.

To create a how-to image, you have to demonstrate visually the required steps. For example, a how-to image of an oil change on your vehicle may involve pictures of the steps required to change the oil. Often, the image alone isn't sufficient for someone to be able to comprehend the task. How-to images are typically used to accompany an article with text explaining the steps in detail.

You can view how-to pictures that are shared on social networks in Figure 17-10.

Figure 17-10:
How-to images used in visual social marketing.

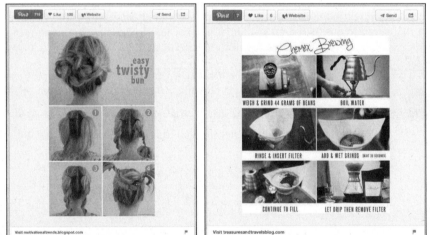

Chapter 18

Ten Types of Videos to Create

Many businesses and organizations struggle when getting started with video marketing, because they aren't sure what types of videos they can create. Businesses and organizations of any type can create appealing videos for visual social marketing.

Whether you're creating videos on Vine, Instagram, or YouTube, this chapter can provide some inspiration. After reading this chapter, spend some time brainstorming to determine which of these videos you can create and start shooting.

Finding Videos for Inspiration

Okay, I fudged this section's content (I don't technically describe a type of video you create) because I want to explain how to find the inspiration to create the types of videos listed in this chapter. After I recently decided to create a new promotional video for one of my businesses, I spent hours looking at similar videos online. I borrowed the ideas and concepts that I liked from other videos to insert into my own, re-creating the best parts of other videos.

Start by looking for videos that inspire you and get your creative energy flowing. Rather than start from scratch, however, you can view videos similar to the one you're trying to create. Make notes so that you can try to re-create parts of the videos that truly stand out.

Search for videos in a variety of places to increase the diversity of the videos you're viewing. The types of videos you find on YouTube, for example, may be different from those you discover on Vimeo or by using Google Video Search.

Here are three places to search:

- **YouTube (**www.youtube.com**):** The most popular video-sharing site on the Internet and the second-largest search engine. Most businesses share their videos on YouTube, making it a helpful place to find interesting new videos.

- **Vimeo (**www.vimeo.com**):** A video sharing site that's preferred by video professionals and creative types. You may find that Vimeo videos generally have higher production quality, which can provide additional inspiration.

- **Google Video Search (**www.google.com/videohp**):** Searches websites for videos. Some businesses and professional sites share their videos only on their own websites — not on sites such as YouTube.

Explainer

An *explainer* video focuses on explaining a topic, and it's often animated. Businesses that offer complex products or unique functionality often use this type of video to communicate with their audiences.

An explainer video generally generates most of its views from the website it's displayed on. Because the objective is to explain the product, service, or organization, this video is typically displayed on the home page or product page on a website. An explainer video, which aims to simplify a concept, is typically less than three minutes long.

If you want to showcase your company, product, or service, shoot an explanatory video to describe how you operate and why you're different from your competition.

Check out these sample explainer videos:

- **"Meet Flipboard"** — http://youtu.be/v2vpvEDS00o
- **"What Is Visual.ly?"** — http://youtu.be/AiVKfNeRbPQ

To find explainer videos (and the other types mentioned in this section), search YouTube for the video's title.

How-To

A *how-to* video shows how to do something. This type of video is popular because it provides true value to audience members, who are usually trying to complete a task. How-to videos are also popular because people often search for terms including the phrase *how to,* as in *how to tie a bowtie.* By creating how-to videos, you can increase your reach and get your business in front of new audiences.

A *how-to* video can be as long or short as needed to demonstrate the topic. As with most videos, shorter is better. Some businesses create how-to videos to show customers how to complete a task — and to reduce the number of questions directed to the customer service department. Others use this type of video to generate awareness while showing how to complete tasks associated with their businesses, products, or services. For example, both Lowes and Home Depot offer a variety of videos showing shoppers how to complete home repair projects, such as "How to Change a Faucet."

When your customers or prospects are trying to learn how to do something that relates to your business, evaluate the search terms they use. Envision the videos you can create to connect with these audiences to build brand awareness and, possibly, drive sales of your product.

Here are some sample how-to videos:

- ✔ **"How to replace and install your kitchen faucet," by Lowes:** `http://youtu.be/HlLF24acHbs`
- ✔ **"Weatherizing doors and windows," by The Home Depot:** `http://youtu.be/n2KDbTx9gVo`
- ✔ **"How to tie a bowtie," by Howcast:** `http://youtu.be/_AyaRGEDXAQ`
- ✔ **"How to do an easy oil change," by Advance Auto Parts:** `http://youtu.be/n2KDbTx9gVo`

Behind the Scenes

A behind-the-scenes video gives people a glimpse of activities and processes and other interesting events that may be going on behind the scenes of a company. If you're interested in creating this type of video, be sure that you have an interesting and unique topic to share.

Some of the best behind-the-scenes videos show how complex products, services, or events are created. These videos give people insight into what it takes to do so.

Behind-the-scenes videos are typically short, less than three minutes; however, videos that showcase particularly interesting topics can justifiably be longer.

Here are some sample behind-the-scenes videos:

- ✔ **"Behold the Locomotive (GE Flyovers)," by General Electric:** `http://youtu.be/dz9Ms65vT4I`
- ✔ **"Behind the Scenes of the Louis Vuitton Women's Spring/Summer 2013 Fashion Show," by Louis Vuitton:** `http://youtu.be/XkaMqzUoACw`
- ✔ **"The Panera Breakfast Power Sandwich Backstory," by Panera Bread:** `http://youtu.be/b2t7kwwelrg`
- ✔ **"Behind the Scenes at a McDonald's Photo Shoot," by McDonald's Canada:** `http://youtu.be/oSd0keSj2W8`

Interview

Interviewing people is an engaging way to make an interesting video quickly. Interviewees can range from employees to industry experts and from celebrities to customers to suppliers and more. Anyone with an interesting story or relevant content to share can make an absorbing interview.

The key to creating a successful interview video is to ensure that the interviewee has interesting information to share that your audience will find valuable. Long personal stories or shameless plugs for a product or service usually don't work well.

As with other types of videos, the best interview videos are normally short and last less than five minutes. You may need to edit a video if the interviewee is long-winded. Stick to quick questions and concise answers (from two to five sentences).

Here are a few sample interview videos:

- ✔ **"Zappos Sam Edelman Interview," by Zappos:** `http://youtu.be/m5JdNEHIzJQ`
- ✔ **"Driving Results with Visual Content: Interview with Krista Neher," by Search Engine Journal:** `http://youtu.be/G5PWnyUUarM`
- ✔ **"Skype at CES 2012," by Microsoft:** `http://youtu.be/2ldGb11XVG8`

Product Demo

If you have an amazing product that performs better than people would expect, a product demo video can be an interesting way to generate new customers. Product demo videos show your product in action.

Many studies have shown that for certain types of products, demo videos can lead to higher sales. People can *see* the product being used and witness the results.

Most product demo videos are short — less than a minute is ideal (if possible). You don't have to show every step of your product being used; simply show the highlights and results.

Check out these sample product-demo videos:

- ✔ **"The Mighty Wallet," by Dynomighty:** `http://youtu.be/a28q356MrR0`

- ✔ **"NeverWet Arrives — Hands-On Product Demonstration," by Lancaster Online:** `http://youtu.be/DZrjXSsfxMQ`

- ✔ **"WD-40 OFFICIAL Product Demonstration," by WD-40 Company:** `http://youtu.be/2imSWDorPeU`

Customer Testimonial

Video customer testimonials are powerful because they're more believable and they have more of an impact than testimonials consisting of text. Some television and radio commercials offer testimonials to increase the commercials' impact.

Testimonials with content that's appealing can also be used in other videos, such as promotional videos. Interspersing short testimonials from customers in a product demo or promotional video can give them much more impact. A testimonial video primarily generates views from your website, and it's a good way to increase the effectiveness of your site.

Testimonial videos should be short — typically, less than a minute. You may have to edit a testimonial to make it the length you want and to edit out pauses or unimportant information. You can also combine multiple testimonials into a single video featuring a few different customers.

Here are some sample testimonial videos:

- ✓ **"Proactive Testimonial — Yasmin," by Proactive:**
  http://youtu.be/sDitrnzPBJw

- ✓ **"Toastmasters International Member Testimonials August 2011,"** by Toastmasters: http://youtu.be/9vGk1J8ZDUg

- ✓ **"Philips HeartStart FR3 Defibrillator Customer Testimonials," by Philips Healthcare:** http://youtu.be/-AfG7V34LrM

Educational

Connecting with your target audience by way of education is a useful way to build your brand equity and awareness. By educating people on your products, or subject areas related to your product, you can build deeper relationship with your target audience. This strategy can require that you educate customers or create general educational assets.

An educational video provides clear value to the viewer because it teaches the viewer something. Many people search on YouTube for educational videos, so a clear demand for educational content exists on video sharing sites. Informative educational videos can generate lots of views on sites such as YouTube.

When creating educational videos, take as long as necessary to clearly educate your audience. As with any video, shorter is better, but when you create educational videos, you have more latitude to make them longer because people are usually interested in, and committed to, understanding the subject area.

Here are some sample educational videos:

- ✓ **"How to Get the Hotel Bed Look at Home," by DownLiteBedding:**
  http://youtu.be/0KQHXc4cBvQ

- ✓ **"What the Internet Is Doing to Our Brains," by Epipheo:**
  http://youtu.be/cKaWJ72x1rI

- ✓ **"Beginner Photoshop Tutorial: 5 Easy Photo Effects," by Photoshop: Tutorials** http://youtu.be/pi_0KAP2Lxc

- ✓ **"Get the Look: 80s Inspired Hair," by HerbalEssences:**
  http://youtu.be/UqSJHbirOPU

- ✓ **"How to Make a Margarita Cocktail," by Epicurious:**
  http://youtu.be/afl4SZljUiU

Promotional

A promotional video can be a helpful way to promote your business, product, or service. Promotional videos can be useful on your website because they can further enhance the experience that visitors have there and lead to their making more purchases. Offering videos on websites can substantially increase conversion rates (the percentage of people who buy) on your site. For example, online retailer StacksandStacks.com reported that visitors were 144% more likely to purchase after seeing a product video than those who did not.

Promotional videos can also be funny or entertaining. They work for businesses of all types and sizes, including those that sell to other businesses and consumers.

Humor is difficult to achieve in amateur videos.

My company, Boot Camp Digital, includes promotional videos in all our products. We use videos to explain each product and to communicate the benefits of our training program. Video allows for a more authentic and energetic description of our products than text alone. Evaluate the products or services you're trying to sell, and look for opportunities to use videos to sell or promote your products.

Make promotional videos short and to the point. The best ones last less than two minutes, but use as much or little time as you need to make your point.

Here are some sample promotional videos:

- ✔ **"Our Blades Are F***ing Great," by DollarShaveClub:**
  http://youtu.be/ZUG9qYTJMsI

- ✔ **"First Visit to the Dentist," by KellermanDental:**
  http://youtu.be/BPAkhoQcT60

- ✔ **"Angry Birds Star Wars Cinematic Trailer," by Rovio Mobile:**
  http://youtu.be/16lYFO_tKlE

Index

• J •

About the Author

KristaNeher (www.KristaNeher.com) is the CEO of Boot Camp Digital (www.BootCampDigital.com), an international speaker on social media and Internet marketing, and a best-selling author.

Krista started her career at Procter & Gamble, where she learned strategic brand building and marketing. She left P&G to run marketing for an Internet startup, where she became a social media marketing pioneer, running one of the first Twitter business accounts. Krista founded Boot Camp Digital in 2009 and has trained and educated thousands of marketers.

In addition to training via Boot Camp Digital, Krista created one of the first accredited social media certification programs when she was the managing director of the Institute for Social Media at Cincinnati State. She also contributes to a number of social media training programs and workshops.

Krista has worked with leading organizations such as P&G, GE, Google, the United States Senate, General Mills, Remax, Prudential, the Better Business Bureau, and more. She is a sought-after keynote speaker and trainer, and she has worked with organizations in North America, Europe, Asia, and South America. She has also been a featured expert in the *New York Times;* on CNN, NBC, and CBS; at Mashable and the Associated Press; and more.

She is also the best-selling author of *Social Media Field Guide, Visual Social Media Marketing,* and the textbook *Social Media Marketing: A Strategic Approach.*

Connect with Krista on social networks — simply search for *Krista Neher.*

Publisher's Acknowledgments

Acquisitions Editor: Amy Fandrei

Senior Project Editor: Mark Enochs

Copy Editor: Rebecca Whitney

Technical Editor: Michelle Krasniak

Editorial Assistant: Annie Sullivan

Sr. Editorial Assistant: Cherie Case

Project Coordinator: Rebekah Brownson

Cover Image: Front Cover Image: © iStockphoto .com/scanrail